UNDERMINING THE JAPANESE MIRACLE

UNDERMINING THE JAPANESE MIRACLE

Work and Conflict in a Coalmining Community

MATTHEW ALLEN

Department of History,
University of Auckland

CAMBRIDGE
UNIVERSITY PRESS

Published by the Press Syndicate of the University of Cambridge
The Pitt Building, Trumpington Street, Cambridge CB2 IRP, UK
40 West 20th Street, New York, NY 10011-4211, USA
10 Stamford Road, Oakleigh, Melbourne 3166, Australia

Printed in Hong Kong by Colorcraft

National Library of Australia cataloguing in publication data
Allen, Matthew (Matthew Francis Elkington), 1957-.
Undermining the Japanese Miracle.
Bibliography,
Includes index.
1. Industrial relations – Japan – History – 20th century.
2. Coal miners – Japan – Chikuho. 3. Coal mines and mining –
Social aspects – Japan. 4. Coal mines and mining –
Economic aspects – Japan. I. Title.
331.76223340952

Library of Congress cataloguing in publication data
Allen, Matthew.
Undermining the Japanese miracle: work and conflict in a
coalmining community/Matthew Allen.
Includes bibliographical references and index.
1. Coal mines and mining – Japan – Chikuho-machi. 2. Chikuho-machi
(Japan) – Economic conditions. 3. Chikuho-machi (Japan) – Social
conditions. 4. Chikuho-machi (Japan) – Social life and customs.
I. Title.
HD9556.J32C483 1994   94–2994
338.2'724'095222–dc20   CIP

A catalogue record for this book is available from the British Library.

ISBN 0 521 45009 8 Hardback

Contents

List of Plates

List of Maps

List of Figures

Acknowledgements

The research on which this study is based was conducted with the generous financial support of the Japanese government's Monbusho Scholarship scheme and with the assistance of the Department of Economic History at Sydney University. The students and staff of Kyushu University provided me with encouragement and sound advice on how to conduct my fieldwork in Chikuho. The first part of this fieldwork took place between April 1987 and February 1989. The second stint was at the end of 1991 and early in 1992.

Fiona has supported me, and we have supported Sam, throughout. Their contribution to the production of this book cannot be under-estimated. My parents have contributed significantly to the enterprise, especially my father, with his proof-reading of drafts of the book.

However, it is to the people of Chikuho that I owe the greatest debt. Their support in providing knowledge, ideas, humour, intelligence and warmth have made this book possible. I hope that I have been able to represent their case in a style of which they will approve.

Glossary

asseiyama   lit. 'pressure mountain'; violent, generally small, mine.
beddo taun   commuter or satellite town.
beddo taunzu   plural of *beddo taun*.
bento   lunch box, usually consisting of rice, *nigiri*, and other oddments of food.
Bon Odori Taikai   celebration of the Festival of the Dead; dancing rally.
bōryokudan   organised crime syndicate; *yakuza*; lit. 'violent group'.
bōsōzoku   young, often teenaged car-driving hoodlums, often seen in gangs.
bota yama   slag-heaps.
buraku   lit. 'village'; more commonly used to describe the villages in which 'special villagers' live; that is those who have been ritually discriminated against by the general public since the thirteenth and fourteenth centuries.
Buraku Kaihō Undō   The Buraku Liberation Organisation, an anti-discrimination movement dedicated to eliminating the widespread stigma of association with *buraku*.
burakumin   the group of people who live in the *buraku*; that is, those who are discriminated against by the general public.
chihō ōte   unions representing the regionally powerful mines such as K-san and O-san, supported by association with *Tanrō*.
chimpira   low-level *yakuza* footsoldiers.
chūko chu   unions representing medium-sized mines, with between 500 and 1,000 workers.
chūko ko   unions representing small mines, with less than 500 workers.
chūkokigyō   small to medium-sized mines (lit. 'enterprises').
chūo ōte   unions representing the large mines such as M-san, N-san, T-san, supported by association with *Tanrō*.
daikigyō   large mines (lit. 'enterprises').
daimyō   feudal lords of the pre-Meiji (1868) era.
danchi   housing development; apartment complex.
fujinkai   women's group.
Fukutanrō   Fukuoka branch of the National Coalminers' Union.
genkan   entrance hall.
giri   debt of gratitude; obligation.

Gisei no Tō 'The Tower of Sacrifice' (manuscript).

Gorika The Scrap and Build Plan; the second Temporary Coal Rationalisation Bill.

goyō enterprise; business.

goyō kumiai enterprise union.

gun county; sub-prefecture.

Haitan Kodan Solid Fuels Distribution Public Corporation.

happi livery coat; *happi* coat.

haramaki stomach-protector (to ward off cold).

honne one's true intentions/feelings.

hōritsu law.

idobata kaigi lit. 'well conference'; women's informal gatherings at the local wells, a common means of disseminating local gossip. *Idobata kaigi* was an institution in most of the *tanjū* until the 1960s, when running water was introduced to many coal villages. However, although the wells are no longer used, the women still get together for regular gossip sessions, and still refer to these sessions as *idobata kaigi*, a term used disparagingly by many men.

ippanjin 'normal' or mainstream people; non-coalminers.

jikatabi split-toed heavy-cloth shoes; traditional workmen's shoes.

jimmu keiki period of 'divine providence' (1956–57), prosperity; economic boom.

jinja Shinto shrine.

jinmyaku contact networks.

jinzai lit. 'human capital'.

kachō section chief.

kakari person in charge.

kakui colloq. 'cool', attractive, appealing.

kami shibai picture show man.

kanji Chinese ideographs.

katana traditional samurai sword.

kawasuji kishitsu lit. 'river-dwellers' character', euphemism for 'rough diamonds'; that is, violent externally, but warm internally.

keigo honorific Japanese language.

kenri a right.

kinrō kakari person in charge of labour (at mines).

kinsaku seido the system of capital raising.

Kōgyō Renmei industry association.

kokumin nenkin national public pension.

kotatsu a table and a quilt over a heated area.

ku-chō headman of a ward.

kumi group of houses into which villages are divided, usually between eight and 16 houses.

kumi-chō   head person of kumi.

Kuroi Hane (movement)   Black Feather movement, coal-collecting charity movement established by housewives.

Kyōsei Renkō   Korean Forced Labourers' Association.

machi-zukuri lit. 'city building campaign' (local government-sponsored).

minseiin   welfare commissioner (volunteer).

mochi ritsu, mota retsu   give and take.

naya seido   long-house; barn-like system of traditional coalminer accommodation.

nigiri   rice balls (eaten for lunch in *bento*).

Nittan   Japan Coal Corporation.

ojisan   uncle (familiar form of address used by children for known adult males).

on   obligation; debt of gratitude.

oyabun   lit. 'parent'; *yakuza* boss.

pachinko   upright, legalised pin-ball-like gambling machine.

rōmu   labour; labour watchers (colloq.); (abbrev.) labour overseers.

rōmu kakari   person in charge of labour; labour overseers.

sake   rice wine.

seikatsu hōgo   public welfare.

shataku   lit. 'company housing'; coalminers' housing.

shiatsu   acupressure.

shimin undo   citizens' movement.

shitaijigyodan   day-labourers' work groups.

shiyō ga nai   'it can't be helped'.

shōchu   potato, wheat, etc. liquor.

shokudō   dining-room; dining-hall; restaurant.

shōgun   feudal leader of Japan pre-Meiji (1868).

shokugyō anteisho   work introduction centre.

sōgo hokken   mutual insurance.

Sōhyō   General Council of Trade Unions.

sura   sled for transporting coal.

taiko   drum.

tanjū   coalminers' village.

tankō-kai   coalmine-employed gangers.

tankōfu   coalminer.

Tanrō   National Coalminers' Union.

tanuki bori   lit. 'badger hole'; small, one- or two-person excavation used largely for digging out coal not of high enough quality for reputable companies.

tatami   straw matting used for floor covering.

tatemae   a principle; front-stage behaviour.

tokushū buraku   lit. 'special village'; village in which *burakumin* live.

tokutsu   random manner in which mines were laid out underground.

toroko tsuaa   tour of massage parlours.

tsunami   tidal wave of epic proportions.

uwasa shakai   rumour-based society.

uyoku   right-wing, pro-militarist activities, often associated with the *yakuza*.

yakuza   organised crime syndicates.

yakuza gumi   specific, local branches of *yakuza*.

yakutoku   a privilege.

yama no Kami jinja   the temple of the mountain gods.

yūrei   ghosts of dissatisfied spirits.

zaibatsu   lit. 'financial cliques'; old-style monopoly capitalist corporations, based around a family holding company, and extending into many important, heavy industries. Arguably the power behind Japan's pre-war economy.

Zengakuren   The National Association of Students.

Zentanko   the right-wing National Coalminers' Union.

zori   traditional leather thongs.

List of Abbreviations

BKD	Buraku Liberation Organisation
CICC	Coal Industry Co-operative Council
CUC	Coal Unemployment Commission
FMSC	Fukuoka Mine Safety Commission
JCP	Japan Communist Party
JSP	Japan Socialist Party
LASL	lowest acceptable standard of living
LDP	Liberal Democratic Party
MITI	Ministry of International Trade and Industry
MOP	Ministry of Propaganda
NEC	newly exporting country
NIC	newly industrialised countries
NNS	*Nishi Nihon Shinbun*
RTSB	River Transportation and Safety Bureau
SCAP	Supreme Command of Allied Powers
TCRB	Temporary Coal Rationalisation Bill
TUCWM	Temporary Unemployed Coal Workers Measure
YWM	Y-san Widows' Movement

Notes on translation and anonymity

Throughout this account, I have attempted to remain faithful in translation to the style of Japanese spoken by the miners and people of Chikuho. It is rough, colourful and highly evocative. In Japan, swearing as such is uncommon, but in Chikuho personal abuse in everyday conversation is almost the norm, and I have attempted to retain this in the translation. I accept responsibility for all translations in this book.

I have changed the names of most of my informants and some of the placenames within Chikuho to avoid causing personal hardship for those who so generously gave of their time and knowledge.

The names of companies have been abridged in the Japanese language convention.

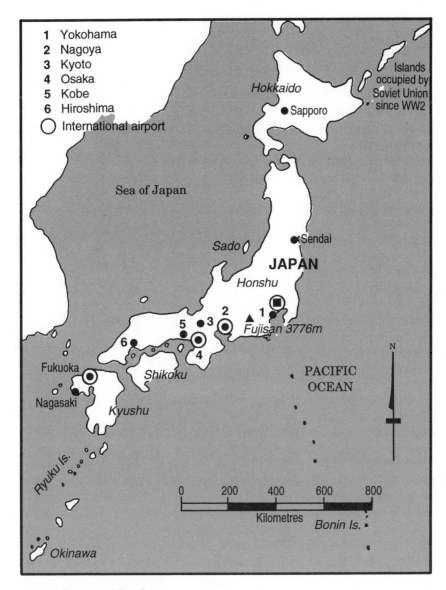

Map 1: Japan and Kyushu

Map 2: Fukuoka prefecture and Chikuho region

Introduction

It is said that it is the peculiar quality of time to conserve fact, and
that it does so by rendering our past falsehoods true.
(Gene Wolfe, *The Shadow of the Torturer*, 1981, p.121)

This is a book about a Japanese coalmining community. In particular it
is a book about the people of the coalmines, and their struggle to
achieve a dignified identity in a rapidly changing society that has no use
for coalminers. Although coal is no longer mined in Chikuho, the
region where the study was conducted, the legacy of the coal years is
omnipresent. People still live in rundown coal villages (*tanjū*), where
slag-heaps abound (many now covered with vegetation), and poverty
and isolation are still characteristics of the existence of those who
worked in the coalmines. In some of the older *tanjū*, where the *naya
seido* (the barn-like 'long houses') still stand, the neighbourhood
structure has remained intact, and although newcomers move into the
villages as former residents die or move away, the social cohesion of the
coal years endures to some extent within this system.[1] This is reinforced
by the impression, transmitted to locals and outsiders alike, that the
coal villagers are different to the rest of society. In turn, this is
reinforced by the geographical isolation of the villages.

At the present time the mining communities are populated by a
cross-section of urban poor. Not only coalminers and their families, but
also welfare recipients, relatives of miners, and some minorities inhabit
the *tanjū*.[2] The economic decline of the region since the end of the
coalmining era has had the effect of gradually transforming the community from a close-knit, hard-working, carousing, lively population to

1

a more diversified and impoverished community with a high degree of welfare dependence. The contemporary dependence on welfare is directly related to both the type of work that the miners performed and the attitudes of government and coal companies when the latter withdrew from the region in the 1960s and 1970s. This book asks why, compared to the rest of Japan, Chikuho is materially impoverished. In order to establish the relationship between coalmining and welfare, it is necessary to examine in some detail the history of the region.

The construction of history is an eclectic process, as Robertson (1991) and others have observed; something that is not the preserve of written sources alone. Attempts to reconstruct history to emphasise certain events, and de-emphasise others, provide alternative understandings not only of the past, but also of the present. In Chikuho, where this study was conducted, the process of reconstructing the past is being undertaken with enthusiasm by a number of people and institutions, each with their own political agenda.

In order to delve into the past, I have asked the question: how do local people, academics, government officials and company employees perceive the past and, through understanding the past, deal with the present and imagine the future?

It became clear to me that issues of powerlessness and dependence are of some importance in understanding how the region changed following the closure of the coal industry. I argue that the region's decline and the limited capacity to provide alternative working opportunities for the population are linked closely to the institutionalised political powerlessness of the miners. A culture of violence dominated relationships between mine management and miners; thus the status quo was maintained and challenges by miners to power-holders and their agents forestalled. The relations of dependence that were fostered by this system removed the capacity of the miners to challenge, with any measure of success, either the legitimacy of the mine-owners during the mining days or the government in the period following the closure of the industry. Only the influence of a group of dedicated philanthropists has provided relief from what was otherwise an almost totalitarian regime. This book explores the ways in which the state, its citizens and private capital have attempted to change and improve these conditions.

Alternative views of history

After the industry ceased operations, many protests emerged about the nature of coalmining work, and the management–labour relations that existed in the industry. Revelations about violence employed by the labour overseers, company corruption, police co-operation with criminal gangs in controlling the labour force, and government–big business collusion in escaping responsibility for their part in the economic destruction of the coalfields clearly illustrate alternative views of Japan's economic development and labour relations. These views, which are becoming more articulate over time, stress the importance of the power relationship of management over labour, and the state over the individual. They challenge the formalised and often-described view of Japanese labour–management relations as harmonious, and of socio-logical structures as classless. Generally, these views are informally expressed, rarely appearing in mainstream publications or in the mass media. Rather they are articulated in discussions between concerned local scholars, ex-miners and leftist activists. They have limited access to the general public, and presumably limited appeal.

Interpretations of Chikuho's mining history that differ so greatly from local government historical accounts, however, require attention. If these accounts are even partially accurate, then surely there is a need to investi-gate the circumstances in which they arose. It is here that the miners' dependence on the coal companies, and the culture of violence and intimidation that prevented them from airing their grievances is of importance. Only after the mining industry ceased operations did widespread condemnation of the industry appear, and in some former coalmining villages there is still reluctance to discuss the past with out-siders, even though close to 30 years have passed since many of the mines were closed.

Although there are formalised outlets for stories of the coal era,[3] most of the stories are anecdotal, informally and orally expressed. It was my intention to collect a series of reminiscences by coalminers and their families to provide some balance to the official historical accounts that portray a benevolent and philanthropic industry. Although I started researching with this aim in mind, it soon became apparent that storytellers had a traditional role in the coalfields, and that many of these raconteurs had the capacity to influence large numbers of people. The existence of the so-called *uwasa shakai* (rumour society) provided the structure through which stories were transmitted to others in towns and villages; that is, through informal gatherings at the wells to collect water for drinking and washing (the *idobata kaigi*), women from the *tanjū* passed on gossip and stories that in turn were passed on to families and other acquaintances. The *kami shibai* men, typically itinerant *burakumin*,[4] regaled villagers with stories of the coal industry, complete with cartoon-like drawings. They were also sources of information about the happenings in other coal villages on their route. Travelling coalminers, either fired from or escaped from some of the more violent mines, passed on stories of their experiences to whoever would listen. The bars were full of gossip, as were the communal baths and *shokudō* (dining-rooms). In the absence of outside knowledge and given the low literacy rate of Chikuho coalminers,[5] the importance of the storytellers in transmitting information to the miners and their families cannot be overlooked, and I emphasise their role in the reconstruction of local history.

Isolation, powerlessness and dependence

The geographical isolation of the mines and the company-provided housing enabled the coal companies to exercise considerable control over the miners. Situated in a basin surrounded by mountains, the coalfields were isolated from the major cities and towns in Kyushu. In a frontier-like environment, which has been likened to Texas in the white pioneer days,[6] a culture that shared some values with mainstream Japanese society, yet possessing a highly esoteric character, arose. Social order in the coal villages was administered not by the police, who preferred not to interfere in 'private' matters, but by the company that owned the housing, stores and bars, through their *rōmu kakari* (labour control office) and their *yakuza* (organised crime syndicates) connections. *Yakuza* organisations were independently active in the villages, towns and cities, providing gambling facilities, protection for bar and club owners, establishing brothels, selling drugs and providing an informal police force with strong mining company associations. The facilities were well used, and the reputation of miners as hard-drinking, heavy gambling, fighting men was often vindicated.

Within this society, values that were distortions of mainstream Japanese social values emerged. Young men aspired to become *yakuza*; the unfettered power, the money, and the status and respect that the job generated contributing to the alluring image. 'It is better to be holding the stick than being hit with it' was how it was explained to me by one *yakuza* informant.[7] Certainly, working for the power-holders was better than working as a miner. Violence was a way of life for most people of the coalmining communities, extant in their work, their entertainment and their social lives. In that anticipation of conflict and inevitable violence dominated many of their social and vocational relations, it is not surprising that miners were themselves inclined to be aggressive, and that violence became a social norm. In stark contrast with the theory of the Japanese vertical society painted by Nakane (1970), which is organised around consensus and avoidance of conflict and confrontation, the coalmining communities were organised around the tenets of conflict and violence.

In the absence of a formal juridico-legal apparatus that could arbitrate in disputes between management and labour, and indeed in the absence of formal social controls, a culture of violence arose within the coalfields. The isolation of the communities from mainstream society contributed to the situation. Although the coal companies supplied employment, housing and living facilities for their miners, they also provided the social control mechanisms already mentioned. In fact, the virtual incarceration of miners in company housing allowed the mine-owners to exert tight social, financial and vocational control over the workforce.

The socio-political structure of the communities was based on the company housing arrangements, the people separated into *kumi* (blocks of eight to sixteen houses facing each other in the *naya seido* (barn-like system)) in which there was an elected *kumi-chō* (head person). The *kumi-chō* was required to meet with the *ku-chō* (the community head person, always a man) and other *kumi-chō* once a month to discuss company directives about maintaining housing, organising community chores and so on. The system enabled the company to monitor the activities of its workforce. Each miner and his family were noted in the company register, and any person could be found at short notice. This was particularly useful in company attempts to track down and deal with 'trouble-makers', especially unionists.

This highly regulated and tightly controlled existence promoted dependence and powerlessness within the miners' ranks; dependence on the company for their livelihood, accommodation and other needs, and powerlessness to improve their standard of living and the conditions of employment. The companies were able to ban independent unions in the (mainly small) mines and invoke physical sanctions against protesters. Either way, the mine-owners were able to forestall challenges to their control of the forces of production. In chapters 6, 7 and 9 I examine this issue in some detail.

The emergence of labour conflict

While the miners endured arduous working conditions, tight social and financial controls, and a regime of violence, the industry was going through a crisis, and this contributed to the stepping up of violent and repressive management methods. By the late 1950s it was recognised by both coalmining companies and the government that there was only a limited future for coal in Japan; the future lay with oil. By the early 1960s most companies had made preparations to withdraw from the industry under favourable conditions provided by the government. It was the closure of the industry more than the repressive working and living environment that led to labour unrest in Chikuho in the late 1950s and early 1960s.

The miners' unions, once totally submissive, became active in disputes to save the mines. A new-found ability, born of desperation, to articulate grievances led to further disputes about violent management methods, the right to organise independent unions, compensation payments to the families of miners killed in accidents, better wages and working conditions, and superannuation and redundancy pay issues. Of these issues, the most pressing became the fight to save the industry, although by this stage their actions were destined to be ineffective.

The revival of independent unions in the late 1950s[8] empowered the miners to disrupt production, and to display openly their dissatisfaction with the status quo. Unfortunately for the unions, because their rise in the late 1950s followed the beginning of the decline of the industry and the subsequent over-supply of miners, the threat of the withdrawal of their labour was easily dealt with by the coal companies. They simply employed redundant coalminers from other regions in the place of the dissident miners and then encouraged all new employees to join company unions, which had been established by companies with precisely this purpose in mind.[9] Miners from independent unions, united under the National Coalminers' Union (*Tanrō*), resorted to opposing the companies physically. The violent confrontations between the miners and company hoodlums supported by the police became the stuff of folklore, especially in the M-san Miike Riots in 1960–61.

For all their efforts, unions were unable to halt the withdrawal of coal companies from the industry or bring about any positive changes in working conditions. In fact, when the actions were over, miners' working conditions had materially deteriorated. Company unions gained ascendancy when the extent of *Tanrō*'s failure was recognised by the majority of the remaining miners. Most miners, it appeared, preferred to work for reduced wages rather than have no work at all. Gradually, militancy was replaced by a conservative resignation about the end of the industry and of coalmining employment. However, the twilight of the industry and the conflict between labour and management led to the involvement in the region of activists from outside Chikuho. Often from politically aligned radical groups, these people took on the roles of ideologue, organiser and motivator within certain mining communities, in keeping with the role that Gramsci (1972) suggested was appropriate for the intellectual in class-based action.

The revivalists

The political activists were first attracted to the region following the increase in the mining-accident rate. Many surmised that the accident rate was indicative of the priorities of the companies in running their operations. While they had no doubt that the mines should remain open, the revivalists, as I refer to the political activists, believed that there was still a need to redress many of the grievances articulated by disaffected miners. In particular, the revivalists were concerned that companies were not spending adequate amounts of money on maintaining safety standards within the mines. Moreover, they were exploiting their workforce, and applying unhindered violence in order to discipline their workers, free from official intervention or sanctions. In short, the revivalists believed that the human rights of the miners had been ignored, and that the mining companies abused their human capital (*jinzai*) to make a profit, even at a high cost measured in human lives.

In the more isolated regions of Chikuho, where small mines were dominant, political activity traditionally had been almost non-existent. But, as the mines were closed down, resentment against the companies increased, and the arrival of the newcomers, with their political skills and acumen, helped focus some of the new-found tensions within the region, as the system of repressive management (and the mining operations) crumbled. Investigations were started into the causes of accidents, community solidarity in the face of company pressure emerged in some mines, and the immunity of companies to legal action was challenged by a conspicuously successful court case initiated by a group of mining-accident widows, with the assistance of outside, leftist organisations. This compensation case, in which the widows were awarded a substantial damages payment, demonstrated that companies were not immune from criticism, and were not omnipotent agencies. They too were required to act within the law.

A renaissance of local interest in coalmining occurred, initially driven by the actions of outsider activists, and then by local scholars, miners and some prominent citizens, as the outsiders moved on to other towns or settled down in the 1970s. The renaissance, or the revival (as I have termed it), is and was based on generating not only interest in Chikuho's coalmining past, but also pride in having survived a regime of terror and violence, and in having a strong, historical sense of community.

Especially targeted today by the revivalists are the young people of the region, the school-aged children, and the young working people, all of whom are too young to have experienced the coalmining days. There are many different political agendas involved in this movement, but across the range not only the cultural revival but also the economic revival of Chikuho is sought. In short, these people were, and are, actively involved in changing perceptions about the region, to make special, rather than stigmatising, the years of coalmining, and to engender dignity within the people. Although this movement has not been altogether successful in changing outsiders' perceptions of Chikuho, the image of the area *within* Chikuho is improving.

Welfare in Chikuho

The transformation of Chikuho from a coalmining community into a welfare community eventually attracted attention from academics and government agencies. These agencies investigated the coal industry, but only peripherally, as they saw it as an unfortunate precondition for the development of new and difficult social and economic problems. The necessity for an economic plan to absorb the unemployed miners, and to improve the material condition of Chikuho's industry was recognised, largely because of the publicity generated on the back of the welfare research being done in the region.

The erosion of living standards following the closure of the coalmines has left many Chikuho people with few options but to attempt to eke out an existence as unemployed people. The isolation of the communities and enforcement by the companies of cast-iron controls over the workforce during the coal era, and the culture of violence together led to relations of dependence and powerlessness in the coalfields, and this endures to some extent. That is, in the continued absence of strong social controls and given the disproportionately high concentration of welfare dependants, *yakuza*, inveterate gamblers and professional *pachinko* players, a strong undercurrent of violence is easily discernible. Few outsiders these days are tempted to intervene in the region, its reputation for 'rough-house' antics, *yakuza* involvement, and high crime rates offering strong disincentives. Yet locals have taken on the responsibility of articulating alternative understandings of the past, to educate other local people and to attempt to reverse the trend of discrimination to which Chikuho people are subjected from many city-dwellers. Today, rather than being dependent on the coal companies, the former mining communities are dependent on the government to provide the basic necessities of life; and once more the miners and their representatives are powerless to alter the situation.

The relatively recent phenomenon of welfare dependence is now being challenged by the establishment of a new welfare directive (the 123 Legislation), which was drawn up with the intention of reducing payments to welfare recipients, so as to curtail a rapidly increasing national welfare budget. Again the coalminers of Chikuho are under siege, as various government agencies attempt to reduce the welfare expenditure, to bring Chikuho's statistics more in line with the rest of the nation. As it stands, the overall region's welfare dependence rate is more than four times the national average, and some towns and villages display up to twenty times the national ratio (Fukuoka Prefecture Social Welfare Statistics, 1989). Chapters 14 and 15 deal with this issue in more depth.

Methodology

Over recent years the links between anthropology and other disciplines have become more substantial, reflecting the anthropologist's concern with a wider range of issues, not necessarily within traditional paradigms. Clifford and Marcus (1986), for example, have concerned themselves with the links between anthropology and literature. I have attempted to link ethnography with history, both oral and written. Further, by imposing a necessarily selective interpretation of events and ideas I have thrust myself into the text, with the aim of documenting the past and the present-day attempts of miners and ex-miners to resuscitate their future.

Rather than employing a conventional class analysis, I have employed an approach that owes a debt to, among others, Walter Benjamin (1977). His concept of the storyteller enables us to understand how people see themselves in society and how they remember the past. Doubtless there are apocryphal elements involved in many of the stories I was told, but it is important to bear in mind that these stories are validated within the community. The tradition of storytelling in Japan is well established, and the role of storytellers in performing a cohesive, binding community function is widely accepted, particularly within coalmining communities, where technology was always slow to penetrate. Within the text I have introduced a number of character portraits of storytellers, each with different, specialised stories to tell. This is to create an effect of montage, in a similar way to Taussig's (1987) book on the South American rubber traders.

The story I present reveals some aspects of Japanese society largely ignored by other writers. It attempts to extract concepts of power that underlie the accounts of the actions of people from the coalmining communities, and of the consciousness that developed from this. It attempts to isolate ideas, thoughts and a sense of purpose that pervaded the region in the wake of the revivalists.

By investigating the circumstances surrounding four flashpoints in the industry, I hope to illustrate the chronology of change in the industry. Moreover, by highlighting instances of conflict between management and labour, I intend to draw out the nature of the work, the environment in which work was performed, and the powerlessness of individuals to change positively their position in society. This leads to an analysis of welfare based on the historical and material conditions of the miners; that is, I examine the proposition that the welfare dependence endemic in Chikuho is a legacy directly traceable to the coal industry's performance and closure. I suggest that the imposition of a culture of violence, and the intimidation of miners prevented challenges to the hegemony of the mining companies (in the Gramscian sense), at least until the industry itself was threatened and mining companies loosened their controls. In the post-mining period the ideological and material conditions in which the miners live and subsist are predicated on this culture of violence. I concentrate on the actions and thoughts of the revivalists to provide critical insights into how the welfare situation developed in Chikuho.

I hope that I will be able to offer some insights into extremes of behaviour within an extreme industry. Just as most positive actions have, at some stage, a negative reaction, Chikuho mining stands out as an example of the manipulation of raw power in an environment that itself was totally manipulated. Like the angel who can no longer beat its wings and fly against the storm of progress in Walter Benjamin's *Theses on the Philosophy of History*,[10] the coal industry was swept towards the future, leaving debris in its wake. This human debris and their children have become the new poor, the welfare dependants of the present.

From a wider perspective, this book deals with some of the issues which mark the other side of the economic miracle. By focusing on the destruction of an industry for relatively short-term gains, and looking at the outcome in terms of human capital losses, the book presents an alternative to interpretations of Japanese society that stress conformity, consensus, vertical integration, homogeneity and the attendant lack of conflict. Further, by exposing the processes of capitalism in the mining industry, and the extremes to which mine-owners were prepared to go in order to maintain their control over the workforce, a picture of regional under-development emerges, one that is considerably different to other studies on Japan. Most importantly I hope to convince the reader that there is a need to reappraise the monolithic representation of 'Japan Inc.' and to galvanise further discussion and study of the phenomenon of Japan's rapid economic growth and of the cost at which it was achieved. Like all other nations, Japan's economy consists of the activities of people. It is critical not to forget the role of the people when attempting to measure the economic changes that take place in any nation.

NOTES TO INTRODUCTION

1   The housing is decrepit and crowded, the facilities negligible, and the monthly rent is extremely low, ranging from 500 yen to about 5,000 yen. The housing provides newcomers with the same rights as the long-term residents to move into new, subsidised, low-cost housing when it is constructed.

2 People living with the *tanjū* include Koreans, *burakumin* and some Chinese. See note 4.

3 There are local newsletters and magazines, and several authors are publishing books about the coalfields. All these approaches are fundamentally critical of the political status quo in Japan.

4 The *burakumin* are a group of people who are racially Japanese, but have been socially, economically and geographically isolated since the imperial adoption of Buddhist doctrines in early feudal Japan. Originally called the *eta* (literally 'full of filth'), they occupied a sub-human position in the social and economic hierarchy during feudal times, based primarily on vocational discrimination. People who worked in professions that were seen as being ritually defiling, such as butchers, tanners, graveyard guards and *zori* (straw sandals) makers were put into this category. Since 1868, when the Emancipation Edict was declared, it has been illegal to discriminate against *burakumin*, but discrimination, especially in relation to work and marriage, continues today. There are more than three million *burakumin* in Japan today, according to the *Buraku Kaihō Dōmei*.

5 Although Japan officially has the highest literacy rate in the world, Chikuho is an exception, according to local high school teachers, citizens' groups and revivalists. These people estimate that, including the elderly miners and their families, the literacy rate in the 1990s in Chikuho is around 70 per cent. My own experiences in the *tanjū*, where I was asked regularly to read the headlines of the papers to my neighbours, suggest that the standard of education, and hence literacy, is still rather low in the coalmining communities.

6 Nakayama, local doctor, interview, 1988.

7 Mori, interview, 1989.

8 The National Coalminers' Union's (*Tanrō*) influence over coalminers had been severely weakened by a series of workplace agreements between employers and employees in the early and mid 1950s. The union was effectively isolated from the process of arbitration, or settling disputes within those mines where the agreements had taken place.

9 Company unions were established by companies to ensure production demands were met, and to define a new orthodoxy in labour-management relations; that is, they were to provide miners with lip-service worker representation to management. These unions ostensibly were apolitical, and were opposed to the leftist, often militant union organisations. Under the Constitution it was made illegal to repress unions, and so at many mines two types of union co-existed: the company union and the *Tanrō*-backed, independent union.

10 Benjamin in *Illuminations*, 1977, p. 259.

CHAPTER 1

Chikuho: A Short Description

The Chikuho region, where this study is based, is situated in the northern central area of Kyushu, Japan's southernmost island. The region lies between Fukuoka city to the south-west and the large industrial cities of Kita Kyushu and Kokura to the north. Chikuho consists of a triangle of three major cities, which in past years were concerned primarily with the production of coal: Nogata to the north, Iizuka to the south, and Tagawa to the east. Lying within imaginary lines joining these three cities are a number of smaller towns that were also primarily coal producing.

Chikuho is situated in what is locally referred to as a 'basin' (*bonchi*), surrounded by mountains. The climate is more extreme than the coastal plains, where the sea breezes tend to be cool in the heat of summer and warm in the winter. Chikuho's geographical position offers little relief from the intense summer heat, and the winters are noticeably colder than in the coastal regions.

Approaching Chikuho from Fukuoka, one drives through the Yakiyama mountains, and from the summit the basin is clearly visible below. The rice paddies dominate the scenery, stretching east toward the Hikosan range and the border with Oita Prefecture, the Onga River winding through the greenery. Iizuka and Tagawa are immediately recognisable by the palls of grey smoke emanating from the cement works and other large industry. The slag-heaps (*bota yama*), which rise incongruously from the predominantly rural landscape, are cone-shaped and perfectly symmetrical, the once-black hills now grassed over, silent testimony to the coal industry's past presence in the area. From the mountains Chikuho looks remarkably green and peaceful. Only the scars of the cities and towns spoil an otherwise idyllic view.

On the plain, however, the scars left from the mining days are ever-present, as the *bota yama* dominate the skyline. The rice paddies, which from the mountains appear to be symmetrical and untainted, have sunk well below the level of the roads they adjoin, as a result of underground subsidence caused by the mines. The soil is bad, and the water in many of the irrigation streams and waterways is badly polluted by waste-products from the coal days. And the smells of the towns are pervasive. There is the putrefying stench of the meatworks in Nogata, the sickly sweet smells from the *sake* factories in Iizuka, and the choking black smoke from the cement works and stench of the open drainage in Tagawa.

The *tanjū*, neglected since the companies pulled out of the industry in the 1950s and 1960s, still stand in many towns, the tiny weatherboard shacks linked together in the *naya seido*. Open drains are evidence of the poor conditions in which the coalminers once lived, and still live in many cases. Gradually replacing these so-called 'eyesores' are the newer concrete apartments, which are generally five-storeyed government-sponsored buildings, most noticeable for the way they are crowded together on narrow plots of land, complete with the message 'Improved' conspicuously etched into the concrete under the eaves.

Huge concrete and lime works, once coal-processing plants owned by the M-san corporation, dominate the landscape, a maze of rusted pipes and conduits criss-crossing the main streets into town. Even a Chikuho symbol, the famous Mount Asahi, has been strip-mined by the lime companies. The top of the severed mountain and the scars from the work, which look like snow-skiing runs from a distance, are visible throughout the region.

The seasons have a marked impact on the impression the region makes on the observer. In summer, with the temperature often in the mid-30s (Celsius; 90s in Fahrenheit terms), and humidity approaching 95 per cent, a greyish haze hangs over the landscape, low pregnant clouds promising the afternoon storm that never seems to come. In winter the clouds are black, this time bringing sleet or occasionally snow, which temporarily purges the brownish sludge from roadways and factories, casting a surreal luminescent glow over the towns. The temperature drops to freezing overnight and the eaves hang with temporary stalactites until the day's warmth melts them in the late morning. The early morning commuter procession of white cars is turned brown by the appalling condition of the roads, churned into a quagmire by the number of drivers who fit their cars with steel-spiked tyres for added winter traction. Both spring and autumn are mild and often clear: the skies seldom cloud over, and the wet season is still far enough away to reduce the humidity to bearable levels.

The Onga River, which flows from Hikosan, the biggest mountain in the region, through Tagawa north to the sea at Kokura is seen as one of the symbols of the area. Many local historians regard the river as the 'lifeblood of Chikuho',[1] primarily because it was the means by which coal was transported to the big industrial ports until the 1940s, when the railways were introduced to replace the system of river barges. However the river still plays an important part in the lives of many of Chikuho's inhabitants in a symbolic and even ritualistic sense. Many local festivals are associated with the river, such as the Tagawa Jinko Matsuri, which is held every May and involves thousands of participants dragging enormous floats from one side of the river to the other, while watched by tens of thousands of spectators and television viewers. The people who live in the area are often classified as possessing the *kawasuji kishitsu*, the ostensible 'riverside-dwellers' character'. The local people are often referred to by this euphemism when they move outside the area, the implications of the name more sinister than they first appear, often implying something 'dirty' or dangerous.

Chikuho is serviced by buses from Fukuoka and Kita Kyushu, and by a railway system that is perhaps the oldest in Japan.[2] In a country where public transport is almost always reliable, the Chikuho line stands out as an example of inconvenience. Trains to the major centres leave only once an hour or so, and the last train runs at 7.30 p.m. As a result, the trains are not well patronised. The local line has been in some financial difficulty over the last few years, and in February 1989 a plan to rebuild the existing system and to cut services to the stations least patronised was approved by Japan Rail. The plan was adopted, and since 1989 rail services in the region have been cut by half.

The bus system is well patronised but expensive. The convenience offered by the bus routes to Fukuoka and Kita Kyushu makes this form of transport the most accessible to Tagawa and Iizuka people, and the only form of public transport available to people from smaller towns and villages in the region.

Chikuho is also accessible by road from Fukuoka. However, serious traffic congestion means that from 7.30 a.m. to 6.30 p.m. a 40-kilometre trip to Fukuoka takes about two hours by car, if one goes by the expensive tollway from Iizuka. Driving on the 'normal' roads increases travelling time to about three hours. The roads to Kita Kyushu and Kokura are also congested, although the relatively new Kyushu Tollway, extending from Omuta to Kokura, has an interchange at Nogata, so local people have access to the expensive expressway, albeit by a roundabout route.

Although the major centres in Kyushu are geographically close, travelling is so time-consuming that the area remains isolated to a large extent. Lack of transportation services is one factor contributing to the depression of certain towns in Chikuho, in particular Tagawa and Kawasaki. Moves to prepare land for industrial development have failed over the years to produce any marked improvement in local economies, primarily because the transportation costs have become so expensive that these ventures have proved to be untenable, according to one official government source.[3]

Within Chikuho there have been some conspicuous post-coal success stories, and many failures. Iizuka and Nogata stand out as two towns that have been able to shrug off the stigma of associations with the coal industry and develop competitive local industries, generally service-sector oriented. Tagawa, Kawasaki, Hojo, Miyada, Sueda, Inatsuki, Shonai and Kurate are examples of towns that have not been able to rid themselves of the economic depression that hit the area in the wake of the rationalisation of the coal industry. It has been argued by some local activists that both Iizuka and Nogata, by virtue of their proximity to Fukuoka and Kita Kyushu respectively, have been able to take advantage of the high cost of land in the big cities to make their towns appeal to workers in the cities as commuter satellites, or *beddo taunzu*, as they are known. Land is relatively cheap in these towns, and it is possible for young people to buy their own homes. In the big cities this is not really possible for many people, unless there is some family property involved and the young people are prepared to accommodate the parents of the husband.

The Iizuka Council has rezoned many industrial and agricultural areas so that they can be developed, and at the time of writing the building sector was the city's fastest-growing industry. Nogata too has bought out many small farmers, and has allowed the development of housing estates in previously rural sectors. Both towns boast good access to the main centres, and modern shopping arcades and consumer services, unlike most of Chikuho. The 'entertainment areas' are thriving in both towns, and the service sector is going through a boom period at the moment. The rapidly growing population figures attest to the way the towns are attracting outside interest.

In stark contrast are most of the towns in Chikuho. Particularly within the Tagawa region, which includes Kawasaki town, poverty and welfare dependence are rife, consumer facilities remain undeveloped, access to the major centres is still poor, and employment opportunities are limited. Tagawa, which lies 25 kilometres west of Iizuka, is too far from the main Kyushu cities to be considered a potential *beddo taun* and has had to rely on outside interests setting up business ventures within the town. Expressions of interest in Tagawa and Kawasaki have been few, and the towns have continued to display the highest unemployment and welfare statistics in the country. Kawasaki, in 1986, had almost 28 per cent welfare dependence, according to official figures.[4] Statistics in 1986 showed that there was less than 2 per cent welfare dependence nationally. This same trend continued into

1988–89, national statistics dropping to less than 1 per cent, while Tagawa-gun[5] and Kawasaki in particular maintained high levels of welfare dependence. In 1989 Kawasaki had the highest level of welfare recipience per capita in the nation with 25.3 per cent.[6]

The welfare dependence of people within the region is in large part a legacy of the coal industry withdrawing when the switch over to oil was in full swing in the 1960s. Largely due to the monopolistic nature of the industry, when the big coal companies closed down there were few alternative industries able to take their place within the local economy. Communities that had been totally dependent on coal were left with few viable alternative economic options and fewer resources. Not only primary, but also secondary and tertiary sectors that had been dependent on the coal industry were forced out of business when the population in the towns decreased and cash flow almost halted in the immediate post-coal period. Government aid was introduced to offer emergency relief, but it is noticeable that the mining companies and local governments neglected to develop any contingency plans for the region, even though the closure of the mines was neither sudden nor unplanned.

Unemployment increased dramatically, and because compensation for the coal companies' damage to farmers' lands was not forthcoming from the mining companies responsible (fields had sunk as they were undermined, water had become polluted and flooding was common), many farmers faced bankruptcy for the first time. Traditionally the agricultural sector in Japan benefits from a gerrymander,[6] and farmers often find themselves well looked after politically. In this case, however, the coalowners' lobby was more powerful, and the farmers' associations were unable to press their own interests. Poorly compensated for mining damage, many farmers were forced off their land. This in turn had the effect of opening up a quite substantial amount of land near the main towns for either industrial or private development, and concurrently added to the welfare statistics.[7] Secondary and tertiary industries have rallied over the past ten years or so in some of the main centres, but this has always been at the expense of the primary sector. In fact the situation has become so serious for farmers that they have been dubbed 'welfare farmers'. The majority of farmers in the region are part-timers who are forced to take what seasonal work there is available: labouring, truck driving, forestry work, for example.

Tagawa City

Tagawa is the largest city in Tagawa-gun, and the smallest city in Japan, with a population of approximately 59,000. Within the city are a number of discrete ex-coalmining villages, which, although once relatively autonomous, are now officially part of the city's jurisdiction. A 'M-san town',[8] Tagawa was almost totally dependent on the coal industry, and on the company's goodwill. The company supplied housing and also finance for consumer services, which were established to service the coalminers and their families. City officials were often seconded from the company, as were police chiefs and other community leaders. A number of former company executives were mayors of the city from the 1920s, when operations started, until 1975.

Although the city is moving slowly into the 1990s, facilities are still relatively undeveloped: shopping arcades have been built, but with the exception of a new complex built in 1991, these offer a limited range of goods at expensive prices. Therefore many shoppers go to Iizuka where the department stores offer wider choices of consumer items at cheaper prices. Some cultural facilities have been developed, such as the Cultural Centre, which was completed in 1982, and in 1985 a new central gymnasium was built on a demolished coalmine site. There is talk of building a new art gallery if the funds can be allocated, but this seems unlikely to be started within the next five years. There is one major hospital and a number of small, specialised clinics, but medical services are strictly limited, so serious cases are taken to Iizuka or Nogata, where the facilities are much better. A public library employs three people, and is in a state of disrepair.

Education facilities are also poor. There are four high schools, which have the reputation of being among the worst in the prefecture academically. Although there is a junior university, which specialises in welfare and kindergarten teaching, in 1988 there were no students from Tagawa at the university. It is a public university and as such is difficult to enter. Because the level of education in Tagawa is so poor, the students who go to the city schools cannot hope to get into such an illustrious, albeit technical, university.

The M-san company's lack of interest in the city has contributed to the retarded revival of the local economy. When the last of the four main Tagawa mines closed in 1970, with the exception of the M-san tile factory, which employed approximately 250 workers, M-san withdrew its financial support from the region. The company, however, has maintained real estate offices to collect rent from the miners and miners' families who live in the *tanjū*, before they are rebuilt (at government expense). Responsibility for the maintenance of the *tanjū* has been delegated to local government as part of an arrangement between the company and the government, which in effect has meant that the miners themselves are expected to maintain the rented housing at their own expense.

M-san has also invested a considerable sum in building a mining museum at the site of the number two mine, which is next to the Ita *tanjū*. This museum is a self-congratulatory tribute to the role of the company in generating employment and building the city of Tagawa. There are no records of the accidents, deaths, violence or crime that accompanied mining. It is so antiseptic that an uncritical observer would assume that the happy miners lived in luxury within a system of paternal guidance, working in only the most modern conditions that technology could provide. The stories of the miners are decidedly contradictory to this official view, and most of the local population have dismissed the museum as an example of M-san propaganda.

Tagawa's local economy

The economy of Tagawa is improving gradually, according to govern-ment figures and reports, as excesses within the system are trimmed and strengths consolidated.[9] However, although the statistics support this position, there have been many conspicuous business failures with-in the city over the past ten years. The appreciation of the yen in 1986 had a particularly damaging effect on export-oriented factories. For example, the Pioneer Car Stereo factory established in 1971 originally employed more than 500 workers, selling its products through an arrangement with Datsun (Nissan) America, but in 1987 was forced to close down as the increasing value of the yen reduced the competitive-ness of the products overseas.

Although a number of clothing and electronics factories have been established within the Tagawa region in the post-coal years, these employ predominantly women as 'part-time' labour, a peculiarly Japanese classification, which means that women are required to work as hard as men, but are paid much less because they are 'casual' workers.[10] The owners have resisted unionisation because unions mean 'trouble', as I was often told, and so the women sell their labour for between 300 and 500 yen an hour,[11] without the benefits received by full-time company workers, such as bonuses in lieu of holidays. There is a large pool of unemployed women desperately in need of work in the area, so they are prepared to take whatever work they can get, and the owners of these factories are prepared to get what they can from the women at the cheapest price possible.

> If you join a union, or even try to join a union the company just fires you. It's as simple as that. At the clothing factory there are more than 50 people employed but no one is in the union. You see it's just asking for trouble, and we're lucky to have any work at all, so we take what we can get even though the men there get more than five times the hourly rate we do. Of course, we don't get sick pay or bonuses like the men do, but we're lucky to have the work so although we know that it's unfair we don't complain about it.[12]

A breakdown of the workforce statistics shows three major growth sectors within the local economy: small business, the service sector and local government. The building industry was hit by a mini recession in the early part of 1984 and has not yet fully recovered. Agriculture figures show that there are still some two thousand or so people officially employed within this sector, but the majority of these are working part-time and are dependent on welfare to tide them over the lean winter months, according to the Department of Welfare Services. The manufacturing industry, which was the industry most likely to succeed in the post-coal period, after an initially strong showing has been severely damaged by the high yen and by the lack of development capital. Only the service sector, small businesses and the local bureaucracy have really developed.

The implications of this are wide-ranging. The number of Tagawa residents who work outside the city is increasing every year, because the local economic infrastructure cannot cope with the size of the working population. As a result, only those businesses sponsored by outside interests and employing predominantly women and those catering to the consumerism of the local population appear to survive comfortably. Bars, eateries, *pachinko* parlours and nightclubs are still viable concerns, many of these being run by women on a part-time basis. Corner shops still abound, as do *sake* shops, and small supermarkets, and in recent years, video stores. There are now also two major department stores in Tagawa.

The marked increase in government personnel coincides with the recent government initiative to reduce welfare spending. It seems as though a large number of additional personnel are required to handle the added burden of cutting welfare payments to local people (see chapters 14 and 15). There is irony here, as one Tagawa City welfare worker says, in that the government is spending more money on wages for welfare workers and establishing complex and expensive procedures to limit government spending.[13] Certainly this is not the only reason that the numbers of local government staff have increased: city officials cite the new medical insurance scheme as being very labour intensive, for example.[14] The rebuilding of the *tanjū* in the city has also resulted in employment within official government ranks for workers who would otherwise have been classified as building industry personnel.

Tagawa-gun and Kawasaki

Kawasaki has a population of approximately 22,000 and lies about 12 kilometres to the east of Tagawa City. Predominantly a rural settlement these days, it was once a major coal-producing town, being the headquarters of the U-san mining company. The infamous H-san mine (see chapters 6 and 7), once regarded as the most dangerous and violent of all the coalmines, was located within the town itself. Laid out like many coal towns with streets barely wide enough to allow two cars to pass and dwellings cramped together on either side of the streets, the town looks like a Hollywood western set. Few buildings are more than two storeys high, dating from the early 1940s, and most are made of weatherboard stained dark-brown. There are *sake* shops, many bars and eateries, and some grocery shops, but although there are general stores, a Seven Eleven, and other 'convenience stores', most locals go into the bigger cities, such as Tagawa and Iizuka, to buy most of their consumer items.

Near the centre of town are a number of the so-called 'improved housing' areas. These apartments fall into two categories: the five-storey concrete and rusting steel slums, and the two-storey concrete and rusting steel slums. Both types in Kawasaki were among the first to be rebuilt under the Coal Slums Rebuilding Program, and the age of the buildings is immediately noticeable. When the buildings were first erected, in the early 1950s, to replace the old *naya seido*, they were no doubt an improvement on the dilapidated U-san-owned company housing, but today they are testimony to the lack of foresight of local and national governments, which seem to have simply built slums to replace slums. Especially in the two-storey apartments, the locals have collected a variety of multi-hued tin sheets and old weatherboards, and added ramshackle extensions to the original design in order to house the increasing number of family members, creating a flamboyant mosaic of shapes, materials and colours. In some of these apartments, which are rented by the residents, more than ten people are crammed together in two bedrooms.[15]

There are three junior high schools, generally used as feeder schools for the Tagawa high schools, and one high school in Kawasaki. The reputation for violence in these schools is second to none. There are a large number of criminal charges brought against students annually, and many teachers have had some sort of violent attack made against their person.[16] Knives, *nanchaku*, *kendo* sticks, and occasionally firearms are confiscated from students during the course of the year, according to the principal of the local high school. Not surprisingly, the level of scholastic achievement is very low.

There is one small, local hospital, which caters primarily for the aged and infirm, and one mental hospital. Because medical facilities have not really been developed since the coalmining days, seriously ill patients are taken to hospitals in Nogata or Iizuka. The ambulance service is unreliable, so local people rely on the Tagawa service, which is both expensive and inconvenient.

The building industry has gone through a revival recently, with the contract to rebuild a local coalminers' settlement awarded to a consortium of local companies rumoured to be associated with the local *yakuza* organisation. Other building projects, generally associated with the Coal Slums Rebuilding Program are also flourishing as the program reaches its nexus (work is scheduled to be completed on this project by 1995) and employment in this sector is relatively high at the time of writing. Also Nishikawa Hausu, a large building firm, has bought some of the old slag-heaps and is in the process of levelling them and building housing estates on the land to cater for the demand for private housing in the area. However, the service sector and other small businesses in the town have yet to experience the growth that is so widespread in the service sector throughout most of the Chikuho region. No figures were available on the breakdown of industry in the town.

Welfare

Although this topic will be treated in much more detail in chapters 14 and 15, it is necessary to outline briefly the situation in Tagawa here. Since the mid-1960s, Tagawa-gun has had the highest per capita ratio of welfare recipients in Japan.[17] This is related not only to the coal industry withdrawing its support from the region, but also to the poor economic infrastructure established during this period. Nagasue (1973) has pointed out that the government was negligent in allowing the coal companies to get away with what he refers to as a 'scandalous abuse of human rights' when they quit the region.[18] He goes on to say that the influence the M-san company was able to exert on the government, supported by the Liberal Democratic Party (LDP), in delegating the responsibility of cleaning up the area to local governments was equal to 'signing the death warrant of Tagawa'.[19]

The onus of restructuring the economy was placed firmly with the local Chamber of Commerce, a group of local businessmen with good intentions, good coal-industry connections and very little experience in dealing with the type of social and economic problems they faced. Rather than trying to foster interest in the region, they concentrated their efforts in getting government grants to support public works programs. The result of this policy was that Tagawa had some excellent roads within six months of the introduction of the plan and huge numbers of unemployed workers receiving the 12-month coal unemployment benefit. Unemployment had reached 45 per cent by 1965, and the unemployed were encouraged to leave town and get work elsewhere, rather than draining local coffers of funds.[20] (The local government was required to subsidise 30 per cent of the unemployment funds, the prefecture 50 per cent, and the national government 20 per cent.)

Although Tagawa was severely affected by the demise of the coal industry, other towns (such as Kawasaki) were even more seriously crippled. Tagawa had some secondary industry, but in Kawasaki there was virtually nothing other than coal and its by-products. This history of unemployment has had a potent effect on the present welfare situation.

Tagawa-gun not only has the highest per capita welfare recipience, but also the highest ratio of drug abuse and violent crime in Japan.[21] Although Tagawa City has recently made inroads into cutting welfare spending, Kawasaki has remained the town most dependent on welfare. In 1984 the national government introduced a new policy, which was aimed at reducing the number of people dependent on welfare. This was to be achieved through the narrowing of eligibility for benefits and a shift of the burden of support to recipients' relatives. For example, if an applicant for welfare had immediate family (father, son, brother, sister, cousin, uncle, aunt, etc.) who was earning more than the designated poverty line, the social worker employed to handle the case was required to write a letter to these family members asking whether they would financially support the applicant, 'for their country'.[22] On top of this, the applicant was required to demonstrate that he or she had no visible means of support, and no property that could be sold for cash (farmers being the exception here).

This policy has had the effect of limiting the number of people who are eligible for welfare, and placing considerable social and financial pressure on the families of the elderly, unemployed, sick and handicapped people who might apply for welfare. In Tagawa-gun, where there is a very high per capita aged population (more than 15 per cent),[23] local people, already low income earners, have had to bear the added financial burden of a government policy that denies them reasonable and equitable pension and welfare payments. According to the head of one welfare office in Tagawa-gun, the government is desperate to reduce welfare dependence statistics to less than 1 per cent nationally to persuade domestic and overseas critics of Japan's limited welfare expenditure that the Japanese people do not need excessive welfare benefits. Tagawa has been identified as the main problem area.[24]

The welfare issue is not confined to the older generations either. In March 1988 I interviewed a number of male and female high school students in the Tagawa region, asking them what they intended to do after they left school. One in three answered that they would be quite happy to go on welfare like their parents, and become what is known in the local parlance as '*pachinko* pros'. That is, they would use their welfare incomes to support a lifestyle based on one of the few methods of gambling legitimately available to Japanese, the pinball-like *pachinko*. Other students were quick to tell me that they were not interested in this rather mindless pastime, and that they would choose to join the ranks of the *bōsōzoku*, or street-car gangs, traditionally the first step towards becoming a *yakuza*.

Some academics from the Japan National University of Welfare Studies in Nagoya recently targeted the region as a prime example of the inequalities of the system of welfare distribution. One of these academics, who concentrated his research in Kawasaki and Miyada, concluded that the welfare dependence of the region has come about through a number of variables which frustrate the efforts of local people to develop an alternative and viable economic framework in accordance with local cultural values. He maintains the system of welfare is both too lenient and inadequate, allowing corruption of the system and the awarding of welfare to people who do not need it, such as the local *yakuza*, while the needy are denied their legitimate right to government support.[25] This opinion is ratified by many welfare recipients.[26]

Many welfare social workers confided in me that they were aware that the system had been squeezed by the parsimonious bureaucracy and the coercive crime syndicates. It is certainly more than coincidence that most official *yakuza* members in Tagawa-gun are also welfare recipients.[27] Yet there is widespread poverty within the region, and in the two years I lived there I heard of two cases of people refused welfare who subsequently died of starvation. These cases were not reported by the press, but the welfare workers were aware of them. In fact two social worker informants confirmed these cases to me individually.

Crime

Crime in Tagawa-gun has been a major problem for police and local administrators since the coalmining days. Organised crime, run by the notorious T-san *yakuza* group, has caused many social problems over the years. In Tagawa-gun, the 300-strong T-san have had a pervasive and destructive influence on local issues since pre-war days. Like other *yakuza* organisations in the region, they have a long history of involvement with coal companies, an issue assessed in chapters 3, 5 and 13.

This group controls the drug trade in the region, and is responsible for the introduction, from Thailand, of narcotics and amphetamines into Tagawa.[28] The amphetamines, taken intravenously, constitute a social problem, although the extent of illegal drug use in the region is not closely monitored. The extent of the problem can be surmised from accounts by youth workers and *yakuza* and from observations, such as in bars and nightclubs, where signs asking visitors to refrain from taking drugs on the premises are in evidence. Many of the older members of the *yakuza* are addicts themselves. The group uses a wide variety of people to distribute the drugs, often through channels selected for being unsuspected, such as hospitals. In the press there were more than 35 recorded instances of individuals arrested for possessing and selling drugs in hospitals in the first six months of my research. In three instances old women over the age of 65 were caught passing the drugs to clients within hospital grounds.[29]

Apart from the drug trade, the *yakuza* are well known for their involvement with protection rackets and gambling. It appears that most, if not all, the nightclubs and bars in Tagawa and Kawasaki pay protection money to *yakuza* to prevent 'unfortunate accidents' occurring.[30] The *yakuza* justify this extortion by depicting it as a form of insurance to prevent gangsters from outside the area coming into town to demand the same sort of protection from the owners of these establishments. *Yakuza* interests also include *pachinko* parlours, the so-called 'love motels', prostitution and building companies.

A number of *yakuza* are well connected politically, and the *mochi ritsu mota retsu* (give and take) principle applies in most political dealings involving these people. In 1985 the Socialist mayor of Soeda was assassinated by the *yakuza*, ostensibly as a response to his plan to outlaw the T-san *guni* in his town by stripping them of their rights to own and operate on local property. The killers of the mayor were never caught, and in the subsequent election a conservative mayor was elected without opposition. Despite the conspicuous nature of the police's anti-*yakuza* campaigns — slogans in place outside town halls throughout Chikuho exhort the population to 'Clean up the city from the *yakuza*' — the police presence seems to be mainly symbolic. For example, twice a year police and the local Tagawa City government mount vociferous anti-*yakuza* campaigns. Trucks emblazoned with signs declaring 'Stamp out the *yakuza* presence now!' and 'Report your local *yakuza* to the police and help your fellow citizen' drive through the city streets blasting out these and other slogans from loudspeakers mounted on the truck roofs. But the people largely ignore them. They seem to be too afraid to rebel openly against the *yakuza*.

I was told many stories by a number of locals about the repercussions of informing on the *yakuza*, most involving violent sanctions, but some entailed the imposition of economic strictures, reinforced by the political system. For instance, an old man told me that he challenged the head of the *yakuza* about some 'low' *yakuza* soldiers (*chimpira*) receiving welfare while he and his wife were forced to live on soy-beans and radishes. The local gangsters called at his home and destroyed the small plot of land on which he grew his vegetables, and then applied pressure to the local welfare workers to make sure that he was unable to claim any welfare benefits.[31]

The Tagawa *yakuza* are also notorious throughout southern Japan for insurance scams. The *modus operandi* seems to be that two or three *yakuza* cars (generally black luxury Toyota Crown or Nissan Cedric saloons) surround a single car on the main local roads, and force the driver to brake suddenly, crashing into the back or side of one of their cars. Because the system of litigation is undeveloped in Japan, parties in accidents where no injury is occasioned must sort out the issue of insurance between themselves, generally employing a third party who specialises in this sort of work. In these instances the *yakuza* use standover tactics to ensure that the insurance policy is paid out to their headquarters, and that their own cars are repaired gratis by using their own paid-up 'third party'. When I was living in the *tanjū* I received in the mail the following notice:

All drivers in the Tagawa region are asked to beware of drivers in the following types of cars, and with the following types of number plates [list of about 30 cars and their number plates]. When drivers see these cars, it is best to pull off the road immediately, and where possible contact your local police station.
[Signed by the local police chief]

Nevertheless, these days most citizens regard the *yakuza* as a weakened and relatively harmless group. This is because they appear to confine their most serious violence to internecine fights, with the occasional venture into mainstream society confined to right-wing political activism, a traditional *yakuza* arena.

Perhaps the most insidious influence that the *yakuza* have had on the region is to blacken the name of Chikuho, and Tagawa in particular, as *yakuza* territory, thus reinforcing outsiders' prejudices towards local people. Even within Chikuho, Tagawa and Kawasaki are regarded as 'dangerous' places. Before I moved into the *tanjū* at Tagawa I was warned by most of my fellow Kurate (a town in Chikuho) residents to 'be careful' when I was driving in Tagawa, to watch out for black Toyota Crown sedans, and to be careful about what I said to the locals for fear of some sort of repercussions. In Fukuoka many carparks will not allow cars with Chikuho number plates in, because they fear for the welfare of their regular customers.

This conviction that the Tagawa people are 'dark' and 'dangerous' is reinforced by the local car mania, which culminates every year with the New Year's Eve parade of 'hot' cars, their mufflers removed, complete with Japanese flags, gaudy paintwork, and half-naked occupants hanging out every window, driving two abreast up the dual carriageways from Tagawa to Kita Kyushu. This procession starts at about 8 p.m. and carries on until 5 or 6 a.m. the next day. The drivers are drunk or drugged and accidents are common, but the police keep a prudently low profile, not having the numbers to deal with the thousands of cars on the roads. These car gangs are referred to as *bōsōzoku*, a generic term that includes bikies as well as young delinquent groups. The police make a point of publicly prosecuting a number of these gangs every year, presumably to reassure the public that they are doing something about this rebelliousness.

Youth gangs, often related to the *bōsōzoku*, have been responsible for some exceptionally violent crimes in the region over the past few years. The most memorable of these was picked up by the national press in January 1989, and concerned a group of five youths, three boys and two girls in their early to late teens, who hijacked a 23-year-old man in his small car after he refused to give them a ride, set fire to his car, and incinerated him on a mountain pass near Tagawa. The public outrage this act engendered was nationwide in scope, and was made worse by the fact that only one of the gang was of an age where he could be brought to trial under the legal system. Because the other members were officially minors, they were held to be exempt from the judicial process and have been exonerated. In February of the same year, in another well-reported case, two brothers, aged 12 and 13, strangled their grandmother in her bath because she would not give them their 'pocket money'. Such incidents help to reinforce outsiders' belief that Chikuho people are 'dangerous', 'violent' and 'social outcasts', and no doubt have some effect on outside interests choosing to ignore the area as having investment potential.

Tagawa-ben

Another aspect of the Tagawa region that is worthy of mention is its local dialect. Although each region in Japan has its own dialect, and some are more obscure and incomprehensible than others, the Tagawa dialect stands out as one of the 'dirtiest' of all of them. Tagawa-ben, as it is called, uses not only *all* the swear words of Japanese, often indiscriminately and liberally thrown into general conversation, but also a peculiar inflection, which has caused outsiders to remark that the participants in the conversation must be fighting with each other.

Surprisingly, the women also use this variation of Japanese in their daily conversation, even with men, something unheard of in most parts of Japan, doing away with the niceties of the traditionally feminine, so-called 'standard Japanese'. Many of my informants were quick to point out that using the local dialect was one way of getting to know people, and that when one used the 'cold and impersonal' standard Japanese one could never get to know the person hiding behind the mask of civility the language erected.

From outside, the Tagawa language appears uncouth in a country where educated people pride themselves on their linguistic standardisation and ability. It has become a social stigma, so that Fukuoka people, for example, are instantly aware of a person's peasant or coalfields background when they open their mouths. Although there has been a revival of pride in the dialect over recent years, largely due to the conspicuous efforts of some locally prominent older people, the young people who move to other cities and towns try to adopt standard Japanese as their means of communication, lapsing into local dialect only when they are drunk or return home to visit their parents. In many ways it is analogous to a situation when a Geordie (from Tyneside in the north of England) gets a job in London, assumes the airs of the business community there, and reassumes the mantle of the Newcastle accent, with all its social loadings, when he or she comes home.

Tagawa-gun is distinguished by a number of factors that makes it a fascinating place to study. Most of the features described above would fit into a pattern of depressed working-class existence in many societies, but what makes it noteworthy is that in Japan, where the government has been conspicuously busy trying to create the impression that society is controlled, well-mannered, and free of many of the social upheavals of overseas societies, Chikuho (and Tagawa in particular) have retained their individuality. The economic depression of the area and the concomitant high incidence of crime and welfare dependency mark the region as anathema to the concept that most Japanese and foreigners alike hold about Japanese society today. Contemporary Chikuho owes many of its problems to the legacy of the coal industry, and it will be one of my aims to demonstrate this in the course of this book

It is at this stage that the introduction of the Chikuho revivalists is in order. This group of people came from disparate backgrounds, with many quite esoteric political aims, sharing a commitment to the region and to the people of the region. Their activities over the years since the coal companies began to withdraw have prompted social change and a reassessment of the value of the industry to the region as a whole.

By focusing on these people the relations of power that existed in the coalfields, and the subsequent modification of these relations over time become apparent. The revivalists acted as foci for dissent towards the state and the coal companies. They also acted as catalysts to bring about a sense of regional identity which was lacking in the face of strong company propaganda that attempted to replace 'region' with 'company' as the seminal concept for social identification.

NOTES TO CHAPTER 1

1 Idegawa, 1984 p.5; Ueno, 1985a, pp.5–6.
2 Oguchi, interview, 1988.
3 Tagawa City survey of transport problems, 1988.
4 *Kotoshi no Tōkei Fukuoka*, 1989, pp.18–20.
5 A 'gun' is a district within the prefecture, which is responsible to the appropriate prefectural bureaucracy. Under the umbrella of the 'gun' are communities not large enough to be called cities. The administration of government services to these communities is the responsibility of the prefectural government, through their agents in the 'gun' representative offices.
6 *Fukushi ni Tsuite no Tōkei*, 1990, p.47.
7 By 1986 the percentage of rural households in Tagawa, for example, had decreased to less than 4 per cent, even fewer than in Fukuoka City. (Source: Fukuoka Prefecture Statistics, 1988: 50.)
8 The M-san company owned the coal franchise for Tagawa City, and also owned many smaller enterprises in town. As a result, in its heyday in the 1950s and 1960s, more than 70 per cent of the workforce was employed by M-san or its subsidiaries.
9 *Tagawa Shishi*, 1979, pp.441–60.
10 See Lebra (1984), Lo (1990), Eccleston (1989) and Saso (1990) for more comprehensive descriptions of the conditions of women's part-time, or full-time labour.
11 This was equivalent to between approximately 20 per cent and 25 per cent of the average wage in 1987, according to figures released by the Ministy of Labour in 1988.
12 Nishiguchi, interview, 1989.
13 Miyoshi, interview, 1988.
14 In 1984 the national government introduced the 123 Legislation, which recommended that welfare costs should be reduced. As the population ages, welfare is expected to be one of the largest items of the budget, so it also recommended that the prefectures and cities actively address the problem of long-term welfare dependence; private superannuation schemes, medical schemes and job retraining schemes were to be encouraged at the city and town level. Chikuho, in particular, was singled out for its statistical waywardness in not reducing welfare expenditure in line with the rest of the nation.
15 Oguchi, interview, 1988.
16 Interview with the staff of Kawasaki Ikeijiri High School, 1988.
17 Kumo interview, 1988; Takashima, 1989, p.2, Mishima, interview, 1989.
18 Nagasue, 1973, p.132.
19 Ibid. p.136.
20 *Kotoshi no Seikatsu Hōgo ni okeru Tōkei* 1980, p.45.
21 Kumo, interview, 1989.
22 Although the form letter sent to the relatives of the welfare applicant is only a 'request' it carries a lot of weight, phrased as it is in nationalistic terms. Kumo and many of his welfare workers objected vehemently to this practice, because they perceive it as demeaning to both the applicant and his/her family.
23 *Kotoshi no Seikatsu Hōgo ni okeru Tōkei*, 1988, p.28.
24 Kumo, interview, 1988.
25 Otoma, 1986, pp.45–8.
26 See Takashima, 1988, for example.
27 Chikara (former *yakuza*) interview, 1988.
28 Chikara (former *yakuza* member), interview, 1988.
29 See Chikuho sections of *Nishi Nihon Shinbun*, 17 January and 6 July, 1988, and *Asahi Shinbun*, 23 February 1988, for example.
30 Sato, interview, 1988.
31 Shiroiwa, interview, 1988.

CHAPTER 2

The Chikuho Revivalists

Recently the 'City Building' (*machi-zukuri*) movement, which seeks to distance itself from Chikuho's past 'negative' experience, has become dominant within Chikuho politics. Many of the past violent confrontations between miners and company officials, police and *yakuza* have been ignored, unions are remembered as 'socially disruptive forces', and the legendary warmth of the coal communities is forgotten as local governments attempt to throw off the stigma of the coal years. This rewriting of history is to facilitate new economic and social plans, which are sanctioned by both the prefectural and national governments. The intention of those who thus rewrite Chikuho history is to soothe the fears of would-be investors in the region.

Analyses of the coal companies' roles in the development of Chikuho's economy have been well documented, especially in academic journals and local histories. However, the withdrawal of companies' economic support from the region and the reasons for the subsequent economic and social decline of the area for the most part have been ignored. And while numerous studies have emphasised the economic role of the companies,[1] studies that deal with the people who worked for the companies are rare.

Although it is reasonable to say that the majority of young people in the area are aware of the region's coal background, few have experienced the coal industry at first hand. These young people are becoming more and more dependent on the education system to teach them about the past. To a large extent this is because the tradition of oral folk history passed on by senior members of the family to younger members is being eroded as society moves away from the extended family, once common in Chikuho, to the nuclear family geared to the electronic media. Television, video and computer games have had a widely felt and powerful influence on the population. Discussion within the family is becoming less common, as the difference between generations is made more formal, something reinforced by the mass media.[2]

Young people are targeted by aggressive television companies, which aim a large percentage of their early evening and early morning programs at them. Rather than relying on the written media, young people usually get news from the television. Reading is, understandably, often perceived as 'study', and the distinction between study and play is well understood in a society that places overwhelming educational demands on its youth, even when the educational standard is relatively low. As a result, reading for relaxation is often confined to reading comics, generally escapist in content, although sometimes the young people I associated with actually read 'educational comics'.

The so-called 'generation gap' has become an abyss with the invasion of the electronic media. Rather than calling it a 'generation gap' it is probably fairer to call this quite tangible separation of values an 'information gap'. The older generation, although self-confessed television addicts and as susceptible to suggestion as the younger people, still read newspapers and books. This is not the case with many young people, especially those who do not go on to tertiary education. Consequently young people in particular are exposed to only three consistent sources of information concerning contemporary and past events: television, comics and school.

For all its working-class background, people living in Chikuho towns and cities have embraced the values of middle-class consumer society with as much vigour as people living in more cosmopolitan regions.[3] Therefore, with education, as with many aspects of society, the system promotes those standards deemed to be necessary to produce 'good' citizens; that is, middle-class standards. Although Chikuho students are not particularly scholarly on average, the value of education is constantly reinforced to students. Without entering into a discussion on the relative merits of the Japanese system, it can be said that the onus is placed on individuals within the education system to learn 'facts', so that these facts can be regurgitated at will in exams. Interpretation of information is *not* necessary to pass examinations in the humanities. Also, by stressing the importance of other subjects at the expense of local history (an understanding of local history is not going to improve a student's chances of passing university entrance exams), educators have been quite successful in diverting attention away from the region's past and focusing attention on the future, 'preparing' these people to become the administrators of the twenty-first century. Those controlling the Japanese education system and the newly emerging 'infotainment' industries can choose what sort of material to present to the youth as 'history'.

History has become a commodity in the hands of a cynical and conservative government. Because there are few sources that refute official versions of history, or even modify accounts, the duopoly of information control would seem to be complete, and it could be assumed that mass perceptions of history have been or will be standardised. Those who *could* criticise official versions of Chikuho history are gradually dying out, and with them will go the last oral histories of the region, seen from the bottom up, as it were. Yet underneath the dominant all-encompassing view of history is an underlying chord of discontent. Although it is only just starting to be articulated, the rumblings of disquiet are being felt throughout Chikuho, as more people come forward to give their versions of their own history.

In recent years there have been a number of attempts by local people to develop an alternative to the 'official' history of the Chikuho region. These efforts have been diverse in scope and content, but have had the common thread that they, like the local governments, are attempting to disperse the dark image of Chikuho. However, the aims of the groups could not be more different. The government appears to be trying to mould the views of young people to conform with their plan to 'attack the future'. In doing this, it seems to indicate that the dark events of the past should be forgotten.

Opposition to this approach to understanding history starts from the basic position that the official coal histories are inaccurate, selective and serve only to protect the interests and reputations of capitalist coalmine-owners and government officials. Only a few have access to, or interest in, these unofficial histories, and although they have no single, formal association with any political party, the individuals involved share the common belief that the LDP is corrupt and the Emperor system of government (based on the assumption that Japanese society is ordered by 'divine decree') is flawed. They have attempted in their own ways to develop a folk history, or series of folk histories, with the intention of creating a counter-culture within the region. To some extent these efforts have not been in vain, although they are complicated by a population diverse in both class and culture.

In recent years one woman has had a powerful influence on the actions of this group: Idegawa, who is an employee of the Kurate town museum is an author of a book on women coalminers and also of many papers published in different journals and newsletters. She has been vocal in her criticisms of how the area is perceived. To a large extent

she owes a professional debt to the writing of Ueno Eishin, a Kyoto
University professor who worked as a coalminer in the region and
published a series of books and photographic collections of Chikuho
coalminers. Ueno, an avowed Marxist, came to the area in the 1960s,
before it was fashionable among leftist scholars to do so, and stayed on
to write about his understanding of the coal industry until his death in
1988. Idegawa became his close friend and has adopted the mantle of
responsibility for carrying on his work, although she has a very different political orientation, steering clear of Marxist academic rhetoric,
while maintaining the integrity of Ueno's philanthropy.

Idegawa is only one of a number of people involved in reconstructing
the history of Chikuho from a humanist perspective. Other people,
from teachers at local schools to an outspoken, often radical group led
by a former Red Army operative, have also attempted to change the
perception of Chikuho people about their own history. I shall look at
the actions of some of these individuals and organisations in later
chapters.

The official view

The official history of Chikuho is that allowed by the coal companies.
Local politicians have been instrumental in publishing official city and
town histories, partly or completely sponsored by the companies,
thanks in large part to the influence of ex-company men in high government positions. Japanese cities and towns traditionally have written
local histories, which are published by the relevant prefectural governments. These histories have been selective about the information
disseminated on controversial and potentially politically damaging
topics, such as the misallocation of company funds, political corruption, poverty, crime, unemployment and social upheavals. Although in
Tagawa's case some of these items are touched upon within the history,
most are either neglected, or hidden within the statistical sections. As
the purpose of these histories is to provide a record of the relevant city's
and town's development from feudal times, it is not surprising that
local governments prefer the authors to concentrate on the more
romantic and positive aspects of their histories, such as local archae-
ological finds and the rapid transition cities have made into the
twentieth century because of the efforts of local industries.

While there is certainly some accuracy in these accounts, they are
selective about the information used. In none of the histories relevant
to my account have I found any indication that there have been social
and economic problems of the magnitude that my informants have
described, although the *Tagawa Shishi* does have references to labour

strikes in the region. There is a large section on the problems that followed the withdrawal of the coal industry from Tagawa in this series, but the relationship between the coal industry and, for example, unemployment is ignored. Comprehensive sections of the history describe in detail the measures introduced by the local and prefectural governments to counter the wide range of social problems that erupted in the wake of the industry's demise, but these sections are primarily concerned with statistics, describing, for example, how much money was paid by which government to which fund.[4] Conspicuously, there are few references to company involvement in the reconstruction of the areas, mainly because there was so little. For entirely different reasons, there are also no specific references to the nature of the work, particularly to accident statistics and incidences of violence, *yakuza* involvement and labour confrontations.

The argument presented by city officials to support the integrity of such official histories is that they are concerned only with concrete 'facts', specifically facts recorded by government sources at the time of the event. Opinions and interpretations are seen as being potentially misleading to the reader, because they represent only what individual authors perceive as the truth. Therefore, in the case of the series of labour strikes that rocked the industry in the 1960s, official histories are restricted to presenting the statistics of how many production days were lost, how many men were in which union, when the strike was settled, and the material extent of any damage to company property by the strikers.[5] Company and police violence, methods employed in breaking a strike, the reasons for a strike, and the number of strikers injured or sacked are irrelevant to the accounts in these publications.

Perhaps the most important neglected data concern the people themselves. Official local histories are concerned with government initiatives, industry planning and economic statistics in the period since records have been kept, and not with any ideological standpoint, as city and town officials explained to me on numerous occasions. In other words, although the histories purport to disclaim individual bias, and concentrate on the macro perspective of the towns, without the need for 'personalised, and therefore subjective accounts',[6] by disregarding the opinions of the people who have lived and worked in the area their entire lives, they have effectively nullified the value of their efforts.

It is to fill these gaps that what I will henceforth refer to as the 'Chikuho revivalists' came into being. This is an artificial construct, which I have employed to encompass a wide range of alternative approaches to 'official' versions of Chikuho history and contemporary society. Although there is an association in Chikuho that goes by this name, its operations are limited, and include a monthly publication of leftist literature. The term 'revivalists', as I use it includes a wider frame of reference. Although many people who belong to this informal grouping of revivalists are bound by ties of history, culture and social motivation, it is only because of the efforts of people such as Idegawa and Oguchi, the *kami shibai* man (see chapter 5), who have acted as 'go-betweens', bringing together, physically as well as in context, people who otherwise might never have met, that there is any cohesion at all within this group.[7]

Within the alternative paradigms that are gradually emerging are the perceptions of people such as Chikara, the ex-*yakuza* member who is now the headman of the village in which Oguchi lives. Chikara has taken it upon himself to make the prefectural and national governments pay for the damage they have done to the area. Oguchi, with his seemingly endless range of stories about the coalmines, and his myriad contacts throughout the area's still numerous *tanjū*, has a permanent, if gradually diminishing audience for his interpretations of Chikuho coal history. Teachers, priests and even a couple of journalists are keeping the alternative view of history alive among the younger Chikuho people.

Of all the people I have grouped together under this umbrella of the Chikuho revivalists, only Idegawa and Ishizaki are today consciously involved in passing on their textual interpretations of local history to the people of Chikuho, through their published writing. Other people are the forces behind the reconstruction of local history, the people who actually experienced it, and who have come forward to express their parts in it. They are integral to the text, involved in the text, but removed from the process of textual construction. Their activities in attempting to change the perception of the area and its history have become part of a new wave of energy directed at a new generation of people. To some extent they are history themselves, and it is their history that is represented in the museums.

The coal museums

Within the Chikuho region a number of coal museums have been established in cities that have had close associations with the coal industry. With the exception of the Kurate museum, these have been funded by the coal companies. In Tagawa, M-san sponsored the building and staffing of a very impressive edifice dedicated to the industry. In Nogata, N-san built and staffed a coal museum on the site of the old number four mine. Only in Kurate has the town council had any influence in appointing people to work in the museum, and it is quite noticeable that the Kurate museum operates on a smaller and less conspicuous scale than the big, company-sponsored institutions. Ms Idegawa is the curator of the museum, and thanks to her efforts it has become an example of an alternative perspective of the influence of the coal industry.

The Tagawa museum

The Tagawa museum is a prime example of company propaganda. It is a four-storey, red-brick building on the site of one of the company's mines, within expansive grounds dotted with statues of the heroic miners at work. There is more than half a square kilometre of paved brick, a park and a ground where local sports days, carnivals and festivals are held. The old elevator towers loom above the buildings, repainted, shining examples of the efficiency of M-san's business. Coal trams and other machinery have been restored to pristine condition within an enclosure at the western end of the reserve. The scale of the museum, the grounds and the machinery are all designed to impress the casual observer of the power that the company was able to exert. The sheer size of the exhibits both inside and outside the museum is overwhelming.

In stark contrast are the *tanjū* that border the museum. Mean, decrepit, mud adobe and wooden huts, their sagging roofs and precariously leaning walls supported by liberal quantities of corrugated iron, extend up the hill to where the new, characterless, concrete, five-storey apartments are gradually creeping down the hill, absorbing the old company housing. The road to the *tanjū* is not accessible to visitors to the museum, as a sign prominently declares that it is 'private property' and visitors should keep out. In stark contrast with the smartly dressed visitors and employees of the museum are the inhabitants of the *tanjū*, who are dressed in clothes that look as though they were picked up in a rummage sale. Men dressed in long underwear and *zori* (straw sandals) with *haramaki* (ribbed woollen bands wrapped tightly around their waists) mingle with women in heavy, dark-coloured kimono or quilted *happi* (coats with overlapping front flaps, like karate jackets) and long grey trousers.

The museum has a series of second-floor and third-floor conference rooms, an archive devoted to coal literature situated on the fourth floor, which is not accessible to the public, and on the ground floor a series of exhibits that are the M-san mining centrepiece. The exhibits are worthy of comment. When one enters the main foyer, immediately ahead is a huge tile mural, which depicts the heroism of the miners as they struggle to carry coal from the mines in the pre-mechanised days of the industry. Further sections show the wheels of progress as the miners move from the 'dark ages' of horses and carts and manual labour to the 'modern age' of M-san, new shining digging machinery replacing the shovels and pickaxes, electric trams and elevators replacing the horses and carts, and sophisticated breathing apparatus and gas-detection devices replacing the cloth masks, candles and canaries. But most noticeable of all is the difference in clothing and the light that permeates the mineshaft, thanks to the introduction of electricity into the mines. Once forced to labour naked beneath the earth, the miners are latterly depicted as healthy, smiling men, clothed in company overalls, their faces glowing with pride.

After paying the 500 yen admission charge, one moves into a spacious hall where memorabilia, machinery, work clothes, gasmasks and a huge three-dimensional relief map of the town and the underground network of tunnels are displayed. The map shows in awesome detail the extent of the underground diggings, giving the observer the uneasy feeling that should an earthquake strike there would not be very much left of Tagawa at all. There are many paintings around the hall, most showing the miners at work, and aerial photographs that graphically illustrate the extent of the mining work over the post-war period. As one moves from exhibit to exhibit, regarding the numerous machines and equipment, it is quite striking that although for the most part the uniforms and equipment on display are designed for rescue work, there is no reference to this equipment being employed. There are plaques describing how the advancement of science allowed the company to be prepared for disasters and explosions within the mines, and how new medical technology was able to supply on-the-spot resuscitation of workers burned or injured in gas leaks, yet there is no mention of any of this technology being used.

Right in the centre of the hall is the highlight of the exhibit. This is a full-sized reconstruction of one of the company *tanjū*, complete with life-sized, Disney-like characters. Within this spotless *tatami*-covered house sit three figures: a husband, relaxing in a suit; his wife, dressed in a beautifully made ceremonial kimono; and a cloth salesman, complete with a bolt of cloth that presumably is to be made into a kimono for the wife. The husband and the salesman are drinking tea, which the wife pours into their cups, as they discuss the sale. All three characters are smiling. The people living in the *tanjū* next to the museum found this exhibit the most amusing of all. As one man said to me:

> Do they really think we are that stupid that we forget how things were? Who in his right mind would wear a suit in his own house, unless someone had died? That's probably what it was, you know. The wife of the man had just lost

a brother in another mining accident, and the salesman was selling her some material to make a decent kimono to wear to the funeral. That would explain why they were wearing their best clothes. No one had more than one suit, of course, and you'd need a really good reason to wear one, that's for sure.

And the state of the house! I have never seen such a perfectly clean *tanjū* in my life. Where are the cockroaches? The mice? The ferrets?! Didn't this mining family have any shoes? There are none of the *jikatabi* that we always left in the entrance hall. It's a joke.[8]

The majority of visitors to the museum are school and community groups, mainly from outside the area, who come as part of a field trip to the mining regions. Guides, and sometimes the director, take groups of more than half a dozen people around the museum, commenting on the nature of the industry, and explaining the exhibits. The standard commentary used by the guides describes the technology M-san introduced to their mines, and the regrettable but inevitable closure of the region's coalmines in the face of cheap, foreign, high-quality imports. They compare working conditions within the mines before and after M-san became involved in high-technology coal production, emphasising the dangerous mining conditions in the pre-war period. I assume this is to highlight the fact that the introduction of high technology from overseas was successful in preventing many of the disasters that earlier affected the industry. The increased production figures per worker are also used to illustrate the efficiency of the system M-san employed.

Although the Tagawa museum has an extensive archival section, this is not available to the public as a reference source. On two separate occasions I approached the curator to ask to be admitted to the archives and was refused on the grounds that only company and government officials were allowed access. It should be said that this reluctance to divulge information about the economic state of the company is not restricted to M-san. N-san, U-san, F-san, O-san, K-san and T-san all had similar policies concerning company records. Figures from the pre-war period have also been classified as restricted information.

The Nogata museum

The Nogata museum, although lacking the degree of funding of the Tagawa museum, follows a similar pattern. Free pamphlets extol the virtues of N-san, and the profound effect the company had on local commerce. Within the museum are some dramatic colour photos showing methane-gas explosions, balls of fire ten metres in diameter spewing hundreds of metres out of the mine entrance. The caption describes this phenomenon simply as 'gas explosion'. The usual relief map of the company's operations stands inside the door, and the exhibits are similar to those of the Tagawa museum, although the scale is somewhat smaller. Gasmasks, safety equipment, photos and paintings of the miners at work, pieces of machinery and mining tools line the walls, and between these exhibits are letters of appreciation from local government and business for the generosity of the company in financing certain projects and helping the local economy. Given the much smaller scale and the comparatively smaller budget, there is no Disney show of electrically operating characters.

The curator of this museum was a little more willing to let visitors have access to the archives, but he stipulated that 'because the books are so old' no one could borrow or copy from them.

The Kurate museum

The Kurate museum, officially designated the Kurate Town Coal Industry Records Museum, is run by three people: Idegawa, Koda (a 25-year-old university graduate from Fukuoka) and a secretary. Because it is sponsored by the town council as part of the 'culturation' of Kurate scheme, it enjoys relative autonomy from company pressure as to what it can display. It is smaller than the Nogata museum.

The museum regularly changes its exhibits to coincide with national holidays, seasons and anniversaries of coal-industry-related events. It displays what Idegawa considers items that reflect the culture of Chikuho: children's essays and books from the war years, describing in detail the loss of parents to the enemy or to the mines; photographs of coalminers returning from work in the twilight; old hand-digging tools used by miners in the 'badger holes'; also commentaries about the high percentage of *burakumin* who were forced to work in these mines. It has a number of documents that the Ministry of Propaganda (MOP) released during the bombings of Kita Kyushu, which exhorted the people to stand firm in the face of temporary adversity. Pictures of children in school uniforms being marched out of schools to volunteer for frontline duty are mixed with conflicting reports of damage sustained at the end of the war in the region. Casualty figures the MOP released to the press, dramatically low after major bombing raids on the industrial centres, are contrasted with local government estimates, which are often 20 and 30 times greater.

Some of Ueno's books and photographs of miners are also exhibited, the dark, heavy monochrome prints conveying the Dickensian gloom that permeated the coalmines. Faces and bodies blackened from the coal dust, men and women miners' images are captured as they emerge naked except for loincloths, from their 'badger holes'. The miners outside their homes with their wives and children are caught by the camera as they relax in their *haramaki* and long underwear, dogs running up the narrow roads between the houses kicking up small clouds of dust as they play with the children. Photographs of men sitting in the communal baths at the end of a shift, smiling and drinking *sake*, their eyes gleaming out of blackened faces, are mounted next to photographs of ex-coalminers and their families standing nervously, dressed in their best clothes in front of their banana-trees and timber shacks in the jungles of Colombia, where they had emigrated as part of the Japanese government's Coalminers Repatriation Scheme in the 1960s. It is these images that Idegawa says best represent the culture of the coalmines, not the rapid introduction of high-technology, scientific production techniques, or economic statistics that illustrate the efficiency, or lack thereof, of the industry. It is the people who lived in the primitive mining housing and who worked in the holes in the earth who are important, who *are* the history of coal, she says.

Access to the library in the museum is virtually unrestricted. In fact, local people went so far as to bring for me to use documents that had not been listed in the archive's filing system. Coalminers' personal diaries, notes from meetings with coal company executives when the mines were closed down, union notes, production statistics, accident statistics and information about the system of welfare introduced following the closure of the mines were all supplied to me by local residents at Idegawa's request.

The difference between this museum and the other Chikuho museums is striking. The Kurate museum stands alone as a record of human actions during the coal industry's prominence in the region. This is due in no small part to the influence Idegawa has been able to exert on the town council to allow her to display local culture. It is also due in part to the declining interest N-san has shown in the town, and the resultant lack of interest in funding the museum.

Meeting Idegawa

The first time I met Idegawa was at the museum in Kurate. I had a reference from an academic who knew her slightly, and I had no idea what to expect from this famous 'radical'. I arrived at the museum at the appointed time, looked in the office window in the entrance hall, and was beckoned inside by a man in his late twenties and a short, neat woman of middle age. As I was explaining who I was and that I had come to the museum to meet Idegawa, the woman disappeared and returned quickly with Japanese tea and biscuits. As she gave me the cup she bowed very low, and asked me to forgive her for not having coffee. She then poured the tea for the man and myself, and waited for us to drink before she introduced herself as Idegawa.

Standing about 150 centimetres (five feet), Idegawa is a slight, bespectacled, somewhat school-marmish woman. Her greying hair, conservative dress sense and the air of reserved modesty would seem more suitable, one would think, for a department store assistant than for a museum curator and firebrand author of repute. She seems to really believe that she is 'just an average housewife', as she told me on occasion. Although she speaks in honorific Japanese (*keigo*) most of the time, the content of her speech is severely critical of many of the institutions that most Japanese seem to take for granted. She is slow to get started on a topic, and always waits to hear what others say before she states, with conviction, her opinions on a wide range of social issues. I never heard her raise her voice, although I have seen her quietly fuming on a number of occasions (often over sexist remarks made by her male colleagues), but always maintaining an air of equanimity.

Idegawa's husband and daughter live with her in a house that lies next to the old Kurate coal railway. The foundations of the house have been damaged by underground mining, so that the house tilts at a crazy angle and looks as though it will collapse in the slightest gust of wind. She says that they do not want to move from the place, because it is standing proof of the inaction of government in dealing with environmental damage claims, on the one hand, and it is a vivid reminder of the coalminers' culture, on the other. Among others, they have groups of students who are interested in welfare issues stay with them over the summer holidays so that they can experience for themselves the way people in the coalfields used to live. The rooms where the young people sleep are on the second floor, where the *tatami* forms a pyramid right in the centre of the house, the result of an earth tremor that shook the house in 1980. Idegawa says that the guests look like kindling on a fire, packed in the small rooms, their heads raised half a metre above their feet, thanks to the 25 degree slope, fanning out from the peak in the centre of the floor, their bright-coloured futon the colour of the flames.

The entire family works in some welfare-related field. Idegawa's husband was the director of the *shitaijigyōdan*, the city- and government-sponsored Special Coal Re-employment Scheme, where he worked for more than 25 years. It was closed down in 1991 after 30 years. Her son is a welfare worker at Kawasaki-machi, and her daughter a librarian and record-keeper at the Miyada town welfare office. Because of their vast number of contacts the house is always full of guests, some over to

discuss specific issues, some over just to visit. At night the noise of many
people talking at once can always be heard in the street outside their
house. Folk guitarists and singers blast out coalminers' songs into the
early hours of most nights, their enthusiasm stimulated by the copious
sake and shōchū they consume.

It is this camaraderie and warmth that Idegawa wants the young
people to remember about Chikuho, not just the soiled, violent image
projected by the publicity about the labour strikes in the 1960s. She says
that coalmining in Chikuho is culture, and culture in Chikuho is
coalmining, and that young people in the area are the products of that
culture. They should be aware of their roots, and not be forced to
identify only with the big city culture, which they see on television and
videos, hear on the radio and read in comics. They should also have
pride in their origins and their own special culture, and not feel
inadequate when comparing themselves with big city people.

Perhaps the strongest motivation for Idegawa's research is that the
people she wants to interview are gradually dying off. The youngest of
the women who worked in the mines are in their sixties these days, and
she feels that it is urgent that she record these women's stories while
they are still alive, while they are still able to remember their experiences. With the passing of these people goes a chapter of the history of
the region.

Idegawa is afraid that the very fabric of Chikuho is being changed at
such a pace that the past will soon be only what is recorded in the
official history books, and that the people who lived and worked here
will be forgotten in the reckless charge towards the utopia of the twenty-
first-century megalopolis, the stated goal of the prefectural government. It is because of this fear that she wants to disseminate an alternative view to the 'dark image of Chikuho' to the young people,
because they are the future. She hopes that they will learn from her
own generation's mistakes, although she despairs of this ever coming to
pass. In particular she wishes to convey the effects of the monopoly of
an industry, and the power that the industry has to control ruthlessly
the lives of their employees. Yet she sees the same processes that led to
the dissolution of the coal industry in Chikuho occurring in other
areas: the decline of Omuta City as M-san extracts its last coal from the
mines, and the wastelands of the North Kyushu shipyards, forced to
close down in the wake of the high yen and cheap Korean technology.

Idegawa is concerned with history not only for its own sake, but also
for the practical lessons it teaches us in the present. To this end she has
become involved in numerous movements, inevitably concerned with
the problems of the present. She maintains that the present is
dependent on the past, and therefore the truth of what went before us

has to be understood if we are to change the present positively. By first recognising that there have been many complex, and rarely confessed, negative problems in society, reasonable steps can be taken to deal with them. Acceptance of the government censorship of the past would lead to a loss of culture, and of the wisdom that comes from learning from history, she says. When asked about her permanently amicable and polite manner she said,

> I think that we can convince people of the worth of our cause only by being rational. Would you listen to a crazy person, who shouts at you, telling you what you're meant to think about things? There are many causes worth spending time on, I think, and you have to be totally committed to these causes if you decide to become involved. But you must approach it in a reasonable and rational manner. Screaming at people does not help.[9]

This calm approach to such emotive issues is very rare among the radical critics of official history in Japan, who typically protest in a strident manner. The radical left and right fringes are good examples of this. They drive around towns and cities in military-style vehicles, loudly proclaiming their points of view through loudspeakers mounted on the roofs of their trucks. These loud messages are inevitably emotive in content, whether they be demanding the return of Sakhalin Island by the Russians as the ultranationalists do, or exhorting the public to remove the LDP from office and throw the Americans out of Japan, as do the Japan Communist Party (JCP). The high-profile *Buraku Kaihō Undo* (Buraku Liberation Organisation) publicly and loudly denounce individuals they believe are guilty of discrimination against them. They rely on inducing fear within the public, so that the process of discrimination is in some ways slowed by the process of intimidation. When a person has been found to have committed some offence against any member of the BKD, crowds of up to a hundred people gather outside the guilty party's home and chant slogans condemning the person, and then demand a public apology.

The examples of high profile protests in Japan are many. Steiner, Krauss and Flanagan (1980) have described environmental protest in Japanese towns, particularly the response to the Minamata mercury poisoning and other pollution issues in the 1960s and 1970s. These movements have had some success in generating widespread support for the victims of certain companies' excessive greed and irresponsible attitudes. Furthermore, the success of victims in the courts, where they have won large compensation payouts, has been encouraging for these movements. However, although protests against what are often seen to be environmentally ignorant developments are increasing, the success-rate of these actions is decreasing. The anti-golf-course movement is a good example of the inability of concerned citizens to bring about change in environmental issues. The rhetoric of the LDP suggests that Japan is environmentally enlightened,[10] yet the practice of encouraging golf courses on rural and densely timbered land seems to contradict this position.

The Narita Airport protest, dragged out over more than ten years of bitter fighting by farmers, supported by radical student groups, has yet to see any material result, apart from delaying construction work. Anti-nuclear protests, vociferous and widely supported, are ignored by the government, which is determined to go ahead with the 'nuclearisation' of Japan at any cost. The annual May Day labour marches are further examples of loud public demonstrations; they are dutifully conducted every year despite the fact that wage levels are agreed upon by company and company union officials before the marches. Public, emotive demonstrations appear to fulfil a ritually cathartic role for disgruntled Japanese, and the government welcomes the opportunity to allow people to 'let off steam' in ways that are not damaging to the fabric of society.[11]

Idegawa, and some of the other Chikuho revivalists are opposed to the public outcry syndrome, and believe that the most effective protest is to subvert contemporary views of history, subtly affecting the educational and then the social infrastructure. Idegawa attempts to correct perceptions about Chikuho through the use of her contacts, and through the power of the written word, though these days this power is being rapidly undermined by the pervasive visual and electronic media. To bring her message home to the youth, she and her colleagues struggle to gain access to radio and television. However, a number of obstacles prevent them accessing these essentially conservative media. Their lack of political affiliations, their lack of cohesion as a group, the 'unnewsworthiness' of their cause, their inexperience with media techniques, and the apparently parochial nature of their subject-matter are some examples of the problems they face. Such handicaps are shared with other groups outside the mainstream of Japanese official ideology.

Notwithstanding the limited audience for her views, Idegawa is still able to deliver a potent message about the nature of Chikuho society, albeit preaching to the converted in many instances. As more older people become aware of the problems in the region and of the debt that the coal industry owes them, particularly in relation to the abuse of farmers' land and human resources, there is a groundswell movement developing that is critical of the coal companies' actions. Idegawa and the other activists in the Chikuho revivalists fulfil a need for information that supports this position.

Idegawa's attitude can best be summed up by the following excerpt from the first interview I had with her in December 1987,

The Japanese government these days is so wealthy, and it keeps getting wealthier, but little of this wealth is distributed to the needy people in our society. According to the government the coalfields have already made an economic recovery. In fact the term 'coalfields' is no longer used when referring to Chikuho, officially. In 20 or 30 years the memory of there having been coalfields here will be lost. There is no need for any government money to be invested in this area any more: that time has passed. We have recovered economically, you see, and money invested in the area would seem strange.

This is *tatemae*.[12] But in actual fact, as you have seen for yourself, there are still many instances of damage, both physical and psychological left from the coal industry. But I think that no matter how long we wait, those responsible for the damage to the area will be able comfortably to avoid having to pay any form of compensation to the people of the region. Rather than accepting responsibility for Chikuho, the government has refused to acknowledge that there is a problem here. This means that they are able to stop relief payments to the needy. Cut the payments, cut the payments. That's all we hear when they discuss what to do with Chikuho.

But, you see, the money that has been coming into the region is insurance money, insurance money that the government has at its disposal to be used for relief work. But even though the country is wealthy, they have decided that there are priorities more important than people. With the money that some of the insurance companies have in trust on behalf of the coal companies we could build a number of schools, rebuild a number of houses and buildings, establish community halls. Nothing is forthcoming.

What about the coal companies, you ask? They were not seen to be liable for any of the damage they caused to the land, the buildings or the people. They had insurance companies, which handled these things, so they have been able to escape by paying less than 30 per cent of the required compensation for the region's land damage. The bottom line is that, as far as Tokyo is concerned, the 'Chikuho problem' is solved. Look at welfare, unemployment, poverty, drug abuse, alcoholism, violence, and crime in Chikuho. The problem is *not* solved. And the country owes Chikuho something for the service we performed for so many years, supplying the national energy needs.[13]

Through her network of similarly minded people, Idegawa has been able to spread her version of the events, which constitute the human side of Chikuho history, beyond Chikuho itself. She has associations with many academics from Honshu and other Kyushu centres, who formerly knew and respected the work of Ueno. Over recent years, she has gradually used these contacts to initiate discussions, situated within alternative paradigms, about the nature of Chikuho and coalmining in general in the universities where these academics work. These discussions have prompted the regular visits by young students to her home. Within the Chikuho region she is well known and her contacts are numerous. Although there is no single paradigm within which all the protagonists of alternative understandings of Chikuho history can be placed, there is a sort of camaraderie between them. Because of her reputation within these circles as a woman of integrity and intelligence, she knows (and perhaps subtly influences the work of) many minority groups. In fact, almost all the informants I contacted in the first 12 months of fieldwork were contacts of Idegawa.

Other organisations and individuals with similar views to those of Idegawa about the 'real' history of Chikuho have had a profound influence on the course of Chikuho events over the years. For the most part, these people have been outsiders, generally Marxist in political orientation, who have heard about the suffering within the region and have come at different points in time to give their expert assistance to the mining communities. The influence of the Y-san Red Flag Organisation in the Y-san Widows' litigation against M-san following the disaster in 1965 (see chapter 12) and the influence of students who came to Chikuho from the Tokyo Students' Movement, in the D-san case (see chapter 10) are two prominent examples.

The Tokyo students' connection

The All-Japan Federation of Student Self-Governing Associations (*Zengakuren*) was formed in 1948 and aligned itself with the JCP. It was a committed leftist organisation, which opposed any curtailment of academic freedom, the strengthening of the powers of central government and the police, rearmament and nuclear warfare.[14] When the influence of the JCP began to wane in the mid-1950s, the students' political autonomy brought about a number of ideological differences within their ranks. Some members, often radical anti-JCP (Red Army and New Left) factions, were keen to continue the violent revolution against central authority, while others chose more moderate means to protest against the government.

The US–Japan Security Treaty of 1960 sparked one of the most virulent protests in which the students participated. After this series of demonstrations, where thousands of students and equal numbers of riot police fought a running battle over many months, the factional-isation of the students became extreme. The fundamental aims of the movement remained fairly consistent, regardless of the means by which different factions attempted to achieve them. Within the movement were Christian elements, radical Marxist elements, intellectual New Left factions, the Red Army factions (dedicated to terrorism) and a large number of esoteric groups.

The miners' action at KNU was reported by Ueno to other university and college academics. In fact, Ueno's influence at Kyoto University, one of Japan's leading Imperial universities, resulted in a number of sympathetic Marxist lecturers discussing with their students the mining communities and some of the problems they faced. By the late 1950s, with the publication of the Energy Revolution policies and the Coal Rationalisation Bills, considerable numbers of students and academics were made aware of the nature of the Chikuho miners' hardships. It was at this time that the Caravan Movement, a Christian-based student organisation that had its origins in the Tokyo University students' movement, first came into the area on what was to be a regular series of visits. They distributed food and clothing collected in Tokyo charity drives to the families of miners who had been retrenched under the terms of the Temporary Coal Rationalisation Bill (TCRB). Some of these people stayed on in the area, using their skills to provide assistance to the communities that were hardest hit by the local recession. They built and staffed kindergartens, schools, soup kitchens and community centres over a ten-year period. Oguchi, the *kami shibai* man, was one of these people.

Other students heard about the Chikuho 'problem' after the Miike riots had started in 1960. The Miike 'Old' union admits that many of their most militant organisers and protesters were from the Tokyo students' ranks. These students were often inclined to be militant, and were generally involved with the extreme left of the movement. Some of these students who joined the protests had become members of radical leftist factions, and had gone to China to undertake special weapons training. They became expert in building homemade explosives and mortars, and in operating a wide range of automatic and semi-automatic machine-pistols. Their aim was to allow the miners to fight back against the system. Sono, the man who was to help organise the Y-san Widows' Movement legal action in the mid-1960s, was one of these people.

A third type of student activist was also living within Chikuho during this period. Some members of the JCP, who were also members of the students' movement, were concerned at how few coalmining unions had been able to win concessions from companies, especially in regard to retrenchment and superannuation payments. The JCP faction of the union decided that the basic problem was that there were not enough knowledgeable union staff, on the one hand, and that the unions that dominated the industry were corrupt, on the other. They thought that the miners needed people who were able to explain to them what their rights were under the laws that had been introduced after the war. As a result, students were successfully able to penetrate the offices of some conservative unions, and work as clerks and office personnel, influencing decisions made by and subsequently actions taken by the union. Mizuno, the organiser of the D-san union action was one of these people.

Although there appears to be some consistency of policy here, it is important to realise that there was no single strategy employed by the Tokyo students. In fact, the students often seemed to just drift into Chikuho, their potential for employment in the cities negligible as a result of their student activities.[15] Some moved back to Tokyo. Some adopted alternative lifestyles, moving into the mountains and isolating themselves along Western hippy lines. Others chose to stay within Chikuho, contributing what they could to the society and becoming accepted.

The Chikuho connection

All of these people are what I refer to as Chikuho revivalists, although the connections are rather nebulous, centred as they are around geographical, political and vocational issues, rather than around any one specific case. They are acquainted with each other, although they do not see eye to eye on all, or in fact many, issues. But the revivalists are not restricted to just these people. Others from inside the area are also members of this network. I have mentioned two of them: Idegawa and Chikara. Other people actively involved in issues that critically affect the day-to-day lives of people in Chikuho, such as the welfare problem, are also aware of the nature of the coal industry and Chikuho's past. Kumo, the head of the Welfare Workers' Union in Tagawa-gun clearly is aware of the esoteric background of the area, something he tries to communicate to the brash young caseworkers from outside the region. I was introduced to him by Idegawa.

Members of the *Kyōsei Renkō*, who are committed to seeing the government apologise for its exploitation of and brutality towards Koreans in Japan during and after the Second World War, have a powerful message to deliver to the community at large, and members of this organisation are also involved in the Chikuho revivalists' network of formal and informal contacts. People from the *buraku* community, also deeply involved in the coal industry, have their own perspectives on the industry and their own, discriminated-against role in the 'badger holes'.[16] The *Kyōsei Renkō* and the *buraku* community groups are closing ranks these days, as they present a more concerted and more committed front to both Chikuho and to the outside world.

Underlying these individual groups are the actions of Idegawa. She has the ability to bring together people who have forgotten their own passions and roles in the past, and to revitalise their interests in local history. She has in mind the reconstruction of Chikuho's history and, as

I have described, the development of a new ethos for understanding the present Chikuho. Of the people she associates with, there are two distinct groups: those from within the region and those from without. However, apart from locality, there is a further element that distinguishes these groups, that of involvement.

The people who moved to the area during the period of labour unrest and extreme poverty were activists. They were people dedicated to trying to ameliorate some of Chikuho's problems. Regardless of their political persuasion, these people were involved in protest, rebuilding, political agitation or distributing charity to the needy. Their positions were clearly marked by their commitment to a course of action. At the time, they may not have seen their actions as being part of history, but they have become that. A number of these activists have stayed on in the area, being absorbed into Chikuho society, and in doing so, adopting the parochial viewpoints of many locals. This has resulted in many of these radicals losing their ability to see the political context in which the area is situated, and developing a form of isolationist myopia. Nowadays they are not very active in any political sense: their enthusiasm seems to have been slowed by the natural processes of age and attrition.

Those from inside Chikuho, on the other hand, have maintained their commitment to the causes they believe in. Idegawa in particular has continued to be outspoken in attempting to generate enthusiasm for reconstructing the past. She has moved to shake people out of their apathy, and to make them realise that the world is still going on outside Chikuho. The slide into welfare dependence, and the indifference that she observes is being engendered by this dependence, is having a more serious effect on the population than anything the government could do. Only through revitalising an interest in the past, and through showing insiders, as much as outsiders, both the positive and the negative sides of human action and thought within Chikuho's history can people's anger, interest, passion and then finally pride in the area be restored.

Other Chikuho people, from Chikara, the *yakuza*, through to Kumo, the welfare worker, have vested interests in revitalising an interest in the region's present, and it is not surprising that they also have an interest in understanding the nature of history. Historical precedent has to be grasped if they are to influence the present and the future, whether it be related to asking for financial assistance from the government for rebuilding dilapidated coal villages where the residents hope to keep the original communal plan of the *tanjū* intact, or whether it be accepting an otherwise unacceptable application for welfare on the grounds that an individual ex-miner deserves to get a break once in his life.

It can be said, therefore, that the makers of history are beginning to retell their stories to people such as Idegawa, who is collecting oral histories from a number of sources, and is publishing them for wider consumption. These versions of history are becoming more widely accepted within local society as people are ascribing value to their own lives. In particular, the posthumous respect accorded to the writing of Ueno has had a profound influence on many local people. Teachers, children of miners and priests, among others, are discussing openly the nature of some labour disputes, and are even discussing the sort of violence that was prevalent within the industry. Conferences and nostalgic tours of the old coalmine sites, normally for the benefit of ex-miners, are organised regularly by people such as Ishizaki and Idegawa, and by groups such as the *Kyōsei Renkō*. A groundswell movement is under way, although it has a long way to go if it is to achieve wider recognition and authenticity as a valid alternative to current official histories of the region.

Whereas it is indisputable that alternative renderings of history are essential if one is to maintain a balance between the official and unofficial realms of the past, it is doubtful that the collective, highly emotional renderings of the revivalists can alone provide the necessary foundations. An approach that looks to place Chikuho's coal industry within broader structural parameters, while recognising the roles of the people of Chikuho, is perhaps better suited to the task of attempting to balance accounts of history. To this end, I document in chapter 4 the rise and fall of the industry in the twentieth century, utilising both 'official' and 'unofficial' sources. A brief biographical note of Idegawa precedes this account.

NOTES TO CHAPTER 2

1 See the local town and city histories, for example. The Tagawa City History, the Miyada, Kawasaki and Kurate town histories are good examples of this type of historical approach, which attempts to quantify positive economic changes over time.

2 See Otoma, 1986, p.55.

3 According to a survey I conducted of 315 households in the M-san Ita *tanjū*, over 85 per cent of the respondents stated that they perceived their circumstances as representatives of a 'middle-class' environment.

4 See *Tagawa Shishi* 1979, pp.414–56.

5 See *Tagawa Shishi*, 1979, pp.450–520.

6 Fujimori, interview, 1988.

7 There is now a substantial amount of information in both English and Japanese available on citizens' movements (*shimin undō*). The revivalists, because of their lack of cohesion as a group, and consciousness of themselves as a single unit, do not fit the patterns described by Krauss, Sugimoto, Robinson and others of citizens' movements. They tend to get together over specific issues, rather than as a formal, regularly meeting organisation. Moreover, there is no clear political agenda immediately discernible, nor is there a single focus. Rather the aims of the group are somewhat

eclectic, reflecting individual activists' interests, rather than the interests of the group as a whole.

8 Iwai, interview, 1988.

9 Idegawa, interview, 1988.

10 See *Journal of Japanese Trade and Industry*, October/November 1992, pp.8–17, for example.

11 Interview with official from Prime Minister's Department, 1990.

12 *Tatemae* refers to the face that is presented to the world, the shallow, public face. The opposite is *honne*, one's true feelings. One does not display one's true feelings except under extraordinary circumstances or to very close family and friends.

13 Idegawa, interview, 1987.

14 Hunter, 1984, p.214.

15 In the 1960s Japanese corporations adopted a policy of not employing ex-student radicals. In fact any person who had been member of the *Zengakuren* was seen to be unemployable. This policy is still used by some companies today.

16 Ishizaki, interview, 1988.

CHAPTER 3

Idegawa

Idegawa was born in Kokura, Kita Kyushu, in 1932, the only daughter of a post office worker. When she was 12, after their home was destroyed in Allied bombing raids, the family moved to Kurate-machi, where they stayed for a period of about six months. At that time Kurate was both a coal town and an agricultural centre. Idegawa told me about her life in an interview in 1987.

My father's family came from Kurate. They were farmers. He had been brought up here, so he knew everyone in town, but I knew no one when we first came here. I looked for children I could be friends with. The school was overcrowded (there would have been more than 60 children in one class), and of these about half were from coalmining families, and half from farmers' families. The children from the coalmining families were open and friendly with me because they were used to moving from place to place and seeing lots of new faces, but the farmers' children were quite cold towards me. They were always so controlled and stuck with their own groups.

Of course I wanted to play with the coalmining children, so I often used to go to the *tanjū* to play after school. The Koyama *Tanjū* in those days was a very primitive place compared with the village where I was staying, and I was shocked by the terrible conditions the people lived in. When my parents found out that I was going to play with the coalmining children they were angry and said that I must not go to that dirty and dangerous place. They were very aware of the difference between 'normal people' (*ippanjin*) and coalminers (*tankōfu*). I was told to stay within the confines of the village, and to play with 'my own kind', not with the 'strange' coalminers' children.

It was at this time that I realised that there was something strange going on. Why did my parents discriminate against the coalminers? They didn't seem any better or worse than everyone else, after all. I soon realised that it was not just my parents, but most of the people in the village community felt this way about the miners. They had the same feelings of unease and otherness about Koreans and *burakumin*, who also lived in separate settlements.

51

It was this period of her life that made the greatest impression on her, and her experience strengthened her resolve to become involved in local work. Living in Kurate opened her eyes to poverty and discrimination.

After graduating from high school in 1946 she took work in the local post office, where she worked until she married in 1956. The man she married was working for the Coal Workers' Relief Organisation in Kurate at the time, so she moved back to the area she had always wanted to return to. She had two children, and when they were at school she became aware of the lack of education they were receiving about local history. When she realised that this lack of education was mainly because there had been little or no research done in the area, she decided to devote her time to understanding local coal-related issues, with the aim of rectifying the situation.

> There were a number of problems at first, the biggest being that people were reluctant to talk about the difficult conditions in which they had lived, and continue to live in. Only after a long period was I accepted as someone who could be trusted.
>
> In the late 1950s and early 1960s, when the small mines began to shut down, there was a lot of hardship and suffering in Kurate. Although some people were lucky enough to get jobs in Kansai, Tohoku and Hokkaido, the majority remained here, unemployed. During this period of extreme poverty I decided to join the *Kuroi Hane* Movement. This was a women's movement dedicated to helping the poverty-stricken miners and their families, by collecting money on the streets of the big cities. By the mid-1960s many of the miners at the small companies were depending on charity handouts just to eat, so I got caught up in the movement. I guess that it was my involvement with the *Kuroi Hane* that allowed people to recognise that I was a serious person.

Following the *Kuroi Hane* Movement's eventual demise, she became an active member of a number of other social reform organisations, including the first Kyushu branch of the Women's Democratic Group, and the *Kyōsei Renkō* (the Korean Forced Labourers' Association). She developed contacts within the populous *buraku* community in Kurate, and it was from these contacts that her interest focused on women coalminers. In order to understand the circumstances in which these *burakumin* women worked, she found it necessary to conduct research into coalmining in general. Because many women who worked the 'badger holes' were from *burakumin* families, she decided that she had to investigate the subject of *burakumin* discrimination, which in turn led to her participation in a number of conferences on the subject.

Collecting verbal histories of the women miners became her first priority in the early 1970s, and by 1975 she had an extensive collection of stories and interviews on tape. She decided to write a book about the women, and in 1984 her first book, *The Mothers Who Gave Birth to Fire*, was released to limited, but enthusiastic public acclaim. In 1972 she took a job in the clerical section of the local town office, a position she kept while she wrote the book and a series of papers, which were published in a variety of journals. The fame that spread before her was instrumental in her obtaining employment in the coal museum.

These days she is busy with her museum duties and researching a second book, this time about *burakumin* and Korean coalminers and the life of miners in 'badger holes'. She also presents papers about her research to interested groups throughout the region, particularly to women's organisations. She is involved in the anti-discrimination movement, the Korean Forced Labourers' Association, social welfare protests, and lobbying national and prefectural governments over their inaction in dealing with the land damages claims made by many residents of the coal-producing areas. She has a wide range of interests, and is constantly searching for new intellectual stimuli. Although not officially a member of a feminist organisation, she has pushed for women's rights to work for equal pay with men for many years, and along with some of the women whose stories she has recorded, is regarded as one of Chikuho's most outspoken feminist critics.

Her stories of the coal era, and her commitment to seeing the people of Chikuho given an appropriate place in Japan's history have lent credibility to the efforts of those seeking to instil in the people of Chikuho a sense of dignity and purpose in confronting the future.

CHAPTER 4

A Short History of Coalmining: Chikuho in Context

Chikuho was one of Japan's major coal-producing areas. During the immediate post-war years and into the 1950s and 1960s Chikuho's coalmines produced between 35 and 50 per cent of Japan's total coal output. When the coal industry went into decline in the late 1950s and early 1960s, Chikuho, which was almost completely dominated by the production of coal and secondary related industries, was left with few economic alternatives. The domination of the coal industry was such that there was a monopoly of the local industrial workforce. When the coal companies started to rationalise operations in the 1950s and 1960s, in response to the first of many Coal Rationalisation Plans, there was widespread unemployment, poverty and general discontent, which culminated in a series of national strikes and protest movements, all of which proved to be of little use in reversing the trend away from coal and towards oil.

In describing this process, I shall first look at the national level. I shall then focus on Chikuho itself, drawing on the accounts of informants from a cross-section of local society. There are significant divergences between the 'official' history and that remembered by the people of Chikuho today, and these differences provide fertile grounds for reinterpreting events in the region over the past 40 years.

Prior to the Second World War: The discovery and use of coal

Coal was first discovered in Chikuho in the early sixteenth century and was exploited at that time by the *daimyō* (feudal lords) of the area.[1] The 'mines' were confined to producing small amounts of domestic coal for the purposes of heating and lighting the homes of the lords. Coal was

54

not really perceived to be a viable source of energy at that stage, perhaps because the lords were reluctant to commit themselves to the concept of capital investment, which in turn would lead to further economic dependence on the *shōgun*. This was because each *daimyō* had to pay tithes to the *shōgun* for profits gained from any enterprise. Also the 'crudity' of merchandising was seen as being below the notice of the feudal lords.

At the beginning of the Meiji period in the late 1860s there was a surge of interest in Western culture, ideology and technology. In order to achieve the potential for industrial development, a locally produced energy source to fuel the proposed industry became necessary. Coal was the obvious choice.

The Meiji Restoration saw the emergence of a more progressive, industrial-oriented economy, determined to restore national pride in the face of the imposition of the Unequal Treaties. Following the 'opening of Japan' by the United States in the 1850s, Western nations had pressured Japan to open its ports and economy to Western influence. Rights of extraterritoriality for foreigners in Japan, unlimited access to some Japanese goods, and the right to trade openly in certain areas in Japan were demanded and received by the United States and other colonial nations.

Two powerful merchant organisations, M-san and T-san, were in favour with the new government, and once the technology and demand for industrial development had been identified, the government invested in the coal industry and then sold its interests to these families when it was unable to run them profitably. Together with the A-san and N-san families, which were younger and more diversified than M-san and T-san, these corporations were known collectively as the Big Four *zaibatsu*. They dominated Japanese industrial development and economic expansion until their official demise at the end of the Second World War. All these companies were heavily involved in the coal industry, controlling the lion's share of the industry from the early days of the twentieth century to the end of the coal era.

The need for fuel, established by the growth of industry, was augmented as the country became involved in the 1894–95 war with China, which ceded Formosa to Japan, and the 1904–05 war with Russia, which led to the Japanese annexation of Korea. Coal was the primary fuel source, powering munitions factories and the steel and shipbuilding industries. The *zaibatsu* companies were all involved in the war effort, expanding considerably during this period, and also running mines in Korea, Manchuria and Formosa. Particularly M-san was active in Manchuria, where coal was produced considerably cheaper than in Japan. In the 1930s and 1940s a large number of skilled men from Chikuho were sent to Manchuria to work in the mines, mainly to train Chinese labourers.[2] Japan could not get too much coal for its military and industrial machines during this period.

Despite overall expansion there was turmoil within the coal industry. The small companies in particular were affected by fluctuations in the market, and in 1931 a representative group protested against the importation of Manchurian coal, which was being mined by a consortium of large Japanese coal companies. Cheap coal was flooding the market, and because it was produced by the large Japanese companies offshore, they were able to come to an agreement with the government over an unlimited import quota. The government meanwhile had asked the smaller companies either to reduce output or to reduce the cost of their product to further the war effort. However, the smaller companies objected to this policy, saying that the imported coal, which was being sold at eight yen a tonne less than cost, was forcing them into bankruptcy. After a lengthy protest movement, which led to a confrontation in Fukuoka with the governor, the big companies agreed to shoulder some of the financial burden of this policy, and the demands that coal production be slowed in the smaller mines were mollified.[3]

The years of the Second World War were characterised by a shortage of domestic labour within industries necessary for the continuation of the war effort. To counter this shortage, two main policies were instigated by the government with the assistance of the major coal-producers. M-san was the first of the big mining companies to allow women back in the pits after the national union, in perhaps its only decisive move before the end of the Second World War, had banned them from this work in 1928. Many other mining companies soon followed suit, and by 1943 fully one-quarter of the coalminers in the large mines were women.[4] The second method employed to counter the labour shortage was the introduction of forced labour. Korean men were the first to be brought over to labour in the mines, following the annexation of Korea in 1910. They were followed by Chinese after the Manchuria invasion in 1931–32.

In the 1920s and 1930s few Koreans were necessary in the coalmines, but as hostilities escalated between Japan and other nations, more and more were brought to Japan to alleviate the labour shortage. By the end of the Second World War it is estimated that there were more than 60,000 Koreans working in the pits nationwide.[5] Of these people, probably 75 per cent were in Kyushu, of whom most were in either the Chikuho or Omuta regions of Fukuoka. Along with the Korean forced labourers, other prisoners of war (POWs) were set to work in the mines as the situation got more serious and the demand for mine labour increased. By the end of the war there were altogether more than 100,000 foreign forced labourers in the pits.[6]

In the early 1990s the Korean Forced Labourers' Movement (*Kyōsei Renkō*) has estimated that there were more than 1,000,000 Koreans brought to Japan to work in mines, factories, and domestic building projects from 1911 to 1945.[7] Many of these men were in the Kyushu mines.[8] These forced labourers worked mainly in the large mines owned by the *zaibatsu*, and in *zaibatsu*-affiliated companies. This is attributable to the strong influence the large companies were able to exert on the government's allocation of POW labour. The importance the government attached to the coal industry is reflected in the labour force statistics. In 1932 there were 140,000 miners employed in coalmines nationally. This figure, which included a large number of women miners, had increased to 440,000 by 1945.

Throughout the Second World War, coal production continued to increase. In the period 1930–45 production was up by 200 per cent.[9] Coal production had in effect become the cornerstone of the economy,[10] a position emphasised by the importance attached to reviving the post-war coal industry under the US Occupation. At the end of the war the coalminers who were forced labourers were freed, and the formerly 'free' women miners were forced to give up their work to make space for the men returning from the war.

The boom after the Second World War

The mining industry was in disarray after the war. The repatriation of forced labourers left a huge gap in the labour force, and in 1945, after the war, there were only 100,000 coalminers working in mines throughout the country. Two typhoons devastated the coalmining areas in Kyushu in 1946, flooding many mines and halting production. Because of labour shortages and mining disasters, production had fallen to 550,000 tonnes in 1945, the lowest coal-production figures since Meiji.[11]

Policy decisions concerning the mines were taken by the new government in co-operation with the US Occupation authorities. They decided that it was essential that the mines be kept open and production increased, for underproduction by the coal and steel industries was slowing an industrial revival. Thus at the end of 1946 the Occupation forces, with the approval of the Diet, passed the Coal Priority Production legislation. This legislation was designed to give the state more control of the coal industry by allowing it direct control of market prices and quotas of coal produced. The venture was capitalised by the Japan Reconstruction Bank at 33.5 billion yen in the first year alone. Ironically *Haitan Kōdan* (the Solid Fuels Distribution Public Corporation), which was the administrative organ of the legislation, consisted mainly of ex-*Nittan* (Japan Coal Industry Corporation) chiefs. In other words, the leaders of the large coal companies were given almost totalitarian control of policy- and decision-making. According to one source, of the 33.5 billion yen that was given to the mines to increase production and improve safety standards, more than half the funding went on building housing for miners and stockpiling equipment for when the market was freed.[12]

Following the war, certain incentives were introduced to swell the labour force in the mines under the Priority Production program. One such was the *bento* (lunch box) ration of rice, which was supplied to coalminers while the rest of the workforce was suffering from malnutrition and a lack of even the most basic daily necessities. Other incentives were free housing, which was offered with work, and relatively good pay in large companies. Partly as a result of these policies the labour force had increased to 350,000 by November 1946.[13]

The first independent coalminers' union (*Tanrō*) was formed during this period under the auspices of the Occupation, and by 1948, 50 per cent of coalminers were members of a union, an unprecedentedly high statistic.[14] This number increased after the government, under pressure from the Occupation, made it the right of all miners to join unions in 1948, and by 1950 most miners were involved in some sort of union. However, like today, most of these unions were in reality company or enterprise unions, with limited power to act on their members' behalf. These unions offered support to the companies, rather than to the miners and were often headed by men supported or controlled by management. They were not officially affiliated with *Tanrō*, and they did not accept the recommendations of that union, which was associated with the Japan Socialist Party (JSP).

The period between 1945 and 1950 can best be described as a boom period for both the coalmines and the people who lived in the mining areas. Production increased dramatically to over 30 million tonnes, and the number of miners also increased. The population in Tagawa, for example, grew from 75,000 to 100,000 over this period (see Figure 1). Other towns and cities in Chikuho, which based their economies on the fortunes of the coal industry went through similarly dramatic population increases as their coalmines attracted a broad spectrum of coalminers and people to work in associated industries, especially service related industry (see Figure 2).

With the population increases came the benefits that are often associated with large settlements: improved roads, service sectors and city facilities, such as public transport. However, the boom period was to

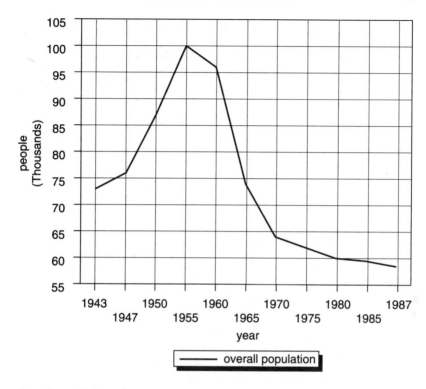

Source: Tagawa City Council Statistics, June 1987.

Figure 1: Tagawa City Population Movement

be short-lived, and by the mid 1950s widespread unemployment had become characteristic of the area as a whole.

The Korean War

The onset of the Korean War in 1950 and the United States' Special Procurements payments led to increased demand for coal in the manufacturing and heavy industries. Although coal production had been steadily increasing since 1946, there was still a relative coal shortage. Once again the government stepped in to encourage the coal companies to increase production. To this end a series of laws were passed making it easy to get interest-free loans to start coalmining operations in any certified coalfield. This was in reality much more complex than it appears because of the nature of the coalfield ownership and leases (see chapter 6). In the years from 1948 to 1960, in

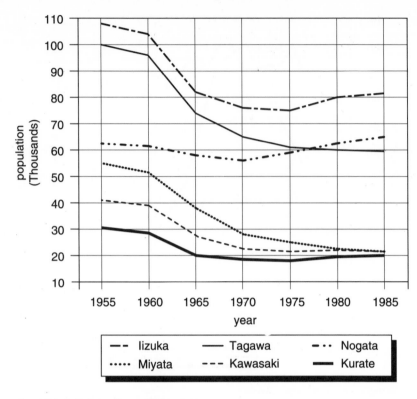

Source: Fukuoka Prefecture Census (1986) pp. 7–21.

Figure 2: Chikuho Population Movement

the Chikuho region alone 559 mainly small mining companies started operations. In the same period 520 companies folded.[15] The market was volatile.

During this period the national coal labour force increased to 370,000, and production reached the highest levels since the Second World War: 48 million tonnes in a single year (1951). Within Chikuho, production increased in line with the national trends (as Figure 3 shows) and output from the three major cities in Chikuho reached close to 15 million tonnes in 1951.

The labour force had been recruited from a number of areas within the economy in the post-war boom period. Returning ex-servicemen filled a large number of the available posts within the industry. Many of these ex-servicemen had been miners or were related to pre-war miners. Other ex-service personnel were too young to have had any

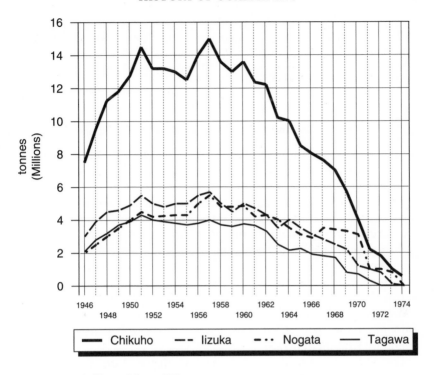

Source: Kyushu Coal Research Centre, 1980.

Figure 3: Chikuho Coal Production

work experience outside of the armed forces, and these people were often trained to occupy positions (such as barrowmen and pit support) that did not require industry experience. People who worked in the depressed rural sector, struggling under carry-over effects of the wartime economic restraints, which had virtually destroyed large sections of rural land through forced overproduction, were attracted by the relatively high wages, the prospect of free housing and the relative job security the coal industry offered.

On top of this, the mining companies had set up a drive to recruit the best of the young academics from the better universities to fill lower management positions. One of these academics from Kyushu University described the situation thus:

> The mining companies sought only the best engineers and economics graduates to work in their companies, which was why they drew their quotas from the imperial universities such as Kyushu, Tokyo and Kyoto universities. The young graduates thought that the mine industry was the industry of the

future, and I suppose you could say that they saw it as the present generation sees the computer and high-tech industries of the 1980s and 1990s. That is, it held a magnetic attraction for the young, go-ahead type of man. The companies had a lot of money and were very powerful, so the young men were very keen to get work with these industrial giants.[16]

The decline and rationalisation of the coal industry

By the end of the Korean War there were massive coal stockpiles. Supply far exceeded demand. This caused many problems for the government, mainly because it had passed legislation after the outbreak of the Korean War encouraging investment in coal, particularly by the small to medium-sized companies, many of which were going bankrupt. The large companies complained that the market was too restricted, and they were faced with increasing competition from oil imports. So they pressured the government to act to remedy the situation. The government response was to establish a Board of Inquiry into the coal industry, which was to report to MITI (Ministry of International Trade and Industry). On the basis of its findings the government decided to implement the first TCRB, which was a three-year plan to go into operation from March 1952.

The TCRB was aimed at fixing production based on locality, fixing prices for the production and fixing the market that was to use coal. By setting the quota of coal to be produced, the government was following the wishes of, in particular, the steel, shipbuilding and electrical industries, which had become more vocal in demanding coal prices be reduced. However, the mining companies rejected a price reduction, because they were not prepared to shoulder any of the financial burden required by the TCRB.

Under the terms of the Bill they stood to receive further tax-free loans, but because they had invested too much money during and immediately after the war in improving production facilities, they were unable or unwilling to undertake the responsibility of further loan repayments. The big companies prepared to diversify their investments and many of them invested in subsidiary interests (offshore opportunities, steel, and oil and petroleum production and importation), relinquishing many of their coal interests. Workers at collieries all over the country were concerned about the probable effects of the TCRB, and a series of strikes occurred in some of the smaller mines in Chikuho during the early 1950s as a protest against the impending closures.

At this stage it should be emphasised that the union response was conservative in light of the severe rationalisations that were taking place within the industry. The mine operators were *not* investing in their mines, and *not* improving safety standards. Rather they were trying to increase production with the facilities and the workforce that existed at the time. The mining accident rate for the years from 1950 to 1960 is remarkably high. It has been estimated that there were 5,000 deaths due to coalmining accidents in the Chikuho area in this period.[17] Because of the nature of the mining structures in operation at the time, it is difficult to calculate the number of deaths from the smaller mines, but other sources have said that this is a conservative estimate.[18] Coupled with the increased danger at the work site, the companies, in their attempts to get what they could from the mines while they were still viable concerns, continued to employ *yakuza*-like overseers (*rōmu kakari*) as they had done during the war, to keep the workers controlled and productive. Violence became a way of life for many of the miners, yet because there was such a poorly developed union consciousness it was very rare that protest against the poor working and living conditions was voiced.[19]

The methods of labour control employed during the war were dependent on the goodwill of the crime syndicates, who supplied the men to work in the roles of overseers, keeping the forced foreign labourers in particular under tight control. After the war, when the large companies had the pick of the labour force, the smaller companies were able to induce some of the Korean labourers to continue working in their mines. The system of forced labour was continued throughout the 1950s and into the 1960s in certain small, notoriously violent mines (see chapters 6, 7 and 9).

As the labour situation grew more desperate, the National Coal-miners' Union (*Tanrō*) stepped in, and in October 1952, when coal stockpiles had reached their peak, *Tanrō*-affiliated unions went on rolling strikes in the bigger mines for two months over wage and job security claims, greatly affecting production. This series of strikes and the violence that occurred in settling the dispute over working conditions became famous in mining folklore. However, the miners won few concessions in this action. Partly as a response to the militancy of the action, market demand dropped, because industries that needed fuel were reluctant to commit themselves to coal in the light of the potential disruptions to supply. This in turn affected the overall production of the mines, which led to a large number of miners losing their jobs. The smaller mines continued to produce, but overall production had dropped by 6,000,000 tonnes from the previous year.[20]

The timing was critical here, because during the months of the strike when there was widespread lack of confidence in the coal industry, the government had moved to relax the tariffs on oil imports in line with other industry demands. The lack of confidence in the coal industry

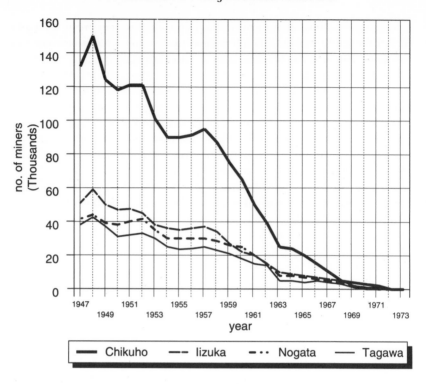

Source: Mizue (1978) p. 237.

Figure 4: Coalminers in Chikuho

was compounded the following year when coal production dropped considerably again as the industry was reeling from the effects of the 1953 recession. The petroleum share of the primary fuel market jumped from 5 per cent in 1950 to almost 18 per cent in 1953.[21]

The national lack of confidence in the industry was reflected in Chikuho, as Figure 3 shows. Production dropped noticeably in 1952 and 1953, but there was a revival, as demonstrated in the artificial peak reached in the late 1950s, during the Suez Crisis. By 1954 more than 90,000 miners had lost their jobs nationwide, and the Chikuho miners in particular were severely affected (see Figure 4). The demand for coal was limited, and because the distribution system favoured the large companies, the smaller companies could not sell their coal. As a result, many companies folded and the unemployment statistics continued to grow.

As the situation deteriorated, industry leaders, manufacturing leaders, local governments, and unions alike put pressure on the government to do something about the state of the mining industry. Unemployment was at the highest levels Japan had seen; there were no job vacancies in the coal areas; and the housing that the coal companies had owned was often left without electricity and water as the companies closed down operations. After the temporary revival provided by the Suez Crisis, when oil imports were threatened, the coal industry was no better off than it was before the crisis started. In response to the cries for help from the mine operators, MITI introduced before the Diet a Bill designed to relieve some of the problems plaguing the industry. A major objective of the Bill was to place the burden of the implementation squarely with prefectural and local governments.

'Scrap and Build'

The second TCRB, or the 'Scrap and Build' (*Gorika*) plan, as it was to become known, was first introduced for discussion in 1954, and after lengthy debate was made law in May the following year. Because the high rate of mine closures in the region was recognised as a serious social as much as an economic problem, the introduction of the TCRB was seen as being an essential step in alleviating some of the pressure from Chikuho and from the other coal-producing areas. The law was a short-term measure and was based around five main points.

1 It was to stretch over five years, and by 1959 total coal production should not exceed 49,500,000 tonnes. There was a condition attached that in order to maintain the high production-capacity coal prices were to be dropped by 20 per cent. This was to make coal competitive with imported energy.
2 The Coal Industry Maintenance Operations Group was to be formed to control the distribution of 3,000,000 tonnes of low-quality coking coal. This would effectively regulate how many new mines would be opened. (The small mines often produced poor-quality coal because of the type of lease that was available in low-quality seams.)
3 As it was necessary to provide some protection for the industry over what was regarded as a temporary period, it was decided that to keep coal competitive with oil, the crude-oil tax would be resurrected. Also the flow of crude oil would be limited by restricting the use of oil boilers.
4 The government would buy out coalmines that were having difficulties remaining solvent.
5 A commission of inquiry was to be established to review the conditions of the present coal industry strategy, with the aim of presenting these findings to MITI. MITI, in turn, would attempt to deal with all future problems in the industry on the basis of this report.[22]

The intention of the legislation was to reduce the overall levels of coal pricing, while still guaranteeing production quotas. This was tied in with the government's commitments to establish oil as the fuel of the future, and to gradually rationalise the coal industry. The coal companies were able to maintain their profitability for the short term, through their ability to manipulate the political agenda, and still be guaranteed the sale of their mines as assets under this legislation. Notwithstanding the Bill, MITI soon adjusted the Oil Boiler Act to suit its own policies, allowing payments of the Oil Tariff to be deferred by industry.

Perhaps one of the most neglected considerations of this Bill is the fourth point. It has been suggested by some local informants that following the establishment of this clause the mining accident rate increased tenfold in the succeeding year.[23] This is certainly difficult to corroborate, because statistics on accidents during this period are conspicuously absent, but from looking through the newspapers at the time, reported instances of accidents increased substantially. One sub-clause attached to this condition stated that if a mine was closed because the conditions had been proved to be dangerous to the miners, the company was entitled to full indemnification from the government. Oguchi, who compiled accident statistics in the region, claimed that certain small mines went as far as to actually precipitate accidents that resulted in the deaths of miners in order to take advantage of this provision.[24]

The coalminers' unions associated with *Tanrō* decided to start a campaign of nationally co-ordinated industrial action against the proposed introduction of the 'Scrap and Build' legislation. Local governments were also concerned that because so many mines were closing down, they would be forced to support financially large numbers of unemployed miners. However, despite their opposition, the second TCRB (the 'Scrap and Build' Bill) became law.

By 1958 mining towns in Chikuho and Hokkaido had opened discussions to protest the drain on local public finances caused by the law, and to demand compensation from the national government to support the rapidly rising numbers of unemployed. They also demanded that outside interference in coalmining matters be stopped.[25] *Sōhyō* (The Council of Trade Unions) supported this stance, and strike action started in many major coal centres, mainly within the big companies.[26]

MITI responded to these demands by establishing a 'mine damages' fund. This allowed for compensation to be paid to local governments for land that was damaged as a direct result of the underground land subsidence caused by the mining. MITI also instigated the National Unemployed Workers' Strategy, which was intended to employ ex-miners in public works programs. There were three parts to this legislation.

1 Sewers, roads and running water services would be improved, which would in turn improve the lot of the average resident of the coal towns.

2 House building and the laying of power lines to the *tanjū* would be started.

3 Unemployed miners would be retrained to work in the salt-manufacturing and other industries that were being encouraged under the rationalisation program.[27]

Unemployed coalminers were to be employed on the public works programs outlined above at local governments' expense, so that not only would the local people benefit from improved facilities, but also the miners would be gainfully employed. The fact of the matter was that there were too many unemployed to fit into the public works scheme, mainly because too many small companies had hastily decided to halt operations under the terms of the TCRB. The third provision was also largely ineffective and the numbers of unemployed rapidly increased.[28]

'Divine prosperity' and new industry problems

The introduction of the TCRB, ironically, coincided with the second post-war boom, the so-called 'divine providence' (*jimmu keiki*). When the Suez Crisis occurred in 1956, the demand for coal rose sharply and the domestic coal industry was once again able to set its own price levels.[29] During the crisis, the industry, rather than being depressed, enjoyed the advantages of having government support. While the government would buy out obsolete mines on the one hand, on the other the mines could control coal prices based on industry demand. The number of coalmines increased by 40 per cent in 1956–57. This was contrary to all MITI's expectations.[30]

However, this was the last real boom period for coal, and from 1959 the figures tell the story of the collapse of the industry in the face of cheap coal imports and the government's promotion of crude-oil boilers for electrical energy. In August that year more than 10,000,000 tonnes of coal were stockpiled throughout the country. Throughout this period large companies were continuing their strategy of investing in other industries, rather than putting more money into an industry that was inherently unstable. To this end they were able to reinforce the leasing system, whereby small companies would work the seams around the main coalmines, pay the production costs, but sell the coal they produced through the network established by the parent company. This effectively reduced the risk for the large companies, but made the smaller companies susceptible to market fluctuations, which ultimately resulted in many of them going bankrupt. The statistics reflect this trend, particularly in the 1950s. The large companies were responsible for 72 per cent of coal-production in 1950, but by 1958 this figure had dropped to 64 per cent.[31]

Scrapped, but not rebuilt

Although one of the aims of the TCRB was to limit coal-production, by May 1959 the total estimated production for the year had already been reached, mainly due to the enormous stockpiles of coal, which could not be sold. In Chikuho 81 mines had been bought out by the government, and between 1956 and 1959 22,900 workers in the region had become unemployed. Earlier, in the first recession of 1953–54, some 31,000 workers had been made redundant in the region, and most of these workers had remained in Chikuho, either looking, often unsuccessfully, for work, or working in the special programs that the government had established. Altogether there were more than 50,000 out-of-work miners by the end of the 1950s, and the prospect of more mine closures was becoming a pressing issue that the government was not prepared to face.[32]

Very little had actually been done to alleviate the suffering that massive unemployment and the erosion of the industry was causing. The promised new roads had not been built. The *tanjū* had not been rebuilt. There were almost no retraining programs. The new railway had been scrapped. Running water was still not available in many homes. The so-called 'Scrap and Build' program was very much a 'Scrap' only program, and to all appearances it seemed as though the government was prepared to write the area off by the end of the 1950s. The only people to have benefited from the program were the mine-owners.[33]

Industries that were related to the coal industry were also hit hard by the closures. Although it is hard to estimate exactly how many people lost their jobs indirectly when the mines closed, some sources have claimed that 70 per cent of the workforce were affected in Tagawa.[34]

> The standard unemployment strategy, rather than creating employment opportunities for the unemployed, was to delegate responsibility for the unemployed to the local governments. This placed a big burden on the local people, who were forced to support the unemployment schemes tabled in Tokyo and passed down through the prefecture. The locals were required to prop up the schemes with their own local taxes.[35]

In Tagawa's case, of the thousands left without work, the national government budgeted for retraining programs for only 337 people a

day, each program restricted to a two-year limit. The rest of the financial burden rested squarely with local governments, which was a major
problem, given the limited resources at their disposal. The national
government extended the program and aid to local and prefectural
governments in 1959, supporting 340 unemployed workers per day.

Under the welfare system, unemployed miners were entitled to 315
yen a day, which was just under 40 per cent of the average mining wage.
In turn, 40 per cent of the financial responsibility for this scheme was
delegated to the city, 40 per cent to the prefectural government, and 20
per cent was supported by the national government. In 1959 49.4 per
cent of all families in Tagawa City were receiving welfare payments.[36]
Unemployment had become endemic, and a long-term solution was
not forthcoming.

Labour unrest — M-san Miike

In 1959, following the lead of the United States, Japan decided to make
a final commitment to switching from coal to oil as the major energy
source. The Japanese government was afraid that the United States
would develop an insurmountable lead in manufacturing through the
implementation of their oil policy, which would effectively cut their
manufacturing costs. Japan then finalised measures to rationalise coal
and transfer its allegiance to oil by signing contracts with Middle East
countries. The oil it contracted to purchase was a third of the price of
United States oil at the time. This was seen as something of a coup
within government circles, and it was widely felt that if the dependence
on coal was transferred to oil, a broad-based manufacturing sector led
economic recovery would be possible.[37]

However, the move to change over to oil was not popular within the
coal industry for fairly obvious economic reasons. The coal companies
wanted to maintain their strong performance, and especially in
Chikuho the need to maintain profitability in the face of declining
profit margins resulted in widespread wage-cuts. The coal unions
responded with some militancy to the reluctance of the companies to
allow their wages to keep up with cost-of-living increases. Stop-work
meetings were held, and many small strike actions were started, protesting both the decline in the relative wage-levels and the impending
closure of the mining industry, which threatened workers' job security.
Mining companies typically refused to negotiate with the disgruntled
miners, citing declining profits and union aggression as being
obstructions to any dialogue.

From the end of 1959 labour strife began to take hold in Chikuho,
organised under the *Tanrō* banner. For the first time since the 101-day

strike at K-san Mine in Kurate, when all members of *Tanrō* went on strike for one day to protest the actions of that company's management (see chapter 9), the concept of class-consciousness appeared to be developing within the national labour movement. This time the focus was on the impending mine closures and the TCRB. Donations were asked for and received from unions in all industries across the country, and a nationwide campaign originating in Miike was started, which attempted to recruit support from members of the working classes. The united labour offensive was launched in 1960, with a budget of two billion yen, and a total membership of 3.8 million workers who subsequently demonstrated their sympathy for the coalminers' position.[38]

In January 1960 the M-san Miike mine had posted a notice stating that 1,300 miners were to be retrenched. These miners were all members of the *Tanrō*-affiliated union at the mine. In the period after the government had finalised its arrangements for rationalising the coal industry, these miners had participated in a number of meetings that condemned the decision of the government. They also denounced M-san management for conspiring to keep wages at below-standard levels and were opposed to accepting a deal that management offered them after the 1959 plan to rationalise the industry was announced. Management in turn accused the miners of being 'industrial saboteurs' and acted quickly to retrench them.

At the time the miners were sacked, of the 40,000 M-san coalminers employed throughout Japan there were 13,500 men employed by M-san Miike Coal, and it was widely felt that if the company could easily dismiss such a large proportion from one mine, then other retrenchments would follow. The *Tanrō*-led union went on strike over these dismissals. It also demanded that job retraining programs be instituted, so that the miners could find work outside the industry, and that there should be wage increases and medical insurance for the remaining period of employment. These demands were met by a 'compromise agreement' put forward by management, in which the company suggested that the union accept a 5 per cent wage increase, with no other benefits, apart from guaranteed work, in return for increased productivity. The union was unmoved by this offer, and because they would not return to work, the company locked the workers out.[39]

On 5 January 1960, two days after the workers were sacked, 30,000 miners from Chikuho marched to the company head office to protest the dismissals. Police and the army were called in, and helicopters were also used to break up the protest. The company instituted another lockout to show their disapproval of the action. This precipitated strike action on a scale previously unseen in Japan. For more than a year the Miike Miners' Union stayed on strike, regularly marching on the company headquarters, demanding their claims be met, and that their workmates be reinstated.

During the time the miners were protesting the actions of the company, the company moved to create a company union within the workforce, to oppose the militant stance of the *Tanrō*-led union. By this stage the company was desperate to get production going again, and a number of material incentives were introduced to entice workers to continue working under the company union's directives. According to some observers, M-san encouraged conflict between the unions, and actively supported discrimination against the striking workers in their efforts to maintain the separation between groups.[40] By March 1960 it was clear that the company was not prepared to mediate with the striking workers, and at the April meeting of *Sōhyō* the union made the commitment to utilise all its strength to mount a series of demonstrations against the new TCRB. The new Bill threatened the livelihoods of more than 100,000 miners nationally, and the M-san Miike case had become a symbol of the mine-owners' refusal to accommodate the needs of its workers. The company's hardline stance against the unions, and the desperation that was bred within miners' ranks, forced the miners to consider using violence if necessary to ensure that their demands were heard.

By August their demands and their high public profile had generated heated debate within local and national government. In September, after a series of violent confrontations with the police and gangsters, reputedly employed by M-san to quell worker unrest, which resulted in many miners being injured, and some losing their lives[41] the union received the official support of all the major political parties except the LDP. The popularity of the miners' stance against the company's rationalisation plan was reinforced in the city election held that month, where support for the JSP increased from 52 per cent to 63 per cent at the expense of the LDP. [42]

Yet, while support for the miners continued to increase, especially among other unions, at the grass-roots level the union split at Miike was beginning to have a profound effect on the miners. Animosity between the two groups developed into all-out war, and there were numerous instances of the groups attacking each other, with the police inevitably siding with the miners from the 'New' union. Gradually M-san was able to increase the relative number of miners in the New union so that only a small percentage of miners in the 'Old' union were left to offer resistance to wage and rationalisation proposals put forward by the company. Although this group from the Old union had plenty of support among the population at large, there was gradually less support from the rank and file, who, as time wore on, became edgy about the lack of a solution. Defections from the Old union to the New union became common, as the reason for the strike was obscured in rhetoric from the company, the New union and the media. The media focused primarily on the problem of the violence and hatred that permeated the mine. The real issues — the impending closure of the mine, the decreasing wage-levels, the lack of available work and the lack of retraining — were neglected in this rhetoric. What became important was individual, short-term survival. No one really considered that the industry would have a future. They were concerned about getting through the next 24 hours, according to one striker.[43]

M-san Miike and popular support

The Miike strike gained a considerable amount of media attention, and in response to this the *Kuroi Hane* (Black Feather) movement began in mid-1960 with the intention of collecting charity for the workers. This movement was started by a collective of women in Fukuoka and aimed to collect from five to ten yen per person throughout the nation.[44] As the *Kuroi Hane* movement began to gain momentum, the press picked up the story, emphasising the humanitarian side of the women's response. Simultaneously the miners' strike and the general depression and unemployment in Chikuho became nationally reported events.

However the press, perhaps in response to mining company and government pressures, soon began running stories denigrating the efforts of the women's movement. These stories claimed that the movement had not been able to realise its aims, and was therefore ineffectual. One series published at the end of 1960 in the *Asahi Shinbun* suggested that the movement had been able to collect only one quarter of the amount it intended in the Fukuoka region, while the Tokyo appeals had been much more successful. The newspaper went on to suggest that the people of Fukuoka, who were physically closer to the problem areas than those in Honshu, were turning their backs on the miners because they really understood the situation; that is, that the miners were not in need of the aid that the public was supplying.[45] This story was picked up in all the mass media and within a month the miners' plight was old news at a national level (outbreaks of violence notwithstanding) and the *Kuroi Hane* movement slowly faded into obscurity. Without public support it was futile to continue.[46] Nevertheless, before the end it had collected and distributed more than 140 million yen to the miners.

M-san was able to break the strike one year after it started, following a series of riots in which hundreds of miners and police were injured. The company adopted a strategy that was the standard in dealing with

labour unrest in the mines. They offered wage and housing concessions, and guaranteed employment to miners who would break from
the Old union and join the company union, while continuing the
'rationalisation' of the miners who opted to stay with the Old *Tanrō*-
affiliated union. The *Tanrō* workers were locked out, and many were
sacked, even though national strike action was threatened. Worker
solidarity was broken as large numbers of miners, unhappy with the
outcome of their union leaders' strategy, defected to the New union.
The strike ended soon after. Other large companies followed suit,
rationalising their workforces in succession, the issue of miners' rights
relegated to being of limited importance by the major coal-producers.
By and large, miners rejected the overtures of *Tanrō* as an organising
body, and by the end of the 1960s the withdrawal of the coal companies
from Chikuho was almost complete.

A temporary truce: the government sells out

The coal unions changed tactics in 1961, protesting to the government
rather than against the companies about the work rationalisations. In
December there was a general protest in Tokyo, where 50,000 miners
convened in front of the home of the Prime Minister to confront the
government with the problems the mining industry was facing. The
representatives made it clear that the shift to oil from coal was causing
large-scale social and economic problems. The government again
attempted to prop up the industry, finally introducing the First Coal
Program. This measure subsidised the industry by guaranteeing production levels of 55 million tonnes a year, with the condition that heavy
industry continue to buy coal. This was to be achieved through an 800
yen per tonne price reduction, which a cartel of big coal companies
agreed on, to be reached by 1963.

Steel and other manufacturing industries demanded a price cut of
1,500 yen per tonne by 1962 if they were to buy the coal that was
produced.[47] MITI intervened and settled on a 1,200 yen per tonne price
cut, with the 400 yen difference to be budgeted for in the form of
indemnification for the end users. A 2.14 billion yen interest-free loan
scheme for the modernisation of the mines and of mining equipment
was also approved. In many cases this money was not used by the companies to improve facilities. Rather, as with earlier government-funded
schemes, it was invested in companies' other diversified interests.[48]

Under the agreement reached, both supply and demand for coal
were guaranteed. But this was not made law. Rather it was a 'gentle-
man's agreement' between the coal, steel and electrical industrial
giants, with the government acting as go-between.[49]

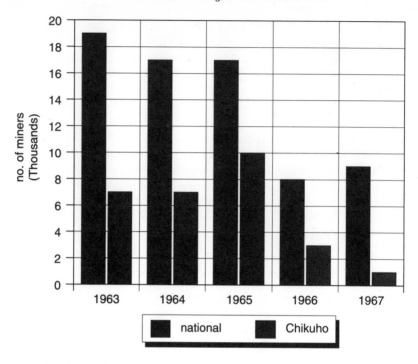

Source: Mizue (1978) p. 237.

Figure 5: Retrenched Miners

In short, this arrangement meant that the government would order
the construction of new coal-fired electrical power generators to absorb
much of the domestic coal, maintain the competitive pricing of coal so
that other industries would continue to use coal, and provide subsidies
for companies that employed ex-miners. However the plan, which
ostensibly aimed to retard the changeover to oil, was largely ineffective,
and social and economic problems with relation to the coal industry
increased at a hitherto unseen rate as mine-owners prepared to leave
the embattled industry.

The government offered to buy out all the obsolete mines at
reasonable prices if the companies were bankrupted for reasons
beyond their control, such as flooding, cave-ins, gas explosions and
serious labour disputes. The closure of the mines was in full swing in
the period from 1956 to 1965. By 1967, when the effects of the TCRB
were being seen nationwide, Chikuho showed the most dramatic
closure rate (see Figures 5 and 6). It should be emphasised here that

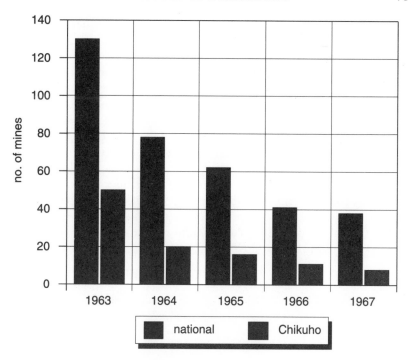

Source: National Census (1975), in *Chikuhō Fukkō Kyhōto Kaigi* (1978).

Figure 6: TCRB Mine Closures

the government was determined to bail out the industry through the 'Scrap and Build' policy. This was to become the hallmark of the government policy on coal. Press releases were full of the news that the 'rationalisation' of the industry was going ahead as planned, and that the competitive mines were now producing coal of better quality at lower cost than in earlier periods.[50]

Cheap coal from Australia, China and Canada, which in some cases was being produced by Japanese-owned companies, provided intense competition for local producers, and the government was under pressure from other industries to relax the restrictions on crude oil. Because the big companies did not want to invest their own funds in developing the mines that already existed, they exploited the sub-contracting system, becoming gradually more dependent on the output of the smaller mines whose coal carried the parent company's name. This allowed the big companies the freedom to close down their major operations and sell out to the government, take advantage of the reduced wages in the smaller mines and invest in other, unrelated ventures.

As a result of these policies, many smaller mines, which to all appearances seemed to be independent, were really working under the control of the big coal companies. They were also receiving financial assistance from the parent company, so that during times of low demand they had some financial security. Many of the small, truly independent companies were forced out of the market by this strategy. They had no financial benefactor, and in the period from 1955 to 1970 90 per cent of the small to medium-sized mines in Japan closed down. The big companies, too, had rationalised their operations, so that by 1970 less than one-third of the number of large mining companies' mines operating in 1955 were still solvent.[51] This trend is reflected in the industrial breakdown of the Chikuho region, where the percentage of workers in individual industries is compared (see Figures 7, 8 and 9).

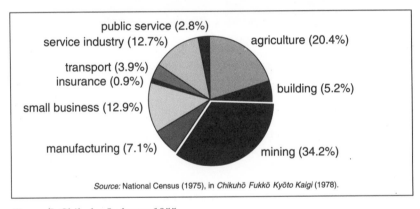

Figure 7: Chikuho Industry 1955

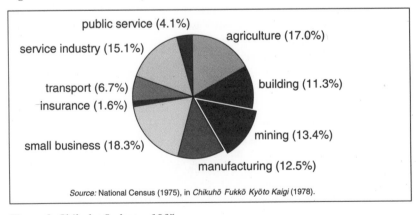

Figure 8: Chikuho Industry 1965

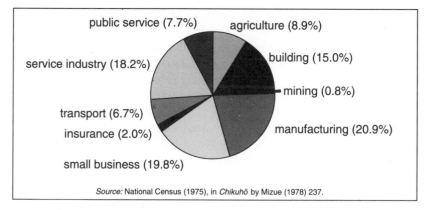

Figure 9: Chikuho Industry 1970

Note, in particular, that the percentage of workers in the mining industry dropped from 34 per cent to less than 1 per cent over this 15-year period.

After the mini-boom brought on by the first oil crisis after the Suez incident in 1956, the coal industry slumped and has never revived, although there were temporary signs of recovery after the 1973 Middle East War. The anti-pollution lobby was also able to exert pressure on the government to restrict the use of coal-powered electrical generators. It was widely touted that oil was cheaper and burnt cleaner. Japan was also being pressured into 'internationalising' by many Middle East countries, which in effect meant importing their oil. Inevitably the Oil Boilers Restriction Act was soon allowed to lapse, and the almost unrestricted flow of oil into Japan from overseas soon followed. It has been said that the only reason coal managed to last as long as it did was because of the heavy influence that the mine-owners had with the central government.[52]

The industry was in disarray, and there were serious problems in the areas where the coal companies had monopolised towns and cities. In the Chikuho region there was mass unemployment, high welfare dependency, major land damage as a result of the mines, polluted water, no work opportunities for many unemployed, no new industry coming into the area and widespread poverty, near starvation and a general deterioration of living standards.

Chikuho and the series of Temporary Coal Rationalisation Bills

The closure of the mines meant that a generation of miners became transient within the industry, constantly looking for whatever work was available in coalmines. This trend was particularly pronounced in

Chikuho, where the mining industry was much more volatile than in other areas. Even at the end of the coalmining era the skilled Chikuho miners would take their trade to towns where the mines were still operating, searching for work. For the Tagawa people, Omuta, where the Miike mines were situated, was particularly appealing. Omuta and Tagawa were M-san towns, and there was a fairly strong relationship between them. When the Tagawa M-san mines closed in 1963 and 1964 many of the young workers went to Omuta to look for work.

One miner at both the Tagawa M-san No. 3 Mine and at the No. 2 Mine at M-san Miike said the following about the process of moving to Omuta:

> I'd lived in Tagawa all my life. My father was a miner, and most of my family were miners too. We'd all worked in Sanko [Tagawa], me since I was a kid. Anyway, in 1964 the mine closed and we all got paid off with a bit of superannuation, which was our right anyway. Well, the money wasn't going to last for ever, so I thought that I'd better go and look for another job. At that time M-san in Miike was still looking for good pit men, and because that was my skill I decided that I'd take my family and go to Omuta. I was one of the lucky ones. I got a job pretty quick, and the work was easier than at Sanko [Tagawa], because there was a lot more new machinery for digging, and we only had to work nine-hour shifts.
>
> But my family was upset at having to leave our relatives. You see we had never been out of Tagawa before, and although there were quite a few other young families from Tagawa, no-one came from the *tanjū*, so we were really isolated. But the thing was that there was no other work that I could do. The only thing I knew was mining, and the only people I knew were miners. I didn't want to go on some work scheme making roads, where my skills would be wasted and I'd be just another labourer. I also didn't want to have to move too far from the rest of my family, who are all in Tagawa, so it was out of the question to go to Osaka or Tokyo to look for work.
>
> So I took the job and the housing that came with it, and I have been working here since then. Well up to last year actually. They retrenched me because I am 53. That's the new cut-off figure, and after 35 years for the company they give me a 7,500,000 yen [equivalent to 2 years' wages] lump sum, and that's it. Now, how am I going to find a job? Who'd employ an old man who has no useful work skills? I guess that I'll have to become a labourer after all.
>
> But, as I said, I was one of the lucky ones. I was young and had a trade, so I was O.K., but none of my brothers got jobs because they were too old or too young. The company wanted only those between 18 and 25 with experience, who were prepared to join the company union. This was after the big strike, you see, and the company didn't want any problems with the workers. So I said O.K., but I reckon they didn't employ anyone with any strength of character. You know, anyone who said that the wages were bad, or that the work was dangerous, or was a member of *Tanrō* or something.[53]

Amid promises that the coal industry could still be saved, the government introduced further new legislation, subsequently establishing the third TCRB. Perhaps this was in response to the lack of success of the

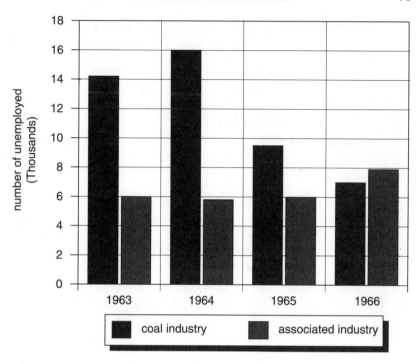

Source: Mizue (1978) p. 237.

Figure 10: Chikuho Unemployed Statistics

previous two TCRBs. The scrapping of inefficient mines had gone ahead at a far greater speed than the government had anticipated, as some mine-owners made use of the legislation to get out of the business with considerable amounts of government compensation in their pockets. The mine accident rate had increased 300 per cent since the introduction of the measure.[54] Unemployment was high (see Figure 10), and local governments were feeling the financial pinch through the unemployment assistance programs they had been forced to adopt. The forecast coal-production figures, which the government had guaranteed in its agreement with steel and electrical industries, were ten million tonnes short in 1964. Although coal prices were being subsidised by government funding, the coal companies had decided that they wanted to get out of the industry as soon as possible. So a situation MITI had not considered arose: demand exceeded supply. By 1964 the numbers of miners in employment forecast by MITI for 1967 had been reached. Smaller mines were closing at a tremendous pace,

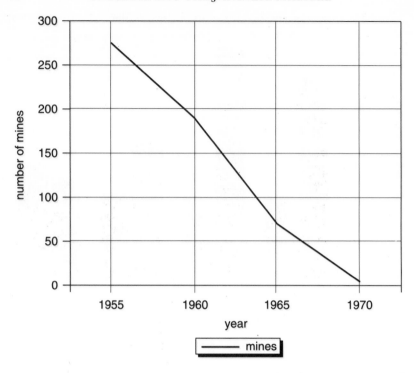

Figure 11a: Fukuoka Prefecture Mines Situation

and the big companies were also attempting to abandon the industry as soon as it was feasible (see Figures 11a and 11b). The owners of the smaller companies were often escaping without paying money owed to the miners from their private superannuation schemes. The super-annuation contribution scheme involved miners paying into a fund, which the company in turn was obliged to pay to the government fund on their behalf. When the miners stopped working, it was their right to get this money back in monthly instalments. It was called the 'private pension scheme', and was open to most workers from most industries. Within the mining industry often the owners did not pay the money into the fund, preferring to invest the money in their own private enterprises.

In these situations the miners had no legal recourse. Their unions were disbanded when the mines closed, and thus had no official or legal status. In the few cases that were taken to court by the unions, the companies in question, with one exception, claimed that they were

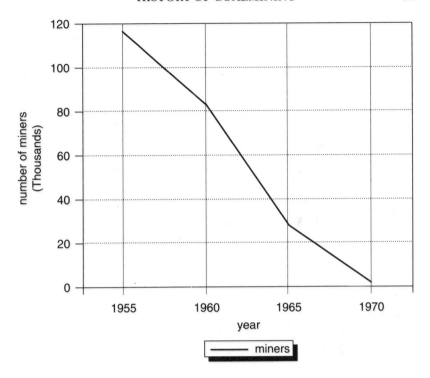

Figure 11b: Fukuoka Prefecture Miners' Situation

bankrupt and therefore not liable for repayment of the superannuation to the miners. So far, there has been only one successful case put by the plaintiffs, according to the Secretary of the Miners' Action Group.[55] As a result of this action, or inaction by the unions, *Tanrō* and the courts, the miners were forced to apply for welfare to survive. The situation was made worse by the problem of final severance pay in the small mines. Few workers received more than a month's severance pay, and many were forced to leave with no compensation at all while the owners pocketed the money that MITI had earmarked for the closure support fund.[56] One informant had the following to say about the system:

> Those bastards just took the money and ran. We had no chance to do anything. One day we were working, thinking that at least when the mines closed we would have some money to look forward to. And then we're all sacked, and all that money that they took from our pay is gone. We were left with nothing. I suppose it couldn't be helped, but we were really angry, and we all wanted to kill A-san.[57]

Further attempts to salvage the industry

One of the effects of the government's plan to salvage the industry by guaranteeing annual 55-million-tonne market levels, was that when supply had not reached the desired levels, MITI was obliged to bail out mines it thought were potentially, or approved, good producers. The K-san mines (incidentally in 1989 the subject of a parliamentary investigation into the misallocation of government funds) were the first to be officially assisted in 1963. The plan was to become a test of MITI's will in keeping the mines operational in the future, in the face of cheap energy imports.[58] But the process of change was firmly under way. The coal industry's 56 per cent share of the electrical generating market in 1965 had dropped to 5.1 per cent by 1975 as the electrical utilities switched almost completely to oil. Despite the ministrations of the government and the compulsory buying of coal, the coal industry was in serious trouble.[59]

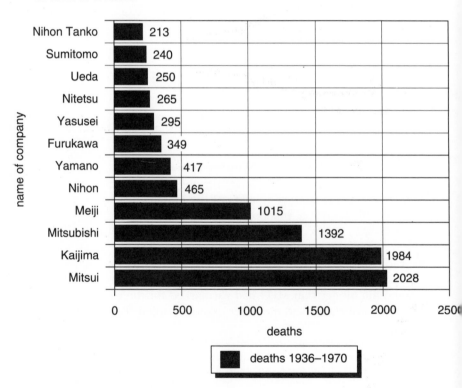

Source: Gisei no Tō (1975).

Figure 12: Chikuho Mining Deaths

In 1964 the unions presented to the government a plan for the nationalisation of the mining industry. The plan stressed the consolidation of the mining districts. By this time *Tanrō* had fewer than 65,000 members and little political influence. The mining companies had generally been ruthless in their dissolution of the unions within the industry, and *Tanrō*-affiliated union members were now unlikely to be given work. The situation in the M-san Miike mines, already described, was perhaps typical. By the end of the 1960 strike the number of miners in the New union was only slightly higher than the Old union, but by 1964, thanks to a policy of conscious discrimination implemented against *Tanrō* members, the New union had fully 75 per cent of the workers on their books.

The attitude of *Tanrō* and the case presented to the government in 1964 can be summarised by the leader of the *Tanrō* union in Miike in January 1989:

If Japan continues to cut resources, what will be left? Like rice, energy is necessary but it's *all* being imported, apart from nuclear reactors, which are crazy anyway. They're dangerous, as Japan is prone to earthquakes. Yet we have the technology, equipment and resources necessary to mine coal here for a long time to come. If we did that, not only would we not be completely dependent on overseas energy, we would also be able to stimulate local economies. But we needed the government's help with this, and the only way we could see this dream coming true was for the industry to be nationalised. They soon put an end to our hopes by forcing the TCRB plans down our throats, and pushing oil at the expense of coal.[60]

The deterioration of the industry continued, with the remaining big companies, notably M-san and N-san, dominating the industry and putting pressure on the government to support coal and to continue the process of providing aid for the companies that they considered worth bailing out: that is, the large companies themselves. They put together a very powerful lobby, which resulted in the formation of the Third Coal Task Force, which was to report to Parliament about the state of the industry, with recommendations on how to save it. This was headed by O-san, the proprietor of one of Kyushu's largest remaining coalmines. On the basis of his committee's findings, the Third Coal Program was introduced in 1966.

The appalling accident rate continued, because the mine-owners were still reluctant to improve mine safety (see Figure 12 for the total number of mining-accident deaths in Chikuho). Unemployment continued to rise as the closure of the mines was accelerated, contrary to the official aim of the program. The mine-owners were now in a rather secure position. They knew that there was guaranteed demand

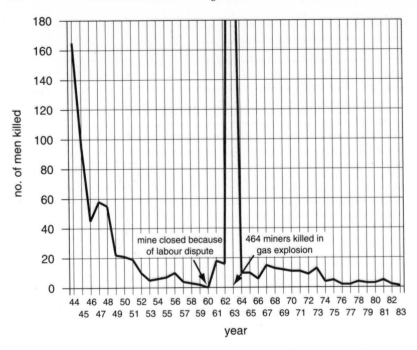

Source: Miike Safety Council, in *Kanashime o Ikari ni Kaete* (1985) *Miike Tankō Rōdhōkumiai*

Figure 13: Miike Mine Accidents—Deaths

for coal over the next five years, and that there were many displaced miners who wanted to work in the mines for almost any amount of money in any conditions. The unions were powerless, their power quashed in the wake of the Miike incidents, so the companies continued to take risks in hastening the production of coal to keep up with demand. One miner, a union member who saw this period out in one of the smaller mines, said of the situation in the late 1960s:

> We were concerned with workers' rights, with basic human rights and with the work conditions. These things were completely ignored by the company. On average we worked in the mine itself from between 12 and 15 hours a shift. The wages were poor. It was hard to maintain even the most basic standard of living. But most of the miners were frightened of the company and of the way the company could not only sack them, but could also cause them physical pain and force them to work. But what could any of us do? We were miners and we needed work, and this was about all that was going so we had to make the best of it.
> Of course the number of accidents increased too, because the company knew that they were going to have to close down soon enough and they

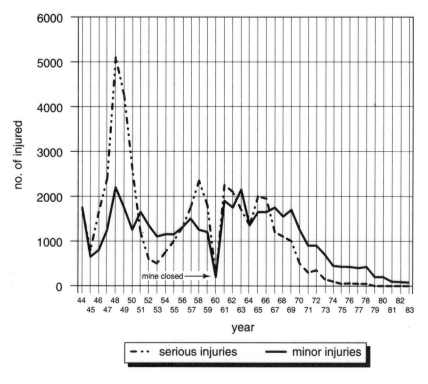

Source: Miike Safety Council, in *Kanashime o Ikari ni Kaete* (1985) *Miike Tanko Rodokumiai*

Figure 14: M-san Miike Mine Accidents—Injuries

meant to get what they could from the mine while they could. That meant they demanded we work long shifts on the quota system, so that a miner could not come out of the pit until he had produced his daily quota. And that quota went up and up as time went by. So tired men were still working the seam 14 or 15 hours after they had come to work, and of course tired men make mistakes. There were a lot of cave-ins where one or two people were killed at a time, mainly through carelessness caused by exhaustion. The company also told us to work under any circumstances. For example, when someone was sick the company would send two or three of the overseers to drag the man out of bed and send him down the mine. If he wouldn't go, he was beaten.[61]

The Miike statistics (Figures 13 and 14) which show the official number of deaths and injuries at this mine illustrate the high accident rate of the safer, large enterprises. Between 1944 and 1983, in the M-san Miike mine alone 1157 miners died, 42,801 miners were seriously injured, and 45,482 miners suffered minor injuries. Unfortunately, with the exception of *Gisei no Tō* ('The Tower of Sacrifice'), which by using media reports of accidents has calculated the total number of deaths in Chikuho mines (Figure 12), there are few records available from the smaller mines concerning accidents. It is unquestionable, however, that the smaller mines suffered higher per capita death and accident rates than large companies, such as M-san Miike, in the post-Miike-strike period in particular.

Responses to the unemployment problem

The time scale of the special public works programs set up under the TCRB had been extended, but the programs were still unable to absorb the huge numbers of unemployed. Local governments were under even more serious financial constraints than they had been, and the prefectural governments were also crying out for aid from MITI. Local citizens' movements had responded to what they saw as an attempt by the government to escape facing its responsibilities caused by the introduction of the TCRB. In Chikuho the Coal Industry Co-operative Council (CICC) had been formed in 1959. This group intended to unite the local coal areas in the fight against the restrictions imposed under the current version of the TCRB. There were altogether 45 cities, towns and villages involved in the movement, which had its headquarters in Fukuoka city. At the first general meeting, in 1959, the CICC passed recommendations that the TCRB was inadequate, and demanded that certain conditions be redressed. The current unemployment benefits were inadequate. The conditions in the coal villages (*tanjū*) were appalling: there was no electricity and no running water in many. More money was urgently needed from the government.[62]

This case was presented to the central government. The Diet gave its response after an all-night sitting. Rather than approach the problem on the premise that the *tanjū* were permanent settlements, and that the workers who lived in them were permanent residents, the government decided that it would attempt to disperse the *tanjū*, and therefore solve the most conspicuous problem the TCRB had caused: poverty. Unemployment could also be solved in this way: that is, by sending the unemployed people from the *tanjū* to other areas to work and live, the government would be able to rid itself of the 'unemployed group mentality'. The people remaining, it was assumed, would be those who were keen to work, and local competition for jobs would decrease in direct proportion to the decrease in population. There was construction work going on in the Kanto and Kansai areas around this time, preparing land and buildings for the 1964 Tokyo Olympics, so the government rightly assumed that there would be much work for displaced miners. Local opportunities for alternative employment were almost non-existent: local industry, which had been almost totally dependent on coal, had dissolved; demand for the service industries had declined in the wake of the diminishing and impoverished population; and alternative business ventures were slow in setting up operations. Consequently, many miners found that their pensions were cut off and that they were being exhorted to leave their homes and go to Honshu to work, in line with the government policies.

> I tell you, when the mines closed, no one could afford to go out and enjoy themselves. You know, drinking and all that. It was because the only people left were ex-miners, and none of us had any money or any future. Some of us in our 40s and 50s were too old to go packing up and looking for work in some strange place where we had never been before. Most of my work-mates left town though, and went to look for work in Kansai, Kanto and Nagoya. Some of them got jobs in construction projects: the Olympics, and in Toyota.
> Everyone was a bit disturbed about leaving (to go to Tokyo), and in my case I couldn't. Many of the men who went up there came home after looking for work and failing. Lots of them hated it away from their friends, and they were treated like outcasts. They lived in groups of Chikuho people, and when they told anyone that they came from Tagawa they were always shunned. Anyway, even if the pay was good I just couldn't go. I was born and bred here, so rather than packing up my family and leaving all my friends I decided that I'd settle for doing day labouring in Tagawa, even though the pay was terrible.[63]

The government went one step further in dealing with unemployment. The policy of exhorting the miners to leave town to work in other areas, or to become unemployed in other areas, had the effect of reducing the unemployment statistics in Chikuho, so after this success the government decided that a larger-scale program was required. In response to the CICC's demands, the government established a seven billion yen fund to help miners resettle overseas, mainly in Brazil, Colombia and Argentina: it decided to export the unemployed.[64] In a political move not unlike Britain's wholesale transportation of convicts to Australia, the government felt that they would be able to solve the problem by moving it elsewhere.

In fact, masses of unemployed did not go overseas, and many of the people who did go soon returned to Japan after 'failing' away from home. Unemployment needed to be dealt with in a more direct manner, and with the exception of the Special Coal Workers' Temporary Re-employment Scheme, there were few mechanisms in place to achieve this. Even this scheme, which was constantly revamped, was hopelessly inadequate, and the numbers of unemployed coalminers increased to previously unheard-of levels in some of the coal areas, notably in Chikuho. In Kawasaki and in Tagawa 45 per cent of the local workforce was either unemployed or living on welfare in 1960.[65]

In the late 1950s *Tanrō* estimated that by 1963 the TCRB would be responsible for the loss of a further 60,000 jobs. The unions demanded that the government take responsibility for the situation, and pass new laws guaranteeing the workers some rights to employment and security. *Keidanren* (the Federation of Economic Organisations) put forward a plan based on the recommendations of the unions, whereby the government would attempt to deal with the estimated 90,000 unemployed miners: 7,000 would be transferred to other mining companies; 34,000 would be retrained to work in other industries; 11,000 would be fitted into community unemployment programs; and 1,000 would be given 'special training'. The remaining workers (about 38,000 of them) would just have to make do as best they could.[66]

The Temporary Unemployed Coal Workers Measure (TUCWM) was made law in October 1959. The main points were as follows:

1 The government would make plans to move the workers from the seriously afflicted areas to other areas, where they could find work. Also, the unemployed coalminers' groups would start up operations where unemployed miners would have their welfare cut off if they didn't take part in the public works programs sponsored by individual local governments.

2 Coal workers would be given preference in employment situations over other unemployed.

3 Retraining in other professions would be given to coalminers who indicated their intention of changing jobs.

4 A Coal Unemployment Commission (CUC) would be established with the aim of distributing benefits to those coalminers who they decided were disadvantaged. Also money and training would be provided to ex-coalminers who wanted to migrate to South America. Money would also be provided for house repairs, and employers willing to employ coalminers would be able to claim special interest-free loans for the expansion of their business.

5 The plan was to have a five-year limit, and there was to be a probationary period of six months, after which the success of the plan would be evaluated, and further aid considered.[67]

This plan, like all the measures that the government came up with, was absolutely inadequate. People could not live on these minimum subsistence levels [under the terms of the CUC] in the first place, and the law didn't address the really important, basic issues, like job creation and compensation for the workforce. This law was purely *tatemae* [lip-service], and was ineffective. The relief that had been promised in all the discussions before the measure was made law was not relief at all in the end. In fact, the law was responsible for escalating the victimisation of many people. People were forced to live off each other, as they do today in this area, because they didn't qualify for the restricted welfare benefits.[68]

The unions complained that the government was not doing enough, and local governments complained that their own financial responsibility was heavy enough without the added burden of the new measure. They maintained that they would not be able to fund the new law. While local government supported the aims of the legislation, they demanded that the national and prefectural governments be more involved with the financing of these projects.

But the biggest problem was that these measures were largely lip-service, and very few workers were actually 'retrained'. The real effect was that there was now a number of ex-miners working on public works projects at minimum wages, others in construction (it has been estimated that there were 100,000 miners involved nationally in construction work), a few miners working in new mines, even fewer miners going overseas, more miners receiving welfare payments, and others living 'hand to mouth'.[69] The TUCWM legislation was a placebo and had the desired effect: it was a piece of legislation designed to show the government's concern with the miners' situation without being too expensive. The government continued with its rationalisation plans for the industry, and the changeover to oil was in full swing as this measure was announced.

The same informant, Idegawa, said this about the situation in Chikuho at the time:

> The situation had deteriorated to such an extent in the smaller *tanjū* that people were relying on food tickets handed out by the company and redeemable only in the company stores. Of course, no one could save any money, and the future looked bleak. In Chikuho, prospects were negligible for middle-aged and older miners, and the kids had little chance of an education. There was large-scale, but temporary, movement out of the area in the early 1960s as workers went elsewhere to search for work. The general feeling was that Chikuho was dead. Welfare recipients outnumbered workers, and many people suffered from malnutrition. In short, the situation was desperate.[70]

Although the smaller companies were the first to be affected by the TCRB, the larger companies also began to rationalise their operations in earnest after consultations with MITI. The government was still actively involved in developing legislation to keep coal companies operational, and it had negotiated with the leaders of the big coal companies and the major coal-purchasers to ensure that production targets and prices be met. With mass closures looming over the industry, the coal-producers were determined to make a stand to reduce the chance of losses.

O-san, the leader of the mine-owners' cartel, pressured MITI into making some hard decisions as to how far they were prepared to go to help out the industry. His taskforce demanded that the government invest 100 billion yen to take over the superannuation payments and the running of all mines slated for scrapping in the near future; that 70–80 per cent of required capital be given to the mining companies interest-free for the modernisation of equipment; and that an additional 500 yen a tonne be paid by the government as a subsidy to the coal-producers. The surprising thing about these demands was that the government seriously considered them, and when the program went through the legislation process, some were met. The final version of the new Coal Program announced in July 1966 allowed for a production target of 50 million tonnes, with funds allocated to the companies set at treble their previous levels. A 100 billion yen interest-free loan scheme was also extended to the industry in an attempt to protect the mine-owners.[71]

Operating deficits had doubled within two years to 200 billion yen, yet the banks continued to extend funds to the coal industry in the expectation that the government would step in and help them out, as they had done many times in the past. The industries that were to buy the bulk of the coal were dissatisfied with the price the cartel of big coal companies had required, and demanded that the price be dropped, and that the government pay compensation to them. The electrical utilities agreed to take 23 million tonnes if the price that they paid was not higher than the price that had been agreed upon in the earlier programs. The steel industry also agreed to take the ten million tonnes they had been slated for only if full government indemnification was included. MITI agreed to supply the steel industry with 53 billion yen as indemnification for taking even this low quantity of domestic coal. Ironically, the steel industry grew so fast, and the coal industry shrank so fast, that they were soon importing large quantities of coking and steam-quality coal from Australia and Canada to fuel the steel industry.[72]

The assumption of mine debts was to prove embarrassing for the government, because no sooner had the announcement of the new program been made than one of the largest mining firms, Dai Nippon, failed. Other firms followed suit, and when the results of the policy had been tabulated it was clear that 13 big companies were responsible for more than 90 per cent of the industry's debt, which the government had assumed. The small companies gained little or nothing.[73] The banks withdrew their support from the industry, and many of the private larger companies were no longer able to provide capital for operations, and fell into receivership. The diversified industrial giants, such as T-san, M-san and N-san, which had associated banks, were not so adversely affected, and used government support to continue operations, although they too had made preparations to get out of the industry.

The industry was on its last legs by the mid-1960s, yet there were still few contingency plans to ease the plight of the displaced miners. Instead of spending public funds on developing industries in areas where there was massive unemployment, and instead of spending money on the retraining of many of the displaced miners and improving conditions in which they lived, the government succumbed to pressure from the mine-owners. Huge amounts of public funds were spent on trying to revive a dying industry with much of this money going into the pockets of the big mine-owners.[74]

Another informant had this to say about the closure of M-san Tagawa, one of the big companies where she worked for 32 years:

When the mines closed, there was only one thing on everyone's mind: what do we do now? There was despair at the way the government had manipulated us, and now they were just ignoring the problem that they had caused. I went to work in a tile factory, because that was all that there was available, and the money was less than one-third of the pay that I got with M-san. I was a foreman with M-san, but when I went to work in the tile factory, which was also owned by the company, I was forced to work for almost slave wages because I was a woman. I didn't know any of the people there, so the camaraderie that we had at the mine was gone, but I had to support my son.

You see, I wanted to send him to high school and that was expensive, so I just had to take whatever work was available, and the job that I got with the tile company was a lot better than the situation of many of my friends. Lots of them didn't get any work, and depended on their families and the government handouts to survive. There was no way that two of us could eat on what the government was paying out so what could I do? I just had to work, and, really, anything would have done at the time.[75]

Throughout this period of disruption and social change the unions were remarkable for their apparent acquiescence to government policy. After the Miike strike, and a number of smaller strikes, the labour situation was resolved in favour of the companies. The unions did not have the political strength necessary to lead the workers in protests at the wage-cuts, the redundancies and the drop in living standards. Although *Tanrō* made a number of demands about retirement pay, the continuation and nationalisation of the industry, and the support of retrenched workers after the industry had become redundant, few of the demands were met. Union support had declined to the extent that by the mid-1960s few active coalminers were members of *Tanrō*. Although the miners were required to be members of unions, the majority chose the so-called *goyō kumiai*, or enterprise unions, over *Tanrō* basically because members of *Tanrō* were unlikely to find work in the industry in the wake of the Miike labour unrest. The most militant unions in Japan's history slowly faded from view with no more than a whimper, and with them went the power of the workers to influence any policy decisions about wages, working conditions or the future of the mines.

By 1970 there were only five mines operational in the Chikuho region. Nationally, only the M-san Miike, the N-san Takashima and Yubari, and the H-san Hokkaido mines employed more than a handful of miners. These mines were still operating at close to maximum capacity in the environment of co-operation and support from government that existed following the demands of the last coal taskforce. M-san, N-san and H-san gradually reduced the size of their respective mining workforces, and when the H-san and N-san enterprises closed in 1985 and 1987 respectively, only Miike was left operating. Today Miike employs approximately 2,000 miners, and these numbers are rapidly decreasing as management further rationalises the labour force and moves toward closure. The miners are concerned only about reasonable retrenchment pay, and the order of the dismissal notices: that is, which age-group is to be pensioned off first. The dream that the industry could still be a viable concern, and that the men would have some say in the working conditions and wage claims was shattered many years ago. The unions involved say they have only the aim of making the severance from the industry as painless as possible for the men.

Conclusion

Violence, subversion and large-scale political and economic manipulation have underlain the history of the coalmining industry in Japan, and hence in Chikuho. It could be said that government bureaucracy, through its close relationships with coal industry leaders, was the active agent in allowing the misallocation of both local and national funds for an industry that was in reality in rapid decline and beyond redemption. Rather than investigating ways in which the allocation of resources could have been made to best alleviate the suffering within communities that were dependent on coal, the government chose to support the companies that had helped to bring about the situation. The government, through implementing policy that relieved the coal companies of financial responsibility for the social conditions they had created, and placing the onus on the local communities to 'restore themselves', maintained its relationship with the ex-*zaibatsu* at the expense of the people of the coalfields.

There were no safeguards on how public money was spent in attempting to resurrect the industry, the parties involved choosing to honour a 'gentlemen's agreement'. In effect, the government was supporting the coal companies' economic diversification of business interests. Although the publicity surrounding the payments made to the companies under various coal programs indicated that the money would be used to improve safety standards and company housing, for example, this money was apparently diverted to other company businesses, such as oil, petroleum, chemicals, textiles and cement.

Equally, the government ignored the implications of their ambiguously worded series of TCRBs and Coal Programs, which allowed coalmine-owners to add to the already onerous demands upon their workforce, forcing them to increase production in increasingly unsafe conditions. These circumstances doubtless contributed to the rapid increase in the number of mining accidents which occurred in the 1960s. The mining companies themselves had been able to avoid paying compensation for damage to body or property as a result of accidents, and were able to remove the concept of the payment of compensation from the political agenda by claiming their inability to pay.

The government, in what appeared to be a form of collusion with the industry leaders, chose not to investigate what had happened to the large sums of money they had invested in the companies, which suddenly declared bankruptcy. Instead, they chose to undertake the process of paying compensation to the mining communities on the companies' behalf through the political process: that is, by supplying *all* of the legislation and *a percentage* of the actual money (usually 30 per cent) and delegating all other responsibility to the communities and prefectures.

The government, through its reluctance to support the coal industry until it was too late, and through its approval of the switchover to oil and imported coal, under pressure from its international trading partners and for obvious macro-economic reasons, facilitated the development of a political structure in which a repressive system of mining practices came to be standardised. By establishing the tone of political conspiracy, the government, through its manipulation of the legal agenda, worked in co-operation with the large mining companies' owners, who were able to manipulate the economic agenda by imposing tight margins for small producers. These, in turn, responded by tightening labour control to retain profitability. So a vertically integrated political and economic hierarchy emerged. Labour control was of key importance, and the development of the strategy to split the unions through coercion and co-option weakened the power of the once all-powerful *Tanrō*, which by the mid-1960s was a rather impotent organisation with a limited number of members.

The companies' ability to organise as a cartel and to fight the imposition of a new energy source was also of importance. Moreover, the pervasive influence of the former *zaibatsu* and the strength of the contacts between this group and the government gave them the tools needed to tackle the new energy regime.

Although all the outward trappings of democracy were present in the political system, in practice an elitist group of very powerful men was able to influence other groups of powerful men that their best interests lay in supporting the coal industry over the short term. By removing political opposition, through reaching agreement with other members of private enterprise who stood to benefit by the actions of the coal cartel, the coal companies were able to maximise profitability over the medium term, in an economically 'safe' environment, with a guaranteed return for any investment they made. The unions were compromised at the national level, and at the local level there was no fear of protest because of the system of labour control using the *yakuza*-like *rōmu*, which the smaller mines had imposed (see chapters 6, 7, 9 and 10).

By gradually reinvesting in other business, and by applying pressure on the smaller companies to produce coal on their behalf and sell it in their name, the large companies were able to honour their agreements with the steel-makers and other industrialists under the final Coal Program, without jeopardising their own profitability. Thus the big companies were able to withdraw from the industry profitably, leaving the problem of cleaning up the local economies to the smaller companies and to local governments.

NOTES TO CHAPTER 4

1 Shinfuji, 1985, p.234.
2 Ogata, interview, 1988.
3 For a full treatment of this topic, see Shinfuji, 1985; Takazaki, 1961; *Tagawa Shishi*, 1979 (all in Japanese) and Samuels, 1987.
4 Takazaki, 1961, p.132; Idegawa, 1984, p.12.
5 Kim, personal communication, 1988.
6 *Kyōsei Renkō* bulletin, vol. 1, 1980, p.3; Kim, personal communication, 1988.
7 *Kyōsei Renkō* documents, 1989, p.44.
8 Kim, personal communication, 1988.
9 Samuels, 1987, p.89.
10 Ibid. p.90.
11 Shinfuji, 1985, p.334.
12 Samuels, 1987, p.94.
13 Takazaki, 1961, p.57.
14 Shinfuji, 1985, p.146.
15 Takazaki, 1961, p.26.
16 Yada, interview, 1988.
17 Onishi, 1975.

18 Idegawa, interview, 1988; Takazaki, 1961, p.15.
19 Ueno, 1985c, p.276.
20 Yada, 1975, p.138; Samuels, 1987, p.105.
21 Sonoda, 1970, p.53.
22 *Tagawa Shishi*, 1979, pp.485–6.
23 Oguchi, Idegawa, interviews, 1988.
24 See *Gisei no Tō* (The Tower of Sacrifice), 1975.
25 The oil companies and steel industry had combined at various points to lobby the government to pressure the coal industry to lower its basic price.
26 *Tagawa Shishi*, 1979, p.487.
27 Ibid. p.490.
28 Ibid. p.490.
29 Ibid. p.487.
30 Yada, 1975, p.122.
31 Samuels, 1987, p.111.
32 Yada, 1975, p.140.
33 Takazaki, 1961, p.143.
34 Takazaki, personal communication, 1988; Nagasue, 1973, p.236.
35 *Tagawa Shishi*, 1979, p.494.
36 Ibid. p.496.
37 Shinfuji, 1985, p.247.
38 *Miike Tōsō no Kinen*, 1985a, p.6.
39 *Miike Tankō Rōdōkumiai Nōto*, 1985b, p.16.
40 Shinfuji, 1985, p.258; *Miike Tankō Rōdōkumiai Nōto*, 1985b, p.20.
41 *Miike Tankō Rōdōkumiai Nōto* 1985b, p.54. According to this document, five miners were killed in direct confrontation with gangsters and police, and more miners were attacked in their own homes.
42 *Nishi Nihon Shinbun*, 12 August 1961.
43 Hanno, interview, 1988.
44 It should be pointed out that the miners were without pay for the duration of the strike.
45 *Asahi Shinbun*, 16 November 1960.
46 Idegawa, interview, 1988.
47 Samuels, 1987, p.115.
48 Yada, 1975, p.224.
49 Samuels, 1987, p.115.
50 See, for example, *Asahi Shinbun* throughout December 1961, especially Chikuho section.
51 Yada, 1975, p.223.
52 Ueno, 1985e, p.36; Yada, 1975, p.120.
53 Hamasaki, interview, 1988.
54 Oguchi, Idegawa, interviews, 1988.
55 Hayashi, interview, 1987.
56 Idegawa, Takazaki, interview, 1987.
57 Sasaki, interview, 1988.
58 Samuels, 1987, p.119.
59 Ibid. p.55.
60 Mori, interview, 1988.
61 Ishiguchi, interview, 1988.
62 *Tagawa Shishi*, 1979, p.403.
63 Sasaki, interview, 1988.
64 *Tagawa Shishi*, 1979, p.506.
65 *Chikuho Fukko Kyoto Kaigi*, in *Yomigaere Chikuhō*, 1966, p.72.
66 *Tagawa Shishi*, 1979, p.506.
67 Ibid. p.505.
68 Idegawa, interview, 1987.
69 Idegawa, personal communication, 1989.

70 Idegawa, interview, 1987.
71 Samuels, 1987, p.122.
72 Ibid. p.123.
73 Yada, 1975, p.225.
74 Ueno, 1985b, p.56.
75 Kazuko, interview, 1989.

CHAPTER 5

The Picture Show Man

3.30 p.m. The quiet of the *tanjū* is shattered by raucous children's songs being played at such a high volume that the melody and lyrics are lost in distortion. Emerging from my house, I notice the small children running out onto the roads in the direction of the carpark, behind the new apartment blocks. I yell at a couple of the children, 'What's all the noise?' They yell back, 'It's the *kami shibai* man', without stopping. Like the flute of the Pied Piper, the 'music' seems to have a desperate appeal to the small children as they race towards the source. I follow them. In the carpark is a cream-coloured Toyota Corolla station wagon, the back opened, surrounded by about 15 children and a couple of elderly relatives. Standing in the middle of the crowd is a man in his late thirties or early forties. Quite large, dressed in jeans and a T-shirt and wearing thick-lensed glasses, his gravelly, high-pitched voice has a remarkable penetrating quality, as he tells the children to calm down.

Set up on the wagon's tailgate is a small wooden frame about one metre square, carved to look like the facade of a theatre stage. Within this frame is a lurid painting of a boy fighting a wolf, blood dripping from the knife in the boy's grasp. The antics of the crowd distract my attention from the painting as I take in the scene that is unfolding around me. The children are all shouting, '*Ojisan* [uncle], I want one of those ones on a stick!', 'I want one of those paper thin ones!' The man is handing out sweets in exchange for ten-yen coins. 'I've finished it. Look! The middle's still OK. Give me a new one!' screams one of the smallest children. The man takes the proffered sweet, critically analyses it, and with a slight scowl says, 'All right, here's the new one. You did it just right', giving the child another sweet.

By this time I am totally bemused. I look at all the other children who are very carefully sucking on their sweets, pulling them out of their mouths every couple of seconds to examine them, and then popping them back in again. More children are clamouring for new sweets by this stage, and the *kami shibai* man examines each one carefully, sometimes giving them a new one, sometimes saying, 'No, look at that. You've eaten some of the middle bit'. or 'You've already had a second one. You're not getting any more, you rat'. The children who have been refused scream that he is a 'tight-fisted old uncle', to which he seems impervious.

After about ten minutes of this, the show starts. The story is about a boy who is the son of a coalminer. He goes into the forest one day, and is met by a wolf who asks him the way to town. The boy tells him, and thinks nothing more of it. When he returns home, his parents are missing, and he sees the wolf running from the house, with his dead and bloody mother between its jaws. He discovers the father lying in a pool of blood on the floor. Angry, his innocence lost, he realises what he has done by showing the wolf the way to town. The ghosts of his mother and father come to him that night to tell him that until the wolf has been killed they will have no rest in the spirit world. The ghosts are just as they were when they were killed: the torn flesh hanging from their wounds, the blood congealed, their faces hideous parodies of the human form. The boy eventually tracks down the wolf, and kills it in a bloody climax. His parents are then able to take their rest in the spirit world and are no longer *yūrei* (ghosts of dissatisfied spirits).

The story is told in a matter-of-fact way, each dramatic event illustrated by the introduction of a new picture into the frame, rather than by the narrator's voice. The violent scenes are particularly vividly portrayed, blood and gore rather graphically painted in vermilion. The death of the wolf is described over four frames, the slow, agonising death being a satisfactory ending. The *kami shibai* man's rough voice every now and then betrays emotion, but generally he seems to be going through the motions as he tells the tale. The children, enraptured at first, gradually lose interest over the ten-minute tale, becoming alert only at certain graphically violent scenes. The ending is a big success, with the children screaming their delight at the hideous death of the wolf.

The story over, the children once more clamour for sweets. The *kami shibai* man obliges, the ritual of the selective sweet-sucking played out again. After this ritual is over, he shuts the tailgate of the wagon and drives off, the dulcet tones of the children's music fading into the distance behind him.

The *kami shibai* man

Oguchi, the picture show man, is an anachronism. From near Osaka, he came to Kawasaki with the famous Caravan Movement, a Christian students' movement organised to bring aid and education to the people of Chikuho in 1968, when the plight of the miners was once again brought to national attention. They were only a small group, about 50 in number, yet they established kindergartens, child-minding centres, playgrounds, informal education centres, nursing care, old people's recreation centres and many other facilities throughout, in particular, the small towns in the Chikuho region.

Oguchi was first employed as a carpenter for this group and, after being involved with them for a couple of years, he moved into a *tanjū* in Kawasaki with his family. In 1970 he took a job with the World Council of Churches, a job that took him to most of the Asian subcontinent in the capacity of construction adviser and general handyman. When he returned to his family in 1973, his wife immediately divorced him because she maintained that he was 'not really a very Christian person, and was more concerned with travel than with his family'. He remarried two years later and, as he says, was 'fortunate' enough to be living in a *tanjū* when it was flattened by a typhoon. The rebuilding of the *tanjū* was sponsored by the local and prefectural governments' Special Relief Fund, which meant that the old buildings were torn down and, at the instigation of Chikara, the ex-*yakuza* boss, new self-contained, three-bedroom houses were built on the site of the *tanjū*. The rental of these places is fixed at the same rates the inhabitants paid for the old *tanjū*: 4,500 yen a month. Interestingly, Oguchi himself had no coal experience, although he had worked in a number of different labouring jobs for coal company subcontractors. Yet he was able, through his first wife's contacts (her father was a miner), to get into the *tanjū*.

In 1974, while on a *toroko tsuaa* (massage parlour tour) of Kita Kyushu, he met an old man who had been a miner and a *kami shibai* man. In a room in a dirty hotel in the red light district of Kita Kyushu the old man showed him some of the pictures he used to display to the children in *tanjū* all over the country. Oguchi was so impressed with the artwork and the stories that went with the pictures that he decided to buy them. Altogether he purchased more than 6,000 pictures at a cost of 300,000 yen. There were enough stories to last for more than ten years, he says. He decided then to become a *kami shibai* man for a living, after being convinced that it was both a money-making proposition, and a worthwhile cause.

The *kami shibai* tradition

Kami shibai is traditionally associated with *burakumin* as a profession. It started in the early 1920s, in the wake of the first full-length silent movies. Originally conceived as an alternative to movie theatres, the *kami shibai* rapidly grew in popularity in poor communities. Using the concept of the silent movies and the narrator, the *kami shibai* relied on a series of pictures, which were displayed in a small, theatre-like frame. On the back of these pictures were the sequential elements of the story to be presented, so that the *kami shibai* man was able to read the stories out loud to his audience, each picture being presented with the relevant dialogue. The pictures were painted in bright colours. Typically the stories were moral or cautionary tales, often graphically violent. The people in the stories were often eaten by wild animals, killed by foreigners, or bashed by soldiers and police if they made mistakes. The tattooed *yakuza* also became the heroes of many of these tales.

Up until the 1930s a wide range of social commentary was possible within this medium: from cautions about how to deal with outsiders, and issues concerning sexual relationships, to criticisms of the policies of government. However, in 1932 the dreaded Thought Police, responsible for the curtailment of unpatriotic thoughts and activities 'not in the national interests', decided to investigate the people presenting the *kami shibai*. After this investigation they decided that all *kami shibai* would have to be licensed and the material censored so that nothing critical of the Emperor or the Japanese status quo would be presented. Moreover, in the strict moral climate of the 1930s, topics relating to sex, poverty and crime were made illegal. During the war, transgressions of the law were punishable by death.

Certain stories and themes were allowed, such as those justifying the invasions of Manchuria and Korea, the inalienable right of the Emperor to rule, the value of the Imperial forces, and the integrity of the farmers' contribution to the Divine Cause of the Emperor. In effect, the medium became a propaganda tool for the government. Standardisation brought a much higher quality of artwork, and by the end of the Second World War the standard was more than just a representation of the authors' imagination. Artists had been commissioned to draw complex and subtle images for the Association of *Kami Shibai* People, and some of these pictures are today worth many thousands of dollars. In fact, many of the artists who drew the *kami shibai* in the post-war era are some of Japan's best-known modern cartoonists.

In the period of liberalisation following the war, the content of *kami shibai* was no longer so tightly controlled, but the popularity of the shows decreased owing to the spread of cinema. Cynical, non-aligned criticisms of the coal industry and stories of greed and usury started to appear, but for the most part the *kami shibai* remained fairly conservative in content. This was mainly due to the declining fortunes of the people who presented the shows. Only rarely were the presenters also artists, so new stories had to be commissioned from good artists. This was expensive, and few *kami shibai* people could afford to buy new stories.

Origins of the *kami shibai* in Chikuho

The *kami shibai* was apparently started by the people who realised that there was a gap to be filled in a society where entertainment was limited. The mining communities, particularly the small ones, were an obvious choice, because of their geographical and social isolation. In Chikuho, the movement started in 1923, according to Oguchi, when the first *kami shibai* people came down from Osaka. These people were from an Osaka *buraku*,[1] and had acquired the skills through a guild of actors and puppeteers. As competition in the Kansai region increased, some of their number decided that there might be a better living to be had in Kyushu, so they moved to the Chikuho coalfields.

The *kami shibai* presenters had a set area within which they performed their shows; territories were established by mutual agreement. Up until the 1960s these men (they were always male) would push their carts around the *tanjū* with the picture show set up on the back of the carts. Their cries were children's songs, with the occasional flute accompaniment, and the beating of a *taiko* (drum). *Tanjū* children and adults would come out of their homes and go to see the show, buying the sweets that were the *kami shibai* man's sole source of income. The sweets were sugar and water, square wafers with shapes of animals impressed in the centres. The children had to try to suck the outside of the sweet away so that only the animal in the centre was left. If they could leave only the shape, with no indentations (the rules were strict) they were entitled to a second, free sweet. The challenge was met only rarely in the days when poverty was endemic in the region. Sugar was a luxury that few could afford, and generally the children succumbed instantly to the sickly sweetness, gulping the sweets down. After the sweets had been bought, the *kami shibai* man would present his show.

Not only were the *kami shibai* men entertainers, they also brought news to the people in the *tanjū*. Calling in at as many as ten or twelve *tanjū* in the course of their rounds, the *kami shibai* men were able to collect news of big events, rumours of trouble, messages from people in one *tanjū* for those in another and so on. They were, then, unofficial but trusted news services in their own right. Their position as 'trusted outsiders' in many *tanjū* was an ambiguous role, but certainly they were able to make and exploit many contacts, finding out controversial information about sensitive issues. Because they were outsiders, they were not subject to the same arbitrary punishments as *tanjū* people for disclosing company 'secrets', such as information about the extremes of violence a company used. However, they were required to be discreet, because the company could ban them from entering company property if they thought that they were spreading dissent.

The fact that many of these men were *burakumin*, the despised and 'different' people who lived in settlements removed from the coal company *tanjū*, meant that there were ambivalent feelings towards them. Many *burakumin* worked in the mines, the majority in the 'badger holes'. Within the *buraku* strongholds, *kami shibai* men were regarded as being somewhat unusual, because their contacts with the outside world were so developed. The *buraku* communities were dependent on the *kami shibai* men for news of the world outside their isolated existence. They brought letters, and sometimes newspapers into the *burakumin* communities, and they also carried word of how the other *buraku* communities were organising themselves, and news of the politicisation of the *buraku* cause, and violence directed at *burakumin*.

Oguchi and his personal cause

These days, Oguchi is one of the last remaining *kami shibai* men in Japan. Driving his Toyota from *tanjū* to *tanjū*, he makes a reasonable living in much the same way the *kami shibai* of old did: telling stories to a new generation of miners' relatives; collecting and passing on gossip; making contacts within *tanjū*. Although the style of his presentations is more modern and in line with contemporary society's mores, he relies heavily on the work of traditional *kami shibai* artists. In fact, the stories he presents are the stories that have been presented for a generation, but they are presented in the Oguchi style: laconic, cynical and inevitably delivered with the gravel-voice trademark. Having a car enables him to reach a wider audience than if he was still reliant on the old hand carts; but with audiences dropping off, he needs to be able to reach more *tanjū* to make the business pay.

It might be expected that a person performing in such a venerable profession would be informed about the roots and history of the profession, and deeply motivated to carry on delivering messages traditionally associated with *kami shibai*. In Oguchi's case, although he is interested in the tradition of the *kami shibai*, it is primarily economic necessity and the need to maintain the quality of life that drive him to continue his work. He says:

I do the work because it pays the bills, gives me time to relax (I don't work when it rains, for example, so I can go mountain climbing) and because it's a better job than carpentry. I was lucky to find that man in Kita Kyushu, because doing this job has made a huge difference to my life. I get to talk to many new people, and have contact with people I have always had an interest in. I'm also able to get involved in social movements, and research what happened in Chikuho in the coal days. I mean, it beats labouring, that's for sure.[2]

Over a year, Oguchi maintains that he makes about 250,000 yen a month, which puts him in the higher income bracket for Kawasaki. His wife is a potter, so they and their two children have a fairly comfortable existence. He is active in local politics, largely thanks to his myriad contacts, and organises children's days, welfare outings for the aged, festivals, dances and many other events within the *tanjū*. Because of the diversity of his contacts, he has also become interested in the development of the Y-san Coal Mine disaster relief organisation, the N-san Takashima accident, and the Anti-Emperor Movement. He believes that Chikuho is being eroded from within and without by the totalitarianism of the elite, and that this is connected with the way that history is represented to the local people. He is always willing to discuss the workings of the power elite in Chikuho.

Not everyone shares Oguchi's enthusiasm for this topic, and this situation is exacerbated by his sometimes ill-informed but very confident comments. He is tolerated by intellectuals with whom he deals, such as Idegawa and Sono, who are described in other chapters. These people are aware of the wide audience he has in his travels, but the majority of people who regularly associate with him have said that he often gets so carried away with the subject that fact and fantasy are sometimes indiscriminately mixed. He also alienates many because of his lack of etiquette, something that is strictly adhered to within coal communities. However, his contacts are many, and it was through Oguchi that I was able to meet a huge number of Kawasaki residents and social activists. This was in part due, no doubt, to the fact that he prided himself on his 'internationalism', and his contacts with foreigners, enhanced by the fact that he spoke some English. In fact he often lapsed into a jumble of English and pidgin Japanese, which was as bemusing to me as it was amusing to any Japanese listeners.

However, he proved to have a fascinating approach to life in Chikuho. As a young man working with the Caravan Movement, he undertook with three others a study of the number of mining accidents in Chikuho in the post-war period. This study has become the seminal study of accidents, not so much for what it discovered about the dreadfully high accident rate, but for what it could not discover. The accident rate statistics issued by the companies were not consistent with the statistics his group collected from looking through the newspaper records. The official statistics were less than 10 per cent of the number his group unearthed. More importantly, small mines were not required by law to disclose their accident records, so the huge number of mining deaths in the more dangerous small mines was never actually recorded.

Oguchi is a powerful singer, and he performs every year in the local *Bon Odori Taikai* (the Festival of the Dead celebrations). He is the Kawasaki MC, and one of the organisers of the event that every year attracts thousands of participants and spectators. He has been responsible for the resurgence of popularity of many of the local festivals, actively promoting them on his rounds, petitioning local councils and government to act decisively to reintroduce 'culture' to the region. Because he has a relatively large amount of free time, he is able to involve himself actively with many of the fringe groups he has contacted during his rounds in the region. The Y-san Widows' protest movement, which he decided was a worthwhile cause in the mid-1970s, has profited through his attention and his ability to bring matters to the attention of influential local politicians. The issues of poverty, welfare and crime in Kawasaki have also been looked at by Oguchi. He has contacts within the police department, and has been instrumental in getting local juvenile delinquents involved in community projects as part of their punishment, rather than having them incarcerated in borstals.

As a motivator, he is successful in convincing many young people to become involved in community life, something rare in the coalfields. He now believes that it is essential that young people be able to understand that they are the products of a corrupt and uncaring government/big business policy. Once this is understood,

> they can throw off their need to be recognised by the city people and concentrate on developing their own character with pride. The people here have a history of being squashed by the powerful who have never cared what happens to them, as long as they performed well in their factories and mines. When the mines got out of Kawasaki, the companies did pretty well out of it. U-san made a lot of money from the government out of H-san mine, for instance. But they were responsible for the scrapping of the town too. And with the town went the people. No wonder we have the highest unemployment and welfare rates in the country. No one ever cared whether Kawasaki people lived or died, and because of this, survival of the fittest became the lifestyle here.
>
> The *yakuza* were around, and because they always drove the biggest, best cars, and wore the best clothes, they became the role model for many young men, who had nothing else to offer the community, and few means of achieving wealth. The *yakuza* and the *yakuza* image are probably responsible for the way the people in this town are hooked on cars and motorbikes. I guess the macho image of the *yakuza* is well established in Kawasaki. I mean,

young men make a big show of talking tough, swaggering when they walk, and bullying some of the shopkeepers. But these guys are really good kids. They're just bored and unmotivated. That's what the Youth Camps scheme we set up is about. We're trying to give these kids some direction, you know, to get them into helping within the community. The big problem is that most of the kids who come from families on welfare think that it is 'cool' (*kakui*) to be tough and on welfare, and that it's 'girlish' to be involved in community problems (unless you cause them yourself).[3]

Oguchi's range of acquaintances and contacts has taken him in many ideological directions. However, he remains consistent in that he is concerned with the way people have been abused by the system, whether it be the mining companies, local government, the courts, the police, the welfare system or local employers.

Although he can be sexist and display anti-Christian values, while ostensibly embracing Christianity, is outspoken and sometimes uncouth, Oguchi is a passionate, larger-than-life person. For all his quirks of character, he has a gentle disposition and is totally unselfish, as one would expect from anyone who dedicated his life to a series of causes. To an outsider it seems as though he desperately wants to be liked and revered by all, and his transparent attempts to manipulate this were sometimes a concern. Yet he was an agitator, a very rare breed in Kawasaki, where apathy has spread to all parts of the town, and thanks to his unlikely pairing with Chikara, the former *yakuza* boss, he has used his position to fulfil and exceed parts of the original charter of the *kami shibai* man. In this sense he is history incarnate.

The violence that is intrinsic to his stories is of some cultural significance to the region. In many ways his stories, while read verbatim from the backs of cards, illustrate some of the moral and ethical qualms of the people of the coalfields. Moreover, the intention of providing both entertainment and relief from the more pervasive violence of the mines in the region is noteworthy.

NOTES TO CHAPTER 5

1 Literally 'hamlet, settlement or village', and the source word for the contemporary *burakumin* expression. To be specific, it had its origins in the expression *tokushū burakumin*, or 'Special Settlement' people. See also note 4 to introduction.
2 Oguchi, interview, 1988.
3 Oguchi, interview, 1988.

CHAPTER 6

A Culture of Violence

A number of discussions about violence have appeared within anthropology over the years. Taussig's discussion of the colonialists' rubber plantations in Colombia is a good example of the way the issue of violence has been made a central theme. Other writers have attempted to situate the topic within the field of the sociology of violence.[1] Yet others have tried to develop a Marxist dialectic, by focusing on the issue of violence in class conflict.[2]

I see violence, and its implementation, as an extreme manifestation of the unequal relationship between the holders of power and the powerless. This position swings around the definition of violence. Riches has said that the commonsensical meaning of violence is 'the intentional rendering of physical hurt on another human being'.[3] He has also said that violence is used when the power-holders in any given relationship are 'confident that their actions command a legitimacy [and] they are able ... to satisfy their ambitions through deploying physical harm'.[4] That is, violence is used to *forestall* challenges to the control of the powerful by the powerless, and this violence is legitimated by employing the rationale that it maintains social equanimity. Violence is seen by the victim, on the other hand, as an unambiguous use of *illegitimate* force.

Therefore, the definition Riches settles on is that violence is:

> an act of physical hurt deemed legitimate by the performer and illegitimate by some witnesses and by victims. The tension in the relationship between performer, victim, and witness consists of two elements: an element of political competition, and an element of consensus about the nature of the violent act ... What marks the contestability of violence is that, as acts of physical hurt unfold, performers, witnesses, and even victims *may be expected to alter their opinions about this legitimacy.*[5] [my italics]

By implication, this definition of violence is inextricably concerned with the concept of power and with the uses of power in society. I think this is an admirable concern and worthy of further investigation. To this end I shall look at the coal industry in Chikuho, placing emphasis on the different forms of violence used and the frequency of these violent acts. Particularly the concept that the victims themselves accepted the legitimacy of violence needs to be examined in context.

Is it unreasonable to suggest that the victims of violence have become immune to some of the effects of violence? When it occurs on a daily basis in some form or other, I think that it is not unreasonable to assume a certain acceptance on the part of the victims to the fact that violence is both a routine and necessary evil. If this is the case, it is probably due in part to the legitimation of violent episodes in the past, which have slipped into folklore. I think the fear of further reprisals by the powerful and their agents has, to some extent, resulted in a form of observed acquiescence among the coalminers, and this has been perpetuated by the knowledge that life is livable if one does not go beyond the bounds of 'accepted' social obligations; that is, one does not challenge the status quo overtly. This is not to say that there exists consensus, because this is a quite misleading label.

This seems to fit into Gaventa's argument that 'the most insidious use of power is that which maintains non-challenge of the powerless, even after the powerful have fallen'.[6] I shall investigate this premise in more detail, with specific reference to the Chikuho mining situation.

Violence in the mines

The history of the Chikuho mines is etched in violent episodes, from the day-to-day violence of the overseers, exhorting the miners to work under pain of reprisals, which often meant death in the smaller mines, to the physical intensity that existed intrinsically in the type of work the miners did at the pit face, to the confrontations between the miners' unions and the police and *yakuza* in the 1960s. These episodes have been obscured over time, but the fear that the violence engendered within the miners' ranks is still well remembered.

To put the violence into context I shall look at the structure of the coal industry from a miner's perspective. It is my view that the smaller the company, the greater the incidence of violence in day-to-day situations, but the threat of violence was still an undercurrent even in the biggest mines.

Local coalminers distinguished three types of mine: *daikigyō* (large companies); *chūkokigyō* (small to medium-sized mines, which were often subcontractors for the *daikigyō*); and *tanuki bori* 'badger holes'.

Daikigyō were mines owned and operated by M-san, N-san, T-san and F-san, and typically employed large numbers of miners and sorters.

The large mines were the most desirable to work in for a number of reasons. The popular conception was that the big companies would 'look after' the employees, by offering secure employment and reasonable housing in the best traditions of the Japanese industrial giants. Also, the working conditions had a reputation for being relatively safe, because the big companies invested a great deal of money in maintaining their operations. On top of this was the popular view that people who worked in the big companies were the best in the industry, real professionals.

The *chūkokigyō* were the next rank down. As the nomenclature implies, a vast number of mines of different size were included in this category. The smallest of these mines employed approximately 60 people, while the U-san mines, which were the largest in the local area, employed more than 500 miners in a number of separate pits. The owners of these mines, like their *daikigyō* counterparts, were also responsible for supplying housing for their miners, although in many cases they managed to make this work to their advantage (see later sections of this chapter and chapter 9). Within this group were mines that the local people regarded as 'reasonable' places of work, and others that were regarded as 'pressure mines' (*asseiyama*). The latter term refers to the high incidence of violence in management techniques usually perpetrated by the feared *rōmu kakari*, men with *yakuza* backgrounds who were employed to ensure that production levels were maintained. The 'reasonable' mines were the ones where management was 'relatively humane', although these mines were less numerous.[7]

The *tanuki bori* were the very bottom rank in the local system and were small digs often worked by husband-and-wife teams. These mines were either leased from a company that had stopped production because of dangerous working conditions, poor quality of deposits, or the inaccessibility of the coal, or alternatively were illegally mined.[8] Typically, they were very small shafts, not big enough to stand in. While the husband dug the coal out lying down, the wife carted it to the surface in *sura* (sleds). The people who worked these mines were often from the *tokushu buraku*, the outcasts who were not considered employable by the bigger companies by virtue of their birth. The term 'badger holes' was used because these mines were small and shallow, and as one deposit dried up, the shaft was abandoned and another dug and exploited. Consequently, the countryside was dotted with old shafts. The accident rate in these mines was extremely high, by all accounts, but because of the informal nature of the leasing agreements there are no figures available.[9]

The aim of this account is to put into context the attitudes of the miners towards the hierarchical system of mines they perceived existed. Many Japanese commentators have concentrated on the idea of monopoly capitalism in respect to analysing the system of land and mining ownership in Chikuho.[10] I think that while this type of explanation provides useful structural explanation, it tends to neglect the way the local people themselves perceived their own working and living environments. The focus of this chapter will be on the comparative uses of violence in the daily lives of people working in the different categories of mines. I shall concentrate particularly on the smaller mines, and on accounts about the nature of the work and of the workers' acceptance of the pervasive violence.

The *rōmu kakari* (labour overseers)

Of the violence in the mines, it has to be said that almost always the direct perpetrators of violent acts were the *rōmu kakari*, or overseers.[11] Although these men were only carrying out their duties, the enthusiasm with which they 'attacked' their work was extreme. Regardless of a mine's size, there was always a *rōmu* (labour office). There is an obvious reluctance to speak out about the *rōmu kakari* in Tagawa, even though the last Tagawa mine closed more than 15 years ago. The few people who were prepared to talk about the past, and about the roles the *rōmu* played, were prepared to do so only on the condition that I not use their real names. Obviously there is still fear, and sanctions that lie below the fear, in evidence in contemporary Chikuho regarding the *rōmu*. This is perhaps because of the number of men from *rōmu* ranks who joined *yakuza* ranks, and still play an active part in instilling fear within the local population.

Describing the *rōmu kakari* he dealt with on a daily basis for nearly 30 years in the pits, one unionist said:

Officially they were there to make sure that we turned up for work, and to take the attendance figures for the day. That is, they were there to force us not to take holidays for any reason. If a miner was sick, they would investigate it, and would accuse the miner of faking the sickness, etc. They would come around to the houses where we lived and wait outside and call out that the miner was slacking, and that he should go to work and stop pretending to be sick. When there were union elections, they would go around to the miners' homes and tell the workers to vote for the company representatives, and not to vote for the alternative union leaders, like us, for example. [He was a member of the JCP.] They'd also watch the voting process and take note of who voted for the non-company leaders.

When there were workers who tried to get going labour movements that would cause trouble for the company, such as genuine trade union movements and movements that would lead to industrial strife, the *rōmu* would go to the troublemakers' houses with pistols and iron bars in hand and threaten the would-be leaders to behave themselves. This was standard for the U-san mines.

If there were too· many of these worker-related 'troubles' the company would simply send in the *rōmu kakari* to sort things out.[12]

Another informant saw the control exerted by the *rōmu kakari* in military terms:

> The same situation occurred in the mines as happened in the Army. You know how there was a *kachō* (section chief)? Well, if we did something the *kachō* didn't approve of, we were hit by one of the strong-arm men in the *rōmu*, who told us that by not doing the right thing by the *kachō* we were 'hitting the president in the face'. For instance, if we had said that we weren't going to work because the water in the mine was too high, the *rōmu* would have just come around to the *tanjū* to make us go. The union wouldn't have done anything about it at all. The fact was that the company was too strong for us, and there was nothing that we could do about it. Just like the Army. The people with the power squash the people without it. And what makes me mad is that the Emperor is the head of the whole lot, and even today we have to support the Emperor as though we were still living in the feudal era. Fuck him.[13]

This opinion that the system of violence and discipline that operated within the mines was very similar to that of the Army was often voiced by people who lived in the *tanjū*. Given that the Emperor was seen as the supreme head of the Army, it is not surprising that the contemporary Anti-Emperor Movement is strongly supported by many people in Chikuho.

Although the level of violence used on the workforce was monitored most of the time by the *rōmu* boss, individual *rōmu* did have a certain amount of freedom in dealing with 'worker troubles'. This freedom depended on a number of factors: the type of owner, the type of *rōmu* boss, and the individual *rōmu's* temperament. In cases where any of the above people were prone to employing violence to combat rebelliousness, *rōmu* were able to pick out certain workers for special treatment if they could justify their actions to the *rōmu* boss as being in 'the company's best interests'.[14]

A rationale of violence

There were two offences that the management of most of the smaller, and in some cases, the larger mines as well, could not tolerate. These were: first, any attempt to start an independent union, that is, one independent of the *goyō* (company) union; and, second, the inability to meet production requirements set through 'discussions' between the company union and management.

The former stipulation was strictly policed, particularly in the smaller mines, where the workforce was contained within highly localised *tanjū*. The miners and their families living in close proximity in recorded addresses gave the *rōmu* the advantage of being able to monitor discontent and *potential* discontent, through informants loyal to the company. When challenges to management's authority were manifest, the *rōmu* were able to react swiftly and efficiently, going directly to the homes of the troublemakers, and dealing with them with whatever level of violence they deemed appropriate.

Ogata describes one such instance at H-san, one of the more renowned mines, in the late 1950s:

> Although there was a union in H-san, the company bosses made sure that we didn't get too strong, by taking the guys who were the leaders aside and telling them that if they were 'good' (that is, if they followed company policy), they would get rapid promotion. This meant that the union leaders were usually the company 'dogs'. So we didn't get any real benefits from the union in the time that I was there. I remember one man who was a pretty strong sort of guy. You know, he didn't take the shit that was put on him at work from the management and all that. Well he was sick of the way the union men pushed the rest of us around, and sick of the way the wages never seemed to go up, so he decided to start a second union.
>
> At first he had a fair bit of support from a lot of other miners like me, who knew that we were being taken for a ride while the management was making lots of money. Anyway, one day when we were about to go down the mine the *rōmu* boss says to us: 'I hear you men are thinking about starting a union. Perhaps you'd like to see someone who had the same idea'. So they trotted out this man who had been so tough, and he was a mess. He could hardly stand up and his face was covered with blood. He looked at us and said that he didn't think that starting a new union was such a good idea after all.
>
> After that we all decided to let it go for a while and make do with what we had. That way we could keep enough food in our bellies and keep our families happy. This guy, though, couldn't do that, for now he was out of work *and* messed up. That was the way that the unions were handled by the company toughs.[15]

Within the *tanjū* and at the workplace the company made the laws and the *rōmu* policed them. The *rōmu* played not only the role of the local police, but also the roles of judge, jury and executioner. Moreover, they were the gaolers of the miners, forcing the miners to stay within the physical boundaries of the *tanjū*. Both at the workplace and within the *tanjū* the miners abided by a set of laws that bore little resemblance to those of the outside world, laws that were in contradiction to the democratic principles of mainstream society. These were the laws the *rōmu* policed, and transgressions were dealt with harshly. The outside police seldom intervened in these violent episodes, choosing to regard the daily violence as a 'company matter'. Because the incidents occurred within the *tanjū*, officially the police accepted the word of the owners that the situation was under control. Doubtless the prominent position the mine-owners held in society and the fact that the police chiefs in the towns I researched were often former employees of the coal companies influenced the hands-off policy the police adopted.

In essence, then, the coal companies were able to exert whatever pressure they felt appropriate in order to achieve desired production levels. Unions were seen as a threat to both their autonomous control and the unimpaired continuation of production, and given the freedom to use violence without fear of redress from the outside world, the *rōmu* were exhorted to quell the rising tide of 'red rebellion', as it was referred to in the press in the 1950s.[16] This policy of attempting to destroy democratic unions was widespread within the coal industry, but its enforcement was particularly brutal in the smaller mines.

The second major offence in the eyes of management was obstructing production in other ways. The most obvious way production can be slowed, short of concerted industrial action, is through worker absenteeism and 'go-slows', and in most coal-producing nations such tactics are used.[17] In Japan, however, through the judicious use of violence, management was able to prevent the use of these tactics.

Traditionally, miners throughout the Western world have had the reputation of being rough, but existentialist in philosophy, choosing to live for the immediate future, rather than saving for the long term. It has been postulated by a number of authors that there is an economic rationale in place here. That is, the long hours and the arduous and dangerous nature of the job could be balanced by the miners taking days off when their savings had reached the point that they could afford not to work.[18] In Britain, absenteeism was the major problem recognised by the National Coal Board in a survey on production problems in 1984.[19]

In Japan the problem of absenteeism was confined to the bigger companies, because their management methods were less forceful than those used in the smaller mines. In the small companies the rational application of violence, and its corollary, psychological intimidation, was used to forestall the problem of absenteeism. From an economic perspective this method was quite successful in maintaining production.

Violence and structural constraints

Miners regarded two coalmines (H-san, a mine in Kawasaki, and S-san, a small Kurate mine) as being particularly violent. People living in Kurate regarded the Kawasaki mine as the worst. On the other hand, those living in Tagawa or Kawasaki regarded the Kurate mine as the worst. Because there was a fair amount of movement between mines, stories of the nature of violence employed in these mines became commonplace as miners discussed their old jobs with their new workmates. The big companies were very selective as to the sort of workers they employed, so a miner who, for whatever reason, was not able to gain employment with one of the big companies, became dependent on the smaller mines for work. Miners in the smaller companies constantly compared mines, discussing the unions, the *rōmu* and the extent of violence used by management, wages, mine safety, company housing and job availability.

In the immediate post-war boom, many small companies had difficulty keeping up with demand and holding on to their labour force. The work was dangerous and not very well paid, and miners typically were forced to work 12–14-hour shifts. They were often beaten if they did not go to work. Many men were not prepared to be treated in this manner, and wanted to look for mining work elsewhere. The companies were aware of the demand for qualified miners and took steps to prevent the labour force from leaving their mines. The first step was to keep the workers in an area where they could be supervised, both at work and at home. This was achieved in part through the structural manipulation of the *tanjū*. Potential troublemakers were usually segregated from the other miners, and the location of any individual miner was always known to the *rōmu*. Consequently when there was any sort of worker strife, the *rōmu* were able to get to the offenders immediately. Through this system management was also able to control the miners' standard of housing, differentiating between those who followed the company's policies without complaint, and those who resisted.

The next step was to restrict both the scope and frequency of worker contact with the outside world. Many people talk about the isolated nature of the Chikuho region, how that, although the area is situated in a geographically advantageous position, the outside world is largely ignored by the local communities, and vice versa.[20] The isolation of the region was a major factor in allowing the development and maintenance of the mine-owners' control of the labour force. As there was so little contact with the outside world, the mine-owners were able to exert illegal and violent sanctions over the workers without fear of recrimination.

Historically there are a number of precedents for the type of management that was practised within the Japanese mining industry. The salt mines of Siberia during the Stalinist purges, and the incarceration of African diamond-miners in South Africa offer similar examples to those employed by the coal companies.

During the Second World War many local mines relied on forced foreign or POW labour to continue operations. It is worth noting that I draw the distinction here between the two groups: by foreign labourers I mean Koreans, who made up the vast majority of the non-Japanese workforce. There were also a number of Chinese, Filipinos and European labourers involved, but these people were usually 'genuine' POWs. The Koreans, on the other hand, were often not soldiers, but young men who had been conscripted by the Japanese to support the Japanese war effort. These days the *Kyōsei Renkō* (Korean Forced Labourers' Society), is quite active in condemning the Japanese government for allowing mine companies to exert violence over the Koreans, both during and after the war.

The forced labourers were closely guarded at all times in the mines. They slept together in a section of the *tanjū* removed from the local workers. There are many stories of atrocities committed against the Koreans during the war by the *rōmu*, but the most insidious use of violence was the pressure placed on individual Koreans to stay on in the mines after the war. During the war, extremes of violence could be justified in a number of ways: the foreigners could be attempting to escape, start a riot or sabotage production. They could be seen to be endangering the security of the country, and the rationale employed was that they should be dealt with severely.

When the war was over, the demand for labour was higher than it had ever been in the industry, in line with the plans of SCAP (Supreme Command of Allied Powers) to revitalise the economy. The smaller mines in particular were desperate for mining staff, because production declined dramatically as the Korean and other foreign workers were gradually repatriated. The solution to the problem of how to maintain a productive workforce was really quite simple. Many Koreans were prevented from returning home.

This was not an original solution to labour problems. The internment system had been used successfully for many years during the feudal periods, in both the East and the West. But in this case the political context was 'democracy', not feudalism. Thanks in large part to the 'hands-off' policies of the authorities, the mine-owners were able to continue the practice of interning Korean workers. The mines were legally, politically, economically, geographically and socially separate from the wider society, so events that occurred within the mines were seen to be the responsibility of the individual mine's management. So long as internal violence did not spill over into mainstream society, the law turned a blind eye. There were no complaints from the miners themselves, apart from the so-called union 'troublemakers', and the police accepted the company's word that these men were untrustworthy and violent themselves — potential criminals.[21] There was no reason for the police to interfere in events they officially knew nothing of, and as contact between the mining communities and the mainstream communities was negligible, the companies were able to continue to abuse the miners. In fact the levels of abuse rose markedly immediately after the war.

In Kurate in the immediate post-war years a frequent greeting between Korean miners was, 'Haven't seen you for a while. What number wife are you on now?'[22] This referred to the outcome of incarceration. That is, when a miner was able to escape from the *tanjū*, he was forced to leave his family behind to fend for itself, because the family would have slowed the escapee to such an extent that he would have been caught by the *rōmu*.[23] As a result of separation from families many miners remarried women from other mining towns.

Retributions against escaped miners who were caught by the *rōmu* were savage. The English word 'lynch' has now entered the local dialect, and also the mainstream language, because of the frequency with which escaped miners were caught and lynched. Escaped miners were systematically beaten and then displayed to the other miners at the workplace. Depending on the mine and the seriousness of the offence, sometimes the escapee was subsequently hanged, or cut to death with a sword or knife in front of the workforce as an example.[24] This process, from capture to punishment and, sometimes, summary execution has become known as 'lynching' in the Japanese language. Even though the miners escaped from the bounded confines of the *tanjū* into mainstream society, the police were still prepared to allow the *rōmu* to hunt down the men and deal with them as they saw fit, as long as the punishment was carried out within the *tanjū*.[25] It was never suggested that the *rōmu* were behaving in an illegal manner. Nor was the authority and legitimacy of the mine-owners challenged.

One informant, talking about the *rōmu*, pointed out the route from the *tanjū* that many miners, mainly Korean, had followed in their attempts to escape from the mines in Kawasaki. It led over a mountain range into a village in Oita prefecture called Otomura, about 40 kilometres away, where mine management had reliable informers who were quick to tell them if new people came to town.

When the miners ran away over the hills, they went to Otomura. You can see that big mountain in the distance. That's called Mount Gonge. If you draw a line from the base of that mountain to the base of Mount Hiko, about half-way along that line you'd be in Otomura. But they never *escaped*. They just ran away. They were soon caught, and of course they were punished immediately after their return, usually killed to show the others what happens to escapees.

These were regular events, the escapes. I suppose that at least one person a week (in the late 1940s and early 1950s) tried to get away from the violence, and was caught. You just can't imagine the sorts of violence used against the miners here.[26]

It can be said, then, that the miners who escaped, or attempted to escape from these so-called 'pressure mines' were desperate enough to risk the wrath of the *rōmu* and the loss of their families for their freedom. Sadly, many were caught and severely punished, losing their freedom, families, employment and, in some cases, their lives in the process. Certainly the fear of failure in an escape attempt was strong motivation for the miners to endure the hardships of work, and for many years the vast majority did just that. Moreover, the fear of the overtly violent nature of the *rōmu* themselves served to encourage the miners to remain quiescent. Although the miners themselves were physically strong people, the *rōmu*, being bound only by the laws of the company, carried weapons that allowed them to assert their physical superiority over the workers without fear of recrimination from either inside or outside the *tanjū*. As one informant, who was associated with the *rōmu* for 25 years in one of Kawasaki's more violent mines, said:

We weren't scared of anyone. The only people we were responsible to were the (*rōmu*) Boss, and the boss of the *yakuza gumi* (gang), if we were in one. We could do anything to anyone in the *tanjū*. The police were all in the mine-owner's pocket, so we never had any trouble with those idiots. In fact, I think they relied on us to keep the peace.[27]

Because the *rōmu* had such unrestricted power on both the group and individual levels, they were an unpredictably violent force, which generated widespread fear within the *tanjū*. This fear was certainly a potent motivation in convincing the miners to stay within the *tanjū* and to be productive for the company.

More discriminating use of violence?

Levels of violence against the miners rose and fell with changes in the economic climate, according to one source.[28] But even throughout periods when there was little actual physical violence, the threat of violence remained, personified in the physical presence of the *rōmu*. With one notable exception (see chapter 9), it wasn't until the mines were threatened with closure that the miners developed some form of organised resistance to the status quo, and even then the resistance was confined to a minority of miners, usually those from the larger companies.

As far as miners in the smaller companies were concerned, the violent day-to-day relationship with the company continued, even after the general strikes and labour unrest of 1960–61 had finished. Working conditions did not improve markedly as a result of the industrial action that *Tanrō* had taken. In fact, the situation became more desperate for many miners, as demand for their labour lessened with the Energy Revolution in the mid-1960s, which saw government policies set to replace the coal industry with oil imports. In response to the lessening demand for the miners' labour, smaller companies were prepared to let some of the workforce they had interned leave, because there were many miners desperately seeking work. Those miners who remained were forced to work for poorer wages in more difficult conditions, living in rapidly deteriorating company accommodation. Protest from the miners about any of the above conditions was met with the comment, 'If you don't like the way the company is run, leave!'[29]

While this was an improvement on the summary violence that would have been the response to protest a few years earlier, the workers were still dependent on the company in a number of ways that did not allow them to leave. Their housing and services, such as gas, water and electricity, were company controlled. Gambling, to which many miners were addicted, was also a problem and the *yakuza* were known to kill bad debtors.[30] The miners could not save coupons, which they received in lieu of wages, because they were redeemable only in the company stores, so general savings were very low. In short, they had become economically dependent on the mine and the *tanjū*. Thus summary dismissals resulted in total destitution. The general feeling was that 'the actions of the *rōmu* can't be helped', and that the best thing to do was to endure the privations, because 'at least you were working, and if you were working you were eating'.[31]

Even with these economic sanctions hanging over their heads, some miners continued to be subjected to daily violence through the 1960s and 1970s. The nationwide labour strife of the 1960s had not solved the basic problem of management–labour relations. In simple terms, the management of the smaller companies were themselves being pressured into increasing production. They were asked to produce cheaper coal than they had before to meet the requirements of the government quota system, which had been designed by the *daikigyō* cartel.[32] They could not compete with the larger companies on the same scale, so they exerted great pressure on the workers to increase production, while simultaneously trying to reduce expenditure on safety measures and cut other production costs. The simplest way of increasing production was to force the workers to work longer hours on a piecework system. One informant describes the work conditions in a medium mine (800 employees) in the early 1960s:

> There were only two shifts that we worked, not three like many of the big mines. Therefore, instead of working eight-hour shifts, we worked 12 hours at a time. We left home at 8 a.m., and worked until 8 p.m. We had to work a total of 300 hours a month to meet our quota, so often we worked 13- and 14-hour shifts. When we were working past the time we were rostered to work, the next shift had to wait until we were finished. The men coming on shift at 8 p.m., for example, were fresh, but sometimes they had to wait until 12 p.m. or even 1 a.m. until we finished. So after working 13 or 14 hours a day, when we came home we had a bath and something to eat and collapsed completely exhausted. On top of that, working in the mines had become very dangerous as a result of the company neglecting safety regulations. Cave-ins, floods, etc. On top of that the wages were incredibly poor. It was hard to maintain even the most basic standard of living.[33]

Sanctions related to the lifestyles of the miners were easily imposed without recourse to physical violence. These coercive measures were implemented by management and concerned basic needs: control of food, shelter, money and water.

Throughout this period the *rōmu* continued to use violence, or the threat of it, on the workers. Particularly if there was the possibility of a non-company union being formed, the *rōmu* would be called out to deal with the leaders with as much force as they deemed necessary to persuade them to desist. When pressure to produce coal cheaply was placed on management from above, notwithstanding government support that was supplied to the mine, the levels of violence increased correspondingly as the *rōmu* coerced the workforce to dig more coal more cheaply.

Ishiguchi, who was a JCP member *within* the company union, refers to the intimate relationship he developed with the *rōmu* at the mine in which he worked:

> As we were involved with the JCP, the company used the *rōmu* to keep us under control. They stood above us and put pressure on us to disperse, by attempting to get the other workers to join together against us in fear of the company.
> The *rōmu* called us all [JCP members] together and said, 'What's the matter with you people? Don't you know that we do our best to help you, and then you go and post bills saying that the mine is terrible and that you are worked too hard'.
> After the mine had closed, these guys approached me directly and said that I was a real troublemaker, and that they were glad that the whole

business was over. They had tried to stab me in the balls once and beat me outside work, but I usually managed to get away. They really had it in for me, though, they did. They said that I was sick, and I told them that I thought that they were complete bastards [after the mine closed].

Today I can talk to them as though they are human beings, but at the time we were real enemies, and any talks that we had were abusive. I was always worried about the violence that they could do to me at the time, and thus regarded them as real enemies who would only do me harm.[34]

Management was reluctant to enrage the official political parties and, because of his official association with the JCP, Ishiguchi was able to avoid being the target of much direct *rōmu* violence. However, pressure was brought to bear on Ishiguchi and his JCP colleagues in other ways. For example:

We were discriminated against very badly. We got poor wages, and were made to work in areas where there was little contact with the other workers. In sum, we [JCP] workers got about half the wages of the usual miners for doing the same work. In other words, the company hoped that by putting the pressure on us in this way, we would quit of our own volition. There was no reason to sack us, because we did the work that was required. But, because the wages were so low, often the workers just had enough, saying that they couldn't live on those wages, and just quit. This was in line with the strategy adopted by the company.[35]

If Ishiguchi, who was to a large degree removed from direct violent confrontations, suffered physically at the hands of the *rōmu*, what was the extent of the violence perpetrated on the non-JCP members? This is an extremely difficult question to answer, simply because the relatives of the dead and injured are still reluctant to talk. However, his account illustrates quite clearly the concept that the *rōmu* used not only coercion and violence to maintain labour control, but also intimidation, which was so successful that even 20 years after the mines closed in Chikuho there is widespread reticence.

Officially there was no violence within the mines, except for inter-miner quarrels, usually over gambling, or so the local histories of the mining towns would like the reader to believe.[36] And it seems that many Japanese are quite comfortable with the 'official facts'. After I had made a speech at a public meeting about the extent of violence in Chikuho, one city-dwelling informant exclaimed:

Surely those prominent, upright citizens of the community [the mine-owners] would never have allowed that sort of violence to go on within their companies![37]

Obviously the coalmines were rough places. One informant goes so far as to call Chikuho 'Japan's Texas',[38] in a reference to the rough and

untamed nature of the place. Most outsiders' perception of Chikuho
was, and still is, that the area is very violent, crime is high, and there are
many *yakuza*. Few are aware of the nature of the violence, and even
fewer are aware of the extent and history of the violence. This is in large
part due to the influence of the coal companies, which have been
ruthless in suppressing reports of the violent nature of the mines and of
labour relations, by instilling fear of economic and physical sanctions
within the local populations. They have also been able to censor the
information going to the mass media through their *jinmyaku*, or contact
networks, in much the same way as they were able to censor information coming into the *tanjū* in the immediate post-war years.

In Ueno Eishin's books are a number of pointed references about
the state of the mining community. As a miner himself, he was
subjected to many of the indignities the men and women of these
communities suffered. In the case of the KNU mine, he describes the
actions of the *rōmu* and places them within the context of social and
production control. Just how were the miners coerced into working the
long hours in such terrible conditions? Particularly in light of the fact
that Japan was modernising at a rapid rate, the position of the
coalminers was anathema to the concept of a free and democratic,
United-States-backed society. Ueno describes the conditions:

> There were no areas for the children to play. No *tatami* in the houses. No
> response from the company if fire broke out. The houses were in disrepair.
> To all this the company turned a blind eye. The goods in the company store
> were two to three times the price of other local stores, but when the people
> complained about any of the above, they were told by the management that
> if they had any complaints they were free to quit their jobs.
>
> In fact, people who complained about the situation were often subjected
> to wage-cuts and special physical cruelty.
>
> The leader of the Women's Group (*fujinkai*) said that on one occasion
> when she complained about the wages not being enough to live on, she was
> told by the *rōmu* boss that, 'All you ever do is complain, saying how hard life
> is, how you don't have enough money. Don't you drink hot *sake* in the
> evenings? Don't you think that it is a luxury to do so? If it's really so hard on
> you, sell your daughters. After all, you have two daughters, right?' This man
> became the police chief the next year![39]

Violence in Chikuho coalmines was widespread and endemic. It
became the *modus operandi* for many small mines, and the concept of
coercion, as opposed to blatant violence, was found in many of the
larger mines as well. The *rōmu*'s position as unofficial police within the
confines of the *tanjū* gave them almost unlimited power over the
miners, something that was conveniently ignored by the authorities.
Their ability to kill or beat miners who were politically militant or were

not prepared to work within the rules established by the company allowed them to maintain control over the workforce. In this way, violence was used to legitimise the ideology of management and to resist workers' challenge to the existing social and economic structures.

In communities where, apart from joining the *yakuza*, mining was the only legitimate occupation, few options existed for local men other than to enter the mines. Those who joined the miners' ranks accepted the strictures that went with the work. Violence was such a common occurrence that people became inured to it. This is not to say that they were immune to it; rather they accepted that it was a part of the job. It is not unreasonable to assume that the majority of miners in the smaller mines accepted equally the dangers of the *rōmu* and the violence of which they were capable and the dangers of the mine itself. The miners knew what was expected of them, and, because there were few occupational choices available, they made the best of the situation.

The values that were forced upon them in the mines became the norm, so that when the mines were closed, the miners, certainly initially, retained those values in most cases. Yet accepting these values as being part of a limited range of occupational choice and accepting them as their own values are rather different. It could be expected that exposure to the wider community following the closure of the mines would expand the range of individual miner's experiences, and with this expansion of experience would come a developing consciousness of the extremes of violence to which they were subjected in the mines. This in turn would generate feelings of animosity towards the mines and the *rōmu*, which would result in a catharsis of aggression and outspokenness. However, in the small mining communities the *rōmu* are still feared today as much as they were in the past, and few people are willing to discuss their role in the mines. This could be related to the movement of many *rōmu* into the ranks of the local *yakuza gumi*, which wield great coercive power in today's society. It is also related to the power that the company held over the ideological indoctrination of the workers.

The consciousness of some miners is changing as their mining days slip farther into the past, but the miners who are openly critical of company policies are still very much in the minority. Because many ex-mining families still live in the *tanjū* where they have lived for many years, there is a subliminal feeling of gratitude towards the company for not destroying the village, according to Ishizaki.[40] Moreover, the understanding that they have survived the ordeal of the mines (that it is over, and that because they are still alive, they have won) is cause to 'let the past rest'.[41] There is no point in reminiscing about the violence they suffered, or the scars they received at the hands of the *rōmu*, because it is demeaning, embarrassing and, they believe, uninteresting. Perhaps more importantly, it is painful to recall these events. Although union activists such as Ishiguchi, who reluctantly agreed to discuss the past with me *because* I am an outsider (and therefore need to be educated), still exist, the majority of the people who worked in the violent mines don't want to, or choose not to, remember the extent of the violent environment in which they lived and worked. Even the intentions of the revivalists today, with their agenda for restoring pride in people's perception of their own past, sit uncomfortably with the historically determined and indoctrinated powerlessness of the miners.

NOTES TO CHAPTER 6

1 See Girard, 1977; Riches, 1986.
2 See for example, Douglass and Krieger, 1983.
3 Riches, 1986; p.4.
4 Ibid. p.4.
5 Ibid. pp.8–9.
6 Gaventa, 1980, p.82
7 Idegawa, Chikara, Sasaki, interviews, 1987 and 1988.
8 When it was no longer economically feasible to run small mines, they were often simply abandoned. After the pit entrances were blocked, some unemployed miners were able to reopen them and effectively scavenge for coal in the dangerous shafts.
9 See Takazaki, 1966, pp.45–9.
10 See, for example, Takazaki, 1961; Yada, 1975, 1981; Ueno, 1985a, b, c, d; Sonoda, 1970.
11 See Takazaki, 1961; Ueno, 1985a,b,c,d; Chikara, interview, 1988; Idegawa, interviews, 1987–8, for example.
12 Ishiguchi, interview, 1988.
13 Ogata, interview, 1988.
14 Ueno, 1985a, p.78.
15 Ogata, interview, 1988.
16 The 1950s was a period where the doctrine of McCarthyism became dominant in Japan, following the example of the United States.
17 See Dennis, Henriques and Slaughter, 1956; Gaventa, 1980; Metcalfe, 1988; Williams, 1981.
18 See, for example, Dennis, Henriques and Slaughter, 1956: chapter 2, on Britain; and Metcalfe, 1988, pp.34–5 and 78–9, on Australia.
19 See National Coal Board (British), 1984.
20 See Ueno, 1985a, b, c, d; Ishizaki, 1987.
21 Kashihama, interview, 1988.
22 Idegawa, interview, 1987.
23 Takazaki, interview, 1988.
24 Chikara, interview, 1988.
25 Takazaki, 1966, p.14.
26 Ishizaki, interview, 1988.
27 Chikara, interview, 1988.
28 Sasaki, interview, 1988.
29 Kawano, interview, 1988.
30 Sasaki, interview, 1988.
31 Interviews: Sasaki, 1988; Ogata, 1988; Tajima, 1989.
32 Takazaki, 1961, p.25.
33 Ishiguchi, interview, 1988.

34 Ishiguchi, interview, 1988.
35 Ishiguchi, interview, 1988.
36 See *Tagawa Shishi* (1979) and *Kawasaki Chōshi* (1951), for example.
37 Nakano (local dentist), interview, 1989.
38 Nakayama (local doctor), interview, 1989.
39 Ueno, 1985a, p.24.
40 Ishizaki, interview, 1988.
41 Ogata, interview, 1988.

CHAPTER 7

H-san Mine: Violence and Repression

H-san (mine) operated from the early 1920s through to 1961, the year after a dramatic mineshaft flood in which 67 miners died. Throughout this period the mine was renowned as one of the most violent of all Japanese mines. The expression *asseiyama* ('pressure mine') was first used in relation to this mine, and referred to the system of indentured, and often forced, labour. The number of workers killed in the mine in incidents concerning the *rōmu* is difficult to estimate, but one source has put the figure at more than 500 over a 45-year period.[1]

When the flooding occurred locals were outraged at the lack of action taken by management to commit the necessary resources to exhume the bodies of the dead miners after it was finally decided that there could be no survivors. The memory of this lack of goodwill is still strong within the local community, and has a powerful impact on the way the company is remembered in Kawasaki.

The power of the press to influence the course of events is an issue that is often neglected in anthropology. Over time, as memories fade, we become more reliant on written accounts of the time to understand the past. In effect these accounts become history. To understand the nature of these historical 'truths', we must deal with the media accounts of the time. I shall use the newspaper reports from the *Nishi Nihon Shinbun*, the largest of the Kyushu newspapers (circulation five million daily), and the newspaper most in touch with local events, to describe the mining disaster at H-san. The newspaper accounts are relevant because they show how news of the accident was communicated to the population.

I shall intersperse the newspaper extracts with comments from three main informant accounts to contextualise the accident and the events that preceded and followed the disaster. These informants are:

1 Ogata, a man who worked in the pits at H-san for 25 years, who is now resident at M-san Ita in Tagawa.
2 Ishizaki, a woman who was born *burakumin* and who laboured in many small mines in the Kawasaki region before she became a nurse. Her husband was seriously injured in a cave-in at H-san. She is the author of a number of books on discrimination and the abuse of power in Kyushu.
3 Kashihama, the head of the mine construction unit at H-san. A conservative man, he will not tolerate criticism of the mine, because he feels that it is counter-productive to the 'rebuilding of Chikuho', the project he is involved with at present.

Background to the accident

The mine is best remembered today for the flooding of the mineshaft. Whenever Chikuho people mentioned anything about H-san in the course of interviews or discussions, the overriding concern was with the fact that there had been a major disaster at the mine. This concern with the disaster was linked in folklore with the idea that the closure of the mine, which followed the accident, was the beginning of the end of the coal industry in the region. Moreover, local people are still resentful of the company's reluctance to exhume the dead bodies after the flood.

For a solid fortnight before the accident, torrential monsoon rain had fallen in Kawasaki. Because the mine was built under the Chukanji River, the supports that held up the ceiling of the shaft were in danger of collapsing. Against the advice of the Fukuoka Mine Safety Commission (FMSC), mine management decided to open the shaft, which eventually flooded.

Twelve months after the accident a decision was made by the company to halt operations at the mine, and to sell out to the government under the favourable terms of the TCRB. The workers were paid little in compensation, but were permitted to stay on in the company housing, even though they were no longer working for the company. This became a critical factor in company policy. It was essential that the company maintain control of the workers' economic circumstances if they were to maintain the public fictions they had painstakingly developed over the years: that the company was not as bad as it was always made out to be by disenchanted workers; that there was very little violence within the company, and what there was was always perpetrated by the miners against each other or against the *rōmu;* and that the miners were a poorly disciplined group of people, who needed to be closely watched (they were gamblers, and had 'unstable tendencies'), hence restrictive practices, when invoked, could be seen to be necessary.[2]

By keeping the miners within the system of *on* and *giri* (that is, by reinforcing the concept that the miners were still beholden to the company for their present lifestyles), the miners would not challenge the status quo. By supplying housing or in reality by *not* evicting the miners, the company maintained its control of the people. It was low-cost (the maintenance of the housing was passed on to the individuals living in them), and the company maintained its power base by allowing only 'sponsored' ex-miners in. When the government decided to rebuild the *tanju*, the company supplied a list of 'genuine' occupants, who were to receive preference in moving into the new housing. Thus the process of manipulation continued.

The newspaper accounts

DAY 1: 21 September 1960

FEARFUL ACCIDENT IN H-SAN
Rescue Efforts Halted
H-san Mine Flooded
Families Stare at the Mine Entrance

(Tagawa) In a matter of minutes 67 miners were lost in H-san mine, as the families of the miners and others who had joined the rescue parties attempted to get into the mine to help them. However, the efforts of the people were in vain, as the black and muddy waters rose minute by minute to levels approaching 15 metres in height, sabotaging efforts to free the men trapped in the no. 2 shaft. About 50 rescue workers worked the pumps, desperately trying to reduce the water levels, but it became apparent that the water level had not dropped even a little. All the families of the trapped miners could do was to stare at the mine entrance and wait.

The people concerned gathered around Yoshida Seijiro (45) who miraculously survived the ordeal. Mr Yoshida said, 'When I was working in the right-hand tunnel on the face, the electricity was suddenly cut off. So there was a call from the *rōmu kakari*, who said that there was an emergency, and he told me to tell the men to get out of there! We rushed to get out, but the water was already up to our chests, and was pushing us under and back down the mine'. With the terror rising in his chest, he concentrated all his efforts to escape from the mine.

Because the muddy waters from the river had flooded into the mine, the efforts of the rescue workers were severely hampered. More than 100 men from the local fire brigade as well as volunteers and the official rescue teams from the mine itself were involved with the attempts to reduce the levels of the water through the use of the three pumps that were available, but it was almost impossible. By midday they had made almost no progress, and the water was still flooding into the shaft. While the men were pumping the water out, one man (Kobayashi, 34), who was miraculously able to make his way to the surface, even though the water was up to his head at times, said the following:

'About midnight someone noticed that something had happened to the mine entrance. The order to evacuate was given by the man in charge of operations, who ran from the mine himself. When we saw him running for his life, we dropped tools and ran for our lives too. Just as I reached the tunnels intersection there was a loud crashing noise, which was accompanied by a wall of water about three metres high, which looked like a *tsunami* bearing down on top of us. In a matter of seconds the water was past our heads. It's on top of us, we thought, and like a nightmare the electricity lines that were on the ceiling peeled away, and I watched as three or four of the men were swept away in the rush of water, just their cap lamps showing in the distance as they disappeared.

'As the water reached our heads we managed to keep treading water until we were swept to the old ventilation shaft, where we were able to climb out. The guys who were in the left-hand shaft, although they heard the evacuation order were probably not able to find any way out, I think'.

(*NNS*, 21 September, p.1)

The sheer volume of water seemed to have overcome a large number of the workers in the initial flood, especially those in a section of the mine where there was no communication with the surface. In effect, the men who were working in the section that could still be contacted by the supervisor on the surface stood a chance of getting out of the mine alive, but those working on the face where the telephone lines were cut had no advance warning of the disaster. Of the men working on this face, 70 per cent or so were trapped within the mine.

The union, in line with its attitude towards the company, made a public announcement that there was to be a meeting to discuss who would pay the funeral expenses. The following is a notice that was posted around the *tanjū*:

MEETING CALLED IMMEDIATELY
A MESSAGE FROM THE LEADER OF THE H-SAN UNION

I wish to hold a meeting to discuss with all those concerned the problems that this disaster has caused us all — from the cost of the funerals, to the issue of whether it was the company's responsibility, to what improvements must be made to the mine before it reopens. These are all items on the agenda for the meeting.

Up till now we have all been concerned about the rain, and we have gone as far as to organise a Rain Period Control Group, but we never imagined that the river banks would give in as they did. It appears that it was a very old excavation, which gave way under pressure.

It is worth noting here that the union did not publicly express criticism of company policy in opening the mine on the day of the accident, nor did it call for an investigation into the disappearance of its members. In fact, it offered partial excuses on behalf of the company for the disaster, and even avoided considering that the miners trapped in the mine could still be alive.

'ALL WE CAN DO IS PRAY FOR THEIR SAFETY'
The H-san Flood Disaster
The Devastated Wives Run to the Mine Entrance

'The War with the Water' — This is what the accident that occurred on the morning of the 20 September at U-san Kogyo's H-san has become. 'Please get the water out, and quickly bring out the 67 men from within the mine safely' are the prayers of those concerned as they watch the attempts of the rescue workers to free the men from the waters of the Chukanji River. These silent thoughts of the families of the trapped men go out to the rescue workers as they work. Under hot autumn skies the men are struggling in extremely harsh conditions to get at the men.

Soon after the accident the names of the missing men were posted in the *tanju* and in front of the Union office. As the people looked at the list of husbands, sons and workmates, they thought as they wrote the relevant names down, 'Him too?' Others commented that, 'He's late coming home tonight, so I guess ... ' Their brows wrinkled in worry, and the strength drained from their faces, the wives of the missing men rushed to the mine, the hot autumn sun beating down on them, mocking them with dramatic irony after the heavy rain of recent weeks.

That afternoon a sign saying 'Entry into the Mine is Prohibited' was erected as the Emergency Rescue crews started preparations to try to get the water out. The two 30 h.p. and the two 25 h.p. pumps are able to pump out 240 cubic metres of water an hour. However, the face of the man in charge of the project is beginning to show signs of impatience, as the work has still not got under way, although they have been desperately trying to get the preparations finished from the early morning.

Because the motors had not been installed properly before, and because the work on the Chukanji River project had not been completed, the work of getting the water out was delayed. The head of the underground repair section in the mine, Mr Tomoda (48), said that according to those who escaped and those who know a lot about the mine, bad luck caused the accident to be much worse than could be expected.

The water started flooding into the mine at midnight on the late shift. The place the water broke through into the mine was about 200 metres from the entrance and couldn't be seen by those on the surface. It was exactly half-way between the face workers and the machinery operators, and neither of these groups had a good opportunity to see the water coming. This was one bit of bad luck. As the whole tunnel was flooded, there was no way for any of the workers to get out of the shaft to the entrance. If the hole had been a little higher, the surface workers would have been able to see it and therefore been able to give early warning to the miners. Although the hole was small, the water that flooded the shaft was so powerful it cut off the electricity in one section and cut off the telephone in the other.

(*NNS*, 21 September, evening edition, Chikuho section)

The embankment walls of the river were originally built in 1922, and were able to cope with the river rising up to one metre from the average. The fortnight's rain that had preceded the accident was exceptional for the time of year. Kyushu typically gets a monsoon season that finishes at the end of July or the beginning of August. As 1960 was a particularly wet year, a number of mines, including H-san, had been investigated by the FMSC to check for high water levels, the integrity of the underground excavations and general safety standards.[3] However, reports made by this body were usually only recommendations, and thus carried little weight. The investigators for the FMSC were ex-coalmining supervisors or engineers, and it has been argued that their interests were in keeping the mines productive at the minimum operating costs.[4]

When the high water level of the river exceeded the one metre limit, enormous pressure was exerted on the earth in the nearby area as the water overflowed the banks. Because the land by the river was undercut with tunnels from present and past excavations, the potential for some sort of cave-in occurring was high. The company management was aware of this, according to Kashihama, yet could not justify the financial outlay to improve the quality of the digs.[5] The rescue attempts were in trouble from the start, because they could not determine where the accident had actually occurred. This was exacerbated by a number of mechanical problems the rescuers had to contend with. Because the pumps were not able to cope with normal levels of water in the mine, according to one worker who was in the mine at the time, and because they were always breaking down due to lack of maintenance, work was delayed from the moment the extent of the disaster was known.[6]

INADVISABLE TO DIG, SAFETY COMMISSION RECOMMENDED

The Fukuoka Mining Safety Commission had recommended to the management of the U-san H-san that operations be stopped after heavy rain made the river embankments unsafe. Because the mine is situated under the river, there were fears that the mine would be in danger, said a spokesman from the FMSC today. Mine management has not commented.

(*NNS*, 21 September, p.17)

This paragraph was placed next to the produce market prices in perhaps the least read section of the newspaper.

The cave-in site was found by the afternoon of the 21st.

CAVE-IN SITE FOUND AT SECOND ATTEMPT

The red-eyed, exhausted families of the missing miners, who had gathered at the mine entrance today, voiced their complaints about the situation at H-san. 'Why couldn't they have told the men about the danger earlier?' they exclaimed. So, what were the problems that led to so many men being trapped? According to sources who are working on the site at the moment, the late discovery of the cave-in and the telephone being cut off to the mine were the fatal errors.

The first problem occurred at about 8.40 p.m. last night, when a large booming noise heard from near the *tanju* was accompanied by a huge wall of water vapour, which came pouring over the retaining walls. To deal with this problem the local fire brigade were called in, and teams from Tagawa also arrived. At this time they could not find a hole in the earth.

But at midnight when they went out to double-check the site, they found the cave-in, and water was pouring into the mine by this stage. Immediately they called the mine, but of the two internal phones, only one was working, so they told the miners there what had happened. This took altogether about five minutes from the time the hole was discovered. There were 154 men in the tunnel where the phone was working, and of these men 25 are missing. In the other tunnel, where 64 men were working, there are still 42 missing.

By the time the telephone call was made to the tunnel, the leak was apparently already bad. According to one of the men who got out of the Yakiso tunnel, when the electricity was cut off they realised that they were cut off from above ground, and that an accident had occurred.

Overall, you could say that if the cave-in site had been discovered earlier, and if there was not a problem with the electricity and telephone, the accident would have been a minor one.   (*NNS*, 21 September, evening edition)

A plethora of errors affected the miners, as even the conservative *NNS* implies in its back-page article, quoted above. The first problem was that all work should have been suspended following the recommendation of the FMSC. The second problem was that, as the company said in its defence, the mine supervisor was not aware of the seriousness of the flood. By the time management did in fact realise the extent of the flood, and the damage that could be caused by a massive amount of water flooding into the mine, the water pressure had already destroyed the telephone connection, the only link miners in one section of the mine had with the outside world. This severely limited their chances of survival. The third problem was that there was a certain complacency about the mine being able to withstand the pressure of the river, even though the earth under the river had been dug out with the observance of only minimal safety standards. This also contributed to the accident. A fourth problem, which was to develop as the rescue workers set about trying to free possible survivors, was that there were no maps of the underground mining regions. This also caused problems later in the excavation process, but its immediate effect was that there was no way of ascertaining where the earth had become weakened. Hence there was no way of either strengthening the weak places or determining where, in relation to the above-ground maps, the miners were trapped.

DAY 2: 22 September

IT MAY TAKE A NUMBER OF DAYS TO PUNCH THROUGH TO THE TUNNEL

It is already two days since the accident that trapped 67 miners in the tunnels at H-san, and the emergency rescue crews have not yet managed to reach the site of the first cave-in, nor start to pump the water out. The outlook is that it will take many more days to get to the site of what appears to be a second cave-in, and even more days to get the water out from there. In fact, it will take another three days or so to get to the workers in the first cave-in site, the head of the rescue operations said. Because they don't know the depth of the water, or how far the water has penetrated into the mine itself, best estimates are that it will take another four or five days before they can start pumping the water out, because they need to shore up the collapsed sections properly. Where the river flows above the mine, there is a huge area to shore up, and so far more than 150 wooden struts have been placed in the mine approaching the site of the cave-in.   (*NNS*, 22 September, p.1)

As the rescue work encountered more obstructions, the tension at the mine mounted as the chances of there being any survivors lessened. The pumping progress was agonisingly slow, and the families of the trapped men were starting to voice their dissatisfaction at the length of time the work was taking.

To be fair to the rescue workers, because of the state of neglect into which the mine and the maintenance work on the river had fallen, their first priority was to make sure that there would not be a repetition of the accident, and this required rebuilding the river banks and shoring up the sections of the mine that had been damaged by the flood. This was a time-consuming process, and given the negligence of the company in not having adequate geographical maps of the area, they were working in extremely difficult conditions.

The other consideration was the weather. There were fears that the rain would return and result in the river swelling, which would endanger the lives of those working in the rescue operation.

HEAVY RAIN MEANS DANGER
Worried Faces As They Watch the Rain

(Tagawa) Two days after the accident, heavy rainclouds were building up over H-san, as the rescue attempts were spurred on to a faster pace. If it rains, the rain will probably wash away the earth-retaining walls that have been especially built. If the rain is heavy, there is a good chance that the river will flood the repaired embankments. The families and colleagues of the trapped men who are watching the 'Devil's Hole' are praying with all the local people that it doesn't rain.

However, the forecast is for heavy rain in the near future. Although the reconstruction of the embankment walls is basically finished, the river has already swollen about one metre, and the height of the wall above the water level is about one metre. However, over the 90 days up to the accident, on many occasions more than 100 mm of rain had fallen on a single day, and the depth of the river had often risen to more than 2.5 metres. In other words, if there is another 100 mm on one day then there will be a repeat of the danger that flooded the mine as the river bursts its banks. If the rain follows the pattern of past weeks, then the river will overflow, and because of the positioning of the new wall, another hole will open in a place that is still exposed, leaving the rescue excavation operations to face the full force of the river.   (*NNS*, 22 September, evening edition, Chikuho section)

PUMPING PROGRESS HALTED
Families becoming anxious and impatient

Although it has been two days since the disaster, the families of the miners trapped in the mine have yet to see the pumping operation begin. Even if the miners were still breathing, the chances of getting them out alive are rapidly diminishing. The news for the families has all been black so far. Not only are their husbands still in dire trouble, but the extent of the damage to the *tanjū* and to the housing where they live is becoming so bad that they have been evacuated from the area. It's been a day characterised by anxiety and impatience at the lack of progress, as the families fear for the men they are separated from.

Today there were so many more people at the mine entrance than the previous day that rescue workers' access to the mine was partially obstructed. However, the families of the missing men didn't for a second take their eyes off the mine and the men working there. Those who had been standing around the mine for a long time were yelling out, 'Oi! Mrs K can't see what's going on! Get out of the way!' showing the concern the miners felt for the wives of their colleagues. A feeling of desperation crept into the excavation proceedings as the men were aware of the urgency of the situation and attempted to get the water out of the cave-in site fast. But by evening they had managed only to get part of the supporting framework erected, and it didn't look as though they had progressed at all from the previous day.

This morning we waited for the embankment walls to be finished to stop the flooding waters. First the earth was brought in to fill the hole, and then work started on getting a causeway built. This has been done by getting fill from within the mine and sending it to the surface with the conveyor belt, with the aim of first plugging the hole. The retaining wall that has been built is only about half the height needed, so if it rains again there is a good possibility that not only will the first hole open up again, but that a second hole will appear, which will wash the mine out completely. To this end the company has decided to fill the hole with cement, because the company housing that is situated on the land by the river will also be endangered if the river overflows its banks. The company does not want to lose any houses to the river so it is proceeding at full speed.

                    (*NNS*, 22 September, Chikuho section)

The company reacted quickly to the threat of loss of property by immediately rebuilding the river banks around the company housing. This was in marked contrast to the speed with which the rescue work was going on underground.

As far as that work was concerned, the fear of a second cave-in was soon realised when there *was* a major collapse in a previously uncharted area directly over the tunnel where the rescuers were working.

DAY 3: 23 September

FEAR OF NEW CRACKS IN THE EARTH
Earth Split Right Above the Tunnel at H-san

The families of the missing men and the rescue workers face new problems and hardship with the discovery of a second rupture in the earth immediately above the tunnel where excavation is proceeding. At this stage the rescue workers are not sure whether it was caused by the original earth movement following the flooding, or whether it is a new and completely unrelated problem. Regardless, it is making the task the men have set out to do much harder. [See Figure 15.]

On the morning of the 22nd, Mr Ishihara (38), who lives in the *tanjū* at the mine site noticed that gaping cracks had appeared in the walls of his house. Because the homes of Ishihara and many others are situated near the cave-in site (between 70 and 80 metres away) there are fears that the whole village will collapse, hence the order for a temporary evacuation.

(*NNS,* 23 September, back page)

This effect of the disaster on the people who lived in the *tanjū* and in the nearby areas was played down by the press, who generally confined their reports to the progress or lack of progress of the rescue work and the pathos engendered by the images of the bereaved families. As a result of the subsidence the people who lived in the company houses by the river were evacuated, and were forced to move into temporary shelters for periods of up to two years. These workers lost not only their incomes but also their homes, and were largely neglected by the media and the company.

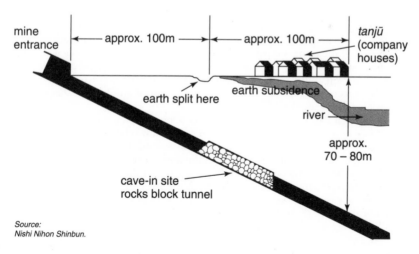

Source:
Nishi Nihon Shinbun.

Figure 15: H-san Accident Site

The farmers who worked the nearby fields were also severely affected by the disaster. One man's rice paddy sank five metres in a matter of minutes when the initial cave-in occurred. The company was not deemed liable for such damages; the government eventually footed the bill.

The discovery of the second rupture above the rescuers compounded the frustration felt by many of the watchers. Ishizaki says that the cave-in occurred because the company had been negligent of worker safety standards when they had excavated the entire region. Hence when the rescuers tried to get to the mine via a non-standard route, the abnormally soft earth from a tunnel built above them collapsed. She describes the problem:

> If you were going to have a mine of this size these days it would be spotless and well laid out, after correct geological surveys had been made. Of course there would be an underground map of the mine. At that time, though, many of the mines were laid out willy-nilly, in a random manner, which was called *tokutsu*. Previous excavations were not marked on the map: the position of any one tunnel was not known in relation to an above-ground position.
>
> Also, MITI had made a law that one couldn't excavate close to, or under, a river. But because there was no map of the underground tunnels at H-san, it was almost impossible for anyone to confirm where, in fact, the mining had reached. The company, then, ignored the law and went ahead with the mining in obviously unsafe conditions.[7]

THE FUKUOKA MINE SAFETY COMMITTEE ANNOUNCES INVESTIGATION INTO ACCIDENT

The second tunnel collapse was unexpected, and there was a need to investigate the circumstances of both cave-ins, the FMSC said today. The earth in this area had been undisturbed for decades, and it was assumed that the roof of the mine was intact and in good condition. If the place where the stones were blocking the tunnel had given in and collapsed under the pressure even a little more, it would have been directly over where the rescue workers were attempting to do their work, and it would have been more trouble than bears thinking about.

Although the investigation has not yet been completed, some points have become clear about the rock fall: (1) it is probably related to part of the roof caving in; (2) the area around the original cave-in site has been structurally weakened, and the earth has been split under pressure, which has contributed to the underground rockfalls occurring. In the case of point (1), one has to consider the possibility that the tunnel is completely flooded, and if that is the case then the water must be pumped out before rescue operations can begin properly. If this is not done, then there is the fear that even a small fall will trigger a further cave-in of the magnitude of the first cave-in.

At a meeting held in the Ikeijiri public hall about the dissatisfaction felt by the families of the missing miners and the people whose houses had been undermined by the cave-in, an unemployed miner, Mr Daiike, said, 'When two houses collapsed after the earth split there was no mistaking the fact that the earth movement had been very close, and the people here were terrified. There is no way that any of the men in the mine could have survived a cave-in of that magnitude. Even if they give us one million yen, those men won't return home'. The representatives of the families of the trapped men also voiced their discontent saying, 'If only they could break through the rocks which have blocked the tunnel, then they will be able to tell whether our husbands and fathers are still alive'.   (*NNS*, 23 September, p. 7)

The fact that the newspaper reported the local people's discontent, rather than just their bereavement, is noteworthy. Although the tone of the article is politically neutral, and no criticism of the mine-owners is implied in the report, there is an air of concern for the people who have been disadvantaged by the disaster. This is consistent with much Japanese media reporting.

DAY 5: 25 September

The following articles appeared on the same page of the *NNS*. The headline for the earlier article was smaller than that of the second, and the respective contents of the reports were rather contradictory.

It is worth noting that in this case the emphasis was placed on finding, and then defending, a scapegoat for the accident. This was done through implying the mine supervisor had acted *independently* of management wishes.

SUPERVISOR WAS NEGLIGENT
Tagawa-gun Council Calls Conference into H-san Disaster

(Tagawa) The Tagawa-gun Council will open a discussion on the H-san mining disaster on the 26 September, taking the view that on the day of the disaster the supervisor was negligent. This opinion, that the blame for the disaster lies with the supervisor of the mine, is supported by the Kyushu head of MITI, and the head of the Kyushu Business and Development Organisation. These men will speak at the conference.

(*NNS*, 25 September, back page)

HEAD OF RIVER TRANSPORTATION AND SAFETY BUREAU INVESTIGATES THE H-SAN DISASTER

The head of the RTSB, who is investigating the H-san disaster, had the following to say after listening to the explanation from the man responsible for opening the mine on the day in question, 'He, the mine supervisor, said that they had intended investigating the old excavations properly, but that the collapse and the accident had happened before they were able to. He was surprised at the scope of the accident. In response to the charges recently made that he was negligent in opening the mine on the day, he said that he had made no mistakes.

'However, although it was true that there was no map of the area where the miners were trapped, for the past three years the company had employed surveyors at a cost of five or six million yen a year to survey the underground region, and the map would be finished in the near future, he said. He went on to say that the Fukuoka Mine Safety Commission had not told him that it was inadvisable to work on that day'.

The investigation is continuing.   (*NNS*, 25 September, back page)

The mayor of Tagawa and the group he represented are shown to be concerned about the accident, and felt the need to affix responsibility for the accident. The mine-owners were really beyond the law, so the supervisor at the mine on the day was charged with negligence, a charge he tried at first to refute.

This is the last article about the investigation to appear in any of the local papers. The tone of the commissioner's report is that the company had acted correctly by instigating action to remedy the poor state of the mine maps, and was certainly not negligent on this count. The forces of nature were just too powerful and too fast to be countered by human action. There is doubt cast on the actions of the supervisor, however, in line with the company's decision that a scapegoat needed to be found. Although the article states that the investigators from the RTSB were interested in his actions on the day in question, the report states only what he had said to the investigator. There is no opinion offered by the RTSB.

This is in line with much media reporting in Japan. Reporters sometimes write an article that can swing either way, depending on the outcome of a potentially catalytic event or decision. It saves face and allows the newspaper to keep its options open, so that it can ride with the tide. In this case, the issue was whether the blame for the disaster was to be attached to the mine supervisor of the day. The newspaper thus reserves the option not to pass an opinion that may be politically damaging to its own interests.

The following investigative article, which appeared in an editorial section of the same newspaper about the disaster, is in marked contrast.

DAY 7: 27 September
'TOMORROW IT'LL BE THE ENTIRE COMMUNITY, TOO'
280 Mine Accidents in Chikuho This Year. The Pain of the Accidents Continues at the Mine

Following on the heels of the H-san flooding disaster, the gas explosion at Momii *tankō* has emphasised the two-sided problem that the people of Chikuho face today. The mining-accident rate has increased, and on top of this there is the problem of the future of the industry in light of the poor economic environment. Decaying with decrepitude, having to dig deeper and deeper in search of coal deposits is the destiny of the Chikuho coalfields.

'Today it's some people at risk, tomorrow it's the whole community' sums up the way the coalfields are reacting to the continual bad news.

Last year, according to the figures released by the FMSC, there were approximately 350 accidents where miners were killed or seriously injured, and there were 221 official deaths. This year already there have been 280 accidents, and 140 deaths, not including the 67 men missing at H-san. September has been called the 'month of disasters'. In Tagawa alone there is a monthly average of 7.5 accidents overall for the nine months, but this September, with the casualties mounting almost daily, more than three times the average number of men have been killed. The FMSC has mounted a campaign to 'Get Rid of the Jinx', but so far that is all they have done.

Mining started in the area in the Meiji period, and a number of small to medium-sized mines especially have not improved facilities at all since that period, according to one source. The fact that the maps of the mines were burnt in the war should have been enough to stop production until the facts of the matter were sorted out.

The second issue that affects the running of the small to medium-sized mines is that as management are forced to dig deeper to recover the coal from their mines, the levels of gas increase, as does the danger of flooding from striking an underground river, or being flooded from above as the ground is weakened from all the underground activity.

The third issue is that the FMSC, which should be monitoring the new excavations, is either not listened to by the companies, or is unaware of the new work. The FMSC says that although they try to apply stringent safety sanctions, which include shoring up new work after it has been properly surveyed, the smaller mines neglect to inform them of new work, so that they can save money by not complying with all the safety instructions. There are obviously a large number of problems that need to be reconsidered. On top of this, the recent long and heavy rains at the beginning of the month, which increased pressure on the earthworks, and on the river itself, should have been ample warning to the mines to apply adequate safety measures. They didn't.

'Rather than thinking about tomorrow, the ticket to the coal industry is thinking about the present', said one coal administrator. The president of a mine in Iizuka said, 'When I heard about this accident, I thought that it was an economic decision that was responsible for the slowness in recovering the bodies'. He went on to say, 'Of course, the FMSC comes to investigate the accident and this is the only time dissatisfaction about the mine surfaces is expressed.'

One miner in Tagawa said, 'Whenever an accident like this happens, I always think that tomorrow it will be me who gets it.' This sums up the attitude of the miners here at the moment.

Some very important and previously neglected points were raised in this article about mining safety, management negligence and the horrific mining accident rate in Chikuho in 1960. In so far as the scope of the article is concerned, these are cogent issues, and each is worthy of fuller investigation.

First, the accident rate and the number of deaths in the mines need to be contextualised. This was the second year after the implementation of the TCRB (Temporary Coal Rationalisation Bill), which allowed mines to be sold to the government if some 'natural' catastrophe halted or severely disrupted production. In this period, following the temporary boom that was prompted by the Korean War, there were vast stockpiles of coal left unsold, and the general outlook for coalmining was not optimistic. In the rush to increase production and cut costs, the smaller mines, which had to compete with the cartel of large coal companies and government-subsidised price cuts, often neglected to consider the safety of the workers. The coal deposits were buried farther underground, so there was a need for the companies to step up the expensive business of excavating new tunnels and faces. The deeper they dug, the greater the risk of cave-ins or methane-gas concentrations.

The unions had been compromised in most cases by management manipulation and were not prepared to interfere on the miners' behalf. The demand for mining labour had dropped concurrently with the drop in demand for coal. There was an abundance of labour available, and the miners were not able to press for improved working and living conditions with any discernible measure of success.

The FMSC's role in policing the safety conditions in the mines was also severely compromised by a number of factors, some of which are indicated in the article. Because the mines were not under any legal obligation to inform the FMSC about new work that was being done underground, very few of the smaller mines actually did contact them, according to one management informant.[8] The FMSC was purely an advisory and investigative body, organised along *tatemae*[9] lines. It was in effect a token body, which the big companies had instituted to placate the growing number of complaints that the industry was dangerous. The FMSC, like similar bodies in other mining areas, was an organ of the mining companies' cartel, and was intimately associated with the mine-owners' federation. One informant suggested that under no circumstances would this body find mine-owners guilty of negligence in the case of an accident.[10] Rather, the process generally employed in these cases was that the person who was in charge of the mine on the day on which an accident occurred was indicted. This person was charged with negligence, or misconduct, was publicly denounced by the company and the FMSC, and then sacked. However, in other cases the responsible individual was transferred within the company to another section and given equal or increased responsibility and salary.[11] This meant the public was able to vent its frustration and anger on a scapegoat, while the company was able to continue operations unchallenged. Thus the idea that the true causes of accidents lay in the type and extent of mining techniques employed by the management of the mines was obscured.

DAY 15: 4 October

The rescue workers continued to push on into the mine in their attempts to reach the miners, although by the beginning of October, even the most optimistic people were resigned to the fact that the trapped miners were dead. There were a number of mechanical problems encountered with the digging and pumping machinery, but the most severe problems concerned the map of the mine itself, as explained in the newspaper reports.

When the rescue team realised that there was little chance of being able to gain access to the mine because of the rockfall that had blocked the main tunnel, they decided to dig towards the elevator tunnel in the faint hope that some of the trapped miners had been able to reach it. Also it seemed to be the most direct access and the least dangerous to the rescuers. Of course, the fact that it took more than two weeks to get to the shaft seriously reduced the chances of rescuing any miners still alive.

THERE IS NO CHANCE THAT ANYONE IS LEFT ALIVE
Elevator Tunnel Reached

The rescue team at H-san, the mine that has swallowed 67 miners, has been making steady progress in working its way to the site where the accident occurred, by digging into the elevator access tunnel. Using a bore, they have come to the point where just two metres separates them from where the access tunnel starts. Using a probe inside the bore, they have been able to determine that there is an exceptionally high build-up of methane and coal gas, both over 12 per cent, on the other side of the rock barrier. This means that there is no chance of survivors left in the access tunnel.

When work began on the rescue operation, they had forecast that after 61 metres they would reach the blocked tunnel, but because of gross errors in the map of the mine, and slight errors in the actual digging, they missed the place. The problem was that they were urged to work with maximum speed to reach the miners in the first four days, and it was carelessness that led to the errors.

While the rescue workers waited at the mine entrance to be equipped with gasmasks after discovering the extent of the gas in the mine, the families withdrew to a place where they gathered together in silence. The atmosphere was tense. Some 25 men who had escaped from the mine came to see the water being pumped out, and they were unanimous in thinking that the miners who were trapped could not have survived in even half the volume of water.   (*NNS*, 4 October, back page)

The families of the miners had had their hopes pinned on the success of the operation to clear the way to get into the elevator tunnel, but when the announcement came that the gas in the mine was at dangerous levels, and that no miners had made their way into the shaft, the community prepared to mourn their dead.[12]

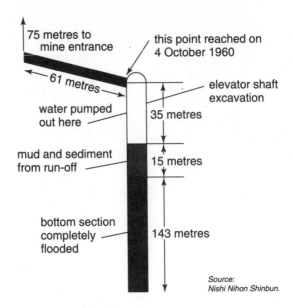

Figure 16: H-san—Rescue Work Progress

According to one source, when the rescuers went to get their gasmasks so they could look into the excavated section of the elevator shaft, the people waiting for news of their men instantly knew the worst. The fears that the men were all dead had been compounded over the weeks since the accident by the public attitude of H-san, who had made it quite clear that he did not regard the company as being liable for the rescue work expenses or funeral costs. This attitude appeared even more callous in the eyes of the bereaved families when the pumps broke down and the rescuers got lost underground, further delaying reaching the cave-in site.[13]

NO EVIDENCE OF ANYONE HAVING CLIMBED THE SHAFT
Excavation Operation To Take a Long Time

Today, 15 days after the flooding disaster at H-san, the rescue workers finally broke through to the elevator access shaft at 5.55 p.m. where they could see the state of the mine [see Figure 16]. But there was no sign that any of the missing men had been able to make it to the shaft. The elevator shaft is blocked with mud and rubble from the cave-in at a depth of about 50 metres, which means that any excavation will now take much longer than was originally thought. The families of the missing men now hold very little hope of ever seeing their men again, and many are becoming more desperate than ever.

The outlook is bleak for a number of reasons. There is an area of about 35 metres where the water has drained through to the next level of about 15 metres of sludge. Under this level there is only water. The thoughts of the rescue workers are that once they reach the lower levels, the pressure of the water will force the sludge up the shaft again, making any attempts to get the men out futile.

The rescue workers will attempt to pump the water out of the shaft, but there will be a delay of at least one day as the men organise the pumps and machinery. And because the pumps are being used to clear the water from three other tunnels at the moment, they are not expected to be able to progress at full speed in the immediate future.

U —, *the president, comments:* 'We have had to cancel this morning's forecast that we would be able to start bringing men out, but the rescue work has been able to proceed according to the plan we made at the very beginning'.

(*NNS*, 4 October)

The normal excuse from the company president that, regardless of the incompetence and excessive time that the rescue efforts had taken, the operation had been able 'to proceed according to plan' is revealing. The implication of this statement is that the management did not care whether the miners were brought to the surface or not. This was in fact the case, as Kashihama states:

> We all knew that the men were dead within the mine, and that there was no need to continue the rescue operation. It was expensive and useless. The problem was that the public needed to know what had happened to the miners, so we were obliged to continue work. This may sound rather crude, but we were in no hurry to get to the accident site because it was a waste of time.[14]

Although the company management may have known that it was a 'waste of time' trying to exhume the miners, the relatives and friends of the missing were not so easily placated. They were desperate that the work continue, according to two sources.[15]

WHERE ARE THE FATHERS AND SONS?
The Families of the Missing Cry with Desperation

Although it is probably a waste of time waiting at the mine entrance, a huge number of people from the families of the missing miners still performed their waiting vigil in silence on the evening of the 4th at the mine entrance. The news that the rescue team had been able to break through to the access tunnel and the elevator was soon spread around the *tanjū* at about 6 p.m. last night. Noguchi, the head of the rescue operation, and the man who had gone into the tunnel first, called a meeting with representatives of the families of the missing men. When the people saw the expression on his face, they knew there was not a lot of hope.

A spokesman for the families said, 'It is difficult to hold out much hope that the men are still alive. We should all start crying now.'

On top of this, there are problems. They don't know where the men in the mine actually are. Consequently, they don't know when the men will be brought out of the mine. After confirming that no one was inside the elevator shaft, the rescue workers are stumped as to what to do next.

(*NNS*, 5 October, evening edition)

It was here that the newspapers dropped the story, and the final chapters of the saga were officially left undocumented. Unofficially, the president decided that the rescue operation was both too costly and too dangerous for the workers, because of the methane gas that had built up in the mine, and he suspended the rescue attempt. In fact, he went one step further, and had the entrance to the flooded shaft, as well as all the cave-in sites, cemented shut. Although this was contrary to the wishes of the families of the missing men, it was typical of the way in which the management of this particular mine dealt with the workforce, and the concreting of the entrance has been used by local activists as a symbol of the oppressive environment of H-san.[16]

Cement the dead

The miners' families were concerned with the recovery of the bodies from the mine, even though the men were dead. There was a great fear that the dead would be left to rot inside the mine, and that their spirits would not be able to rest. This attitude is consistent with standard Japanese perceptions of death and the need for a decent Buddhist burial, particularly among the miners.[17] There was an overriding concern that the men would become *yūrei*, the ghosts of those who are not laid to rest properly. Although this may seem implausible in contemporary Japan, there is still a widespread belief in the concept of *yūrei*. In fact, some Japanese anthropologists conducted research into the concept after the atomic bombs were dropped on Hiroshima and Nagasaki. According to these studies, many people believed that *yūrei* were with them for many years. The idea was that the *yūrei* would go away only when their souls had been laid to rest. Similar attitudes were apparent at H-san.

Within a very short time the shaft was concreted shut, you know, with all the dead people inside. It was because of the danger of a gas explosion in the shaft, or so the management said. That was pretty bad as far as we were concerned, but management said that it was dangerous to leave the mine as it was, and it was impossible to get the dead out.

The relatives and friends said that the company's attitude was terrible, and that it was disgusting that they could ignore the presence of the dead,

especially as the rats that you would have expected to come out of the shaft
when it flooded didn't. Why the rats didn't come out was pretty obvious: they
had enough to eat in the mine. One of my friends, who was the same age as I
am, a really good artist, and a man with soul, died in the accident. Some of
my relatives also died. I was worried that they would never rest properly.[18]

As Ogata has said, with the shaft concreted shut, the matter was
officially closed. This act alone caused a great deal of resentment
among the workforce at H-san, who had lost their friends and
workmates in the disaster, and also their own employment.

However, the circumstances surrounding the cementing of the mine
were not as straightforward as Ogata has described. One of the more
important issues was the issue of compensation for the families of the
dead, and of course for the miners who had been put out of work. Here
the company used its standard methods of dealing with their
employees. Ishizaki is quite succinct about the situation that developed:

They [the miners' families] were told that there was no chance of getting the
dead men out of the mine; then the decision was taken to shut it permanently. The union told the men to be tolerant, saying that it couldn't be
helped. And when the question of what sort of compensation would be paid
out to the families of the dead was raised, the company that had been unable
or unwilling to pump the water out of the mine made the people an offer.

They offered to pay out between 200,000 and 500,000 yen per miner to the
families of the dead (one to three years' wages depending on the length of
service of the individual miner),[19] on the condition that the families of the
dead accept that there was no way that the company would be able to
exhume the bodies. 'If you're not satisfied with the amount we're offering,
then we'll dynamite the mine, and blow the bodies into mincemeat', they
said.[20]

This type of coercion was no different from the style of management
the mine had used since the war years; threats of destruction and
violence, which were softened by offers of monetary compensation far
below the amounts needed for people to survive. The families were
then placed in the position where they had to make either a moral or
an economic choice. The union encouraged them to take what they
called the 'generous offer',[21] and in desperation the vast majority of the
people concurred. The mine shaft was concreted and, although work in
the no. 2 shaft continued for another 12 months, the majority of men
were made redundant.

Ogata describes his feelings about the accident:

I was cut. I'll never forget what happened. Yamanaka, who was like my brother,
died, and every year when we go to visit the graves of our ancestors I think of

him, and wonder what he would have been doing if he hadn't been killed. His children have all grown up now, but at the time I was really concerned for the welfare of his family, because they had almost nothing to live on at all. All the money that they had went on the kids, and there was no one to help raise them, with their father gone. Yamanaka-san dying like that was just terrible. I tried to help them out for a while, but it was hard for us too. We were like brothers, and when they told me that he was dead, well I was devastated, and then they said that his body would not be brought up. Well, it was the last straw. Even if the mine was operating I would have quit anyway.[22]

The newspaper reports were written with a tone of concern for the miners and the families, but with one or two exceptions were roundly convinced that the accident was unavoidable. This accident was the 280th accident of 1960 in Chikuho alone. Yet inquiries into the accidents failed to link the responsibility of the disasters with the company involved in any single case.

The disaster at H-san was followed four days later by a major gas explosion at Momii, another local mine. However, comments about safety considerations, which had been largely ignored by the companies involved, with the exception of the article quoted on pp.136–7 were restricted to small paragraphs hidden away in some of the more 'liberal' newspapers. By early October most newspapers had relegated the disaster stories to the less-read pages, or had confined themselves to editorials on the 'human side' of the disaster, although the *Nishi Nihon Shinbun* sporadically reported the progress of the rescue work.

The union's public statement (see page 127) was revealing in that the nature of the company union mentality was quite apparent in the bland style of the press release. There was no hint of miners' resistance, nor of the movement for compensation for widows and families of the dead. The union also ignored the poor organisation of the rescuers, the lack of proper maps and the number of mechanical breakdowns, which reduced the chances of reaching possible survivors. Rather, they were more concerned about whether they would continue to be employed with the company. I shall discuss the union in more detail below. It is only today, 30 years after the event, that criticism of the company has been publicly aired. Why has it taken so long for people to say what they think about a situation that was emotionally and economically untenable? The brutal way in which the mine was run is a major contributing factor in understanding this.

Violence and repression in H-san — more context

To contextualise this comment, I shall look at some of the accounts of men who worked in the H-san mine about the nature of violence that accompanied them in everyday situations. The issue of mining safety that, although moot in the eyes of the government, was a critical issue in the eyes of the miners, was something that both the management and the union had ignored at H-san up to the time of the flood.

One informant who lost a close relative in the H-san flood had the following incisive comment to make about the disaster:

> The H-san disaster is locally the best known incident that involved mismanagement; at least that is what is said about it.
>
> When the flood occurred, the electricity was suddenly cut off. The men in the mine who got out were the ones who heard voices shouting, 'Get out of there!' But the ones who died had probably not heard the shouts, and *because there had been so many cases when the electricity was suddenly cut off in the past they were prepared to wait until it was restored.* [my emphasis]
>
> If you've done physical labouring work, I'm sure you'll understand this. They started at 10 a.m. and sometimes worked through until 10 or 12 p.m. When they had worked until eight or nine in the evening they had only an hour or so left until they were officially entitled to a full day's pay. So the workers were prepared to hang around and wait for the time to pass.
>
> Therefore, when the electricity was cut off, the workers who were waiting around to get their full day's pay would likely have stayed where they were because they thought that it was only another one of the many incidents that had happened over the years, and if they waited then there was a good chance that they would get their pay for no work with no problems. However, the men who survived were the ones who got out as soon as the electricity was cut off. I've heard this story on a number of occasions. This is what the people who made it out alive had to say about the accident.[23]

The frequent occurrences of electricity being cut off in the past was one fact that was largely ignored by the investigation into the disaster, which found that the company was within its rights to operate as it had on the day in question. The accident was judged a 'natural occurrence' and out of the hands of men.[24] The fact that the mine management had misjudged the conditions in the light of the FMSC's recommendation to abandon mining because of the danger of flooding was perhaps indicative of the way management viewed the workforce. Ogata recalls that many times the men were told to work in water up to their waists, sometimes even when it had reached their chests. Consequently, they may not have noticed the height of the water.

So, what sort of mine was H-san to work in? I shall draw on Ogata's account of his own experience.

Work at H-san

Ogata is 65 years old and, apart from being blind in one eye, is in remarkably good health. He started working in H-san when he was eight years old, in 1933, following his father into the pit, as did many of the pre-war generation of coalfields children. At that time he was employed to look after the horses, and to help the driver with his duties, in a similar manner to the work the young apprentices did in the Yorkshire mines in the early twentieth century. He is an outspoken critic of the unions and of the government, refusing to vote or take part in what he considers a travesty of justice, the unions themselves.

Although he is retired, he still lives in the company housing at M-san Ita in Tagawa, the last mine he worked in. He came to this mine when, after more than 20 years with H-san, that mine was closed down following the flooding disaster. He told me of the hardships of the pre-war miners in an off-hand manner:

> I went to H-san in 1933, and Father was injured in 1936. That was when the economy was in trouble. At that time the mine wasn't really such a violent one, the violence came after the war really. The wages weren't wages though. They used to pay us in ration coupons, not in real wages, so that we were forced to buy all our food through the company stores. On average, no matter how hard you worked, you never got more than 10–20 per cent of your wages in cash. The rest was in those coupons.
>
> This was because the coal economy wasn't really working very well, and there was a general shortage of cash, I guess. The companies couldn't afford to pay the miners their wages in cash, so they gave us the coupons. Transportation was poor at that time, too. Hardly any trains came to the local stations, so we were pretty isolated.
>
> The miners used to take their rations and move from house to house, combining what they had with the others so that they could eat. You see the problem was that the rations weren't enough, so we had to combine our rice, with say, someone's fish so that we could eat properly. You'd look for smoke coming from someone's chimney, and you'd go to their place with your rations, give them to the person who was cooking, and share the food that they served up.
>
> The company houses were very small, you know. Four and a half *tatami*[25]. Of course there were no toilets either. We had to use the public toilets. The people here all used to wash together at the wells, which is where the *idobata kaigi* (discussion at the well) started. There was usually one well per *kumi* (block of ten to twelve houses), which the residents shared. The same applied with the toilets.[26]

Ishizaki, today an active Chikuho revivalist, and member of the Anti-Emperor Movement, was married to an H-san miner. She worked as a cleaner at the hospital in H-san and lived in the company housing at H-san for 25 years with her husband. She explains that the living standards within the *tanjū* were sub-human:

> Before this place was rebuilt, it used to be a U-san *tanjū*. It was not a place in which people could realistically be expected to live. It was an abysmally poor

place. There were open sewers, and the roads turned to mud after the slightest rain. There was no clean water except at the wells, and that water was always a little dangerous. There was never enough to eat, and the food that we did get was rarely fresh. We were lucky to get enough rice to make *bento* (lunch boxes).

The houses were only one or two rooms, and in many places there were more than three generations living under the one roof. The houses were so small that we lived in each other's pockets, and because the walls were so thin all the neighbours knew exactly what was going on in the house next door. There was no privacy of any sort. I am talking about the post-war situation here. It was much worse for the Koreans, the other foreign labourers and even us Japanese during the wars.[27]

This was in many ways a typical, small, Japanese coalmining village, by all accounts.[28] As in many other *tanjū*, there were community toilets, baths and water supplies, and the families of the miners lived in cramped quarters, which were supplied by the company. However, H-san was distinguished from other Kyushu mines by its exceptionally repressive management policy.

Union compromises

Following the war, management was able to exert pressure on the workers either through the union or, if the union was not persuasive enough, through the *yakuza* personnel they employed as *rōmu*. In one way or another, miners were forced into conforming. Complaint and resistance must have seemed impossible. Ogata describes the way he saw the process that took place after the flood at H-san. He emphasises two very important points: first, that the accidents became more frequent as the pressure to increase production became greater; and, second, the passive and compliant attitude of the men to the demands that were placed on them.

After the flood the closures of the mines proceeded at a rapid rate, because the companies were trying to get out of the business as cheaply as possible. The heads of the companies also tried to get away with as much as they could: they didn't want to pay out money if they could avoid it.

To this end they charged their subsidiary companies fines of up to 2,000,000 yen if they could not keep up with production. The accidents were worse and worse as the companies tried to push us to work harder, even though there were almost no safety measures. This economic pressure was transferred directly to us, the workers. This was really bad. But it was typical of the way Japan has treated its people. The people at the top ordered the people at the bottom to do things that affected their homes and their work negatively, while the elite never suffered at all.

But the strange thing about the business was that when the workers heard that the company was going to get fined so much if they didn't improve output, they [the unions] said that we should just forget about the safety standards and get to work. That's the way this country works.

Industry comes first, and the workers believe that human life isn't worth much at all if the bosses tell them that it is so. Down the mines the same thing happened. The miners believed what they were told and always did what the bosses ordered. When we were forced to work naked because water came up to our waists, no one complained. They just did it because they were told to. I used to see this happening all the time. In fact I was one of these monkeys.[29]

The union leadership at H-san was made up of men who had been handpicked by the management to control the workforce. This union employed its own gangs of overseers, usually recruited from local *yakuza gumi*, who exerted pressure on the workers to increase production. The close ties the union had with management were manifest in the day-to-day running of the mine.

We used to see rice delivered to the union leaders, but the workers never got any. It was always kept by the people at the top of the chain.

Around here, the union was a company union. It supported whatever the company said about the workers' position. The union was useless. It was like a babysitter really. It didn't do anything at all for the workers, just supported the capitalists. For example, when we asked union men to ask the company to lower the rents, they just ignored us completely.

The problem was that there were a number of men from the union who wanted to get on in the company, and these men would ignore anything we said that could have jeopardised their status within the company. It was quite surprising how many of the leaders made it to *kachō* [section manager] rank.

It's just like today. They are prepared to back the company over the workers at any cost. The leaders follow orders from the company, and they gradually work their way up the ladder to the top of the lower management. The rule was that the company was always first for these guys, and the workers were always second — after themselves, of course.

These guys were really the eyes and ears of the company within the union. They would tell the president who were the bad workers and who were talking about how bad the company was, and these men were always fired. They didn't work for the men: they worked against the men! They prepared a list of the 'Best Five', which was really the worst five men on the job in their eyes. It didn't matter if you were good at your job. They were concerned only with company loyalty.[30]

The idea that the union officials were able to 'cement' ties with the company so that they would be promoted to the lower management levels was already in evidence at H-san. There was no other organisation that the miners could turn to at the mine for help, so the attitudes of the vast majority seemed to be that they should just endure the situation as best they could.

Further evidence of the nature of the relationship between the union leaders and the company was witnessed in the way the mine fell into receivership after the flood. When the accident occurred, the owner of the mine was in Tokyo. He flew back to Fukuoka immediately and was interviewed by a reporter for the *Nishi Nihon Shinbun* at the airport. The president said that the company was not going to be liable for any damages, that the accident was 'an act of the gods', and that he was sure his staff were blameless. He went on to say that although it was unfortunate, the fact that so many men were injured or killed 'could not have been helped'. He blamed the FMSC for not taking sufficient precautions in their surveys of the mine.[31]

The mine-owner's comments attracted quite a lot of attention, and in the uproar that followed he declared he was going to sell the mine within twelve months, because the accident and the delays in production that followed were effectively bankrupting the mine. The FMSC and MITI together decided that it would be fit and proper for the management to appoint an advance auditing body to check the company's records before it was sold to the government. The H-san Mine Union was asked to carry out this task by U-san. The ties with management were so strong that U-san had complete confidence in the union's 'independent' assessment of the financial state of the mine.

Conclusion

H-san was an extreme case of a trend within the industry to push workers to the limits of their endurance. The closure of the mine was a dramatic event, which has become symbolic of the way the mine was run. The power of the company over the workers was so complete that even some 30 years after the mine closed, the majority of miners are still not prepared to discuss either their work in the mine or the accident. This is related to the control the company exerted over not only the people within its employ, but also over local government and political institutions. Largely through both the isolation of the mine and the company president's manipulation of the political agenda, it was able to consolidate its power base with a respectable political presence, and a responsible public image, which the publicists for the company worked hard to maintain.

By making worker rights, company violence and legal transgressions non-issues, the company was able to maintain its control over the workers, even in the more democratic post-war period. This leaves an impression that the miners were acquiescent about the conditions under which they worked. However, if one digs a little deeper, it becomes obvious that the methods employed to keep issues from becoming issues were nothing short of coercion and violence. Violence became so embedded in the fabric of the *tanjū* that people became inured to it to a large extent. In effect, then, the politics of violence became the politics of the mundane.

Workers knew how far they could push the authorities without being punished, just as they knew that they had to feed their families. Although many men were consumed by anger at the way the company used them like commodities, rather than as humans, they were still aware of the imperative of working in a society that did not support its unemployed for very long. Given the complicated and discriminatory classification of mines and mining types and the difficulties the industry was going through, many of the people who worked for U-san had few options other than to continue work if they wanted to remain solvent.

Isolation, fear, hunger and ignorance all worked against the miners from the start, and by the time they were aware of the nature of the work they had undertaken, it was too late to back down. Following the endemic attitude of *shiyō ga nai* (it cannot be helped), they continued to work and suffer at the hands of the overseers. It wasn't until the mine was actually closed that any real criticism of the mine was publicly aired, and even then it was aired by independent people and groups, not by the miners. Most miners were concerned only about not being thrown out of the *tanjū* when the closure came into effect. To a large extent the fear of the H-san days is still quite tangible in the town. Few people discuss the past, and most choose to forget what happened. Those who are now living in the public housing blocks think that they are there because the company president allowed them to be, and are not keen to risk expulsion by saying what they think about the company.

However, rumours are, and have always been, in evidence about the mine. Even in the big mining *tanjū*, people discuss what a 'tragedy' the H-san case was, and how sad it was that

> the bodies of the miners were all eaten by rats, but the miners have no one to blame for this but themselves. It was bound to happen some day, because U-san was such an evil man. He was only ever concerned about money, and he pushed the men harder and harder to produce more for him. No one apart from the management, government and police really benefited from this mine. He didn't care whether men died, just as long as they were making money for him.[32]

The H-san case, and the lack of action by the union in presenting any opposition to the company either before or after the accident can be contrasted with the Y-san case, which is described in detail in chapter 12. At Y-san, probably largely because of the influence of outside radical groups, the families of men killed in the mine were able to commence litigation against the company for compensation far in excess of the inadequate amount offered.

However, it is not simply outsider intervention that made the difference. Management techniques, and in particular the violence that was a day-to-day occurrence, had a profound influence in maintaining worker acquiescence in H-san, both during and after the mining era. The capacity of the company to maintain the fictions developed during the coal era some 30 years after the mine closed is particularly noteworthy. In many ways this parallels Lukes' (1974) perspective, where he suggests that the most insidious use of power is that in which relations of relative power and powerlessness are maintained even after the powerful have fallen. In mines such as H-san, where unions had been compromised by management intervention, challenges to the status quo have yet to emerge.

NOTES TO CHAPTER 7

1 Ishizaki, personal communication, 1988.
2 Kashihama, interview, 1989.
3 Fukuoka Mine Safety Commission Report, 1961, pp.1–3.
4 Oguchi, interview, 1988.
5 Kashihama, interview, 1988.
6 Ogata, interview, 1988.
7 Ishizaki, interview, 1988.
8 Kashihama, interview, 1988.
9 See chapter 2, note 12.
10 Sono, interview, 1989.
11 See Y-san disaster, 1965; M-san Miike, 1964, for examples of cases where those formally indicted with responsibility for disasters were able to receive advancement with the company.
12 Ishizaki, interview, 1988.
13 Ogata, interview, 1988.
14 Kashihama, interview, 1988.
15 Ogata and Ishizaki, personal communications, 1988.
16 See, for example, Ishizaki in her book, *Less Than the Dregs of Life*, 1987, pp.32–50.
17 See Idegawa, 1984, pp.114–20.
18 Ogata, interview, 1988.
19 The companies were required by law to contribute superannuation and life insurance premiums on behalf of each worker. In the case of an accident, the workers' families were to be paid out the full value of the insurance policy. In H-san, however, although the company maintained that it had paid the contributions to the relevant funds on behalf of the workers, the workers' families were offered only a small part of the compensation that was their legal right. The remainder of the money went to the union and to company management, which incidentally owned the life insurance company to which the mining company contributed.
20 Ishizaki, interview, 1988.
21 According to Kashihama, it was a 'generous offer', although this was hotly disputed by my other informants. Kashihama maintained that the company was not 'really' required to pay out any compensation, and that they were co-operating with the FMSC, which had suggested that it would be the humane thing to do under the circumstances.
22 Ogata, interview, 1988.
23 Oguchi Hanako, interview, 1988.

24 Fukuoka Mine Safety Commission Report, 1961, p.3.
25 Although the size of each *tatami* is getting smaller these days, one *tatami* equals approximately 1.8 metres by 90 centimetres.
26 Ogata, interview, 1988.
27 Ishizaki, interview, 1988.
28 See Ueno's collection of stories, 1985 a–e; Hayashi 1987; Idegawa, 1984.
29 Ogata, interview, 1988.
30 Ogata, interview, 1988.
31 *Asahi Shinbun*, 3 September 1960, p.3.
32 Oguchi, K., interview, 1988.

CHAPTER 8

The Bathing Master

I arrived home at around 7.30 that night. The streets and lanes in the *tanjū* were deserted. As usual, the street lights were not working, and as I rode the motorbike through the maze of housing, the exhaust echoed from the concrete walls and culverts. The fronts of the houses were in darkness: the residents had obviously moved into the main room to eat and watch television, and only the muted sounds of conversation and game show music disturbed the cold, clear night. As I dismounted, I was approached by my neighbour.

'Matt-san, Ogata-san is still waiting in the baths for you. He's been there since five o'clock. By now he'll look like a prune. Go on, get over there,' she urged me. Groaning under my breath I realised that I had forgotten that it was Tuesday, and that the baths were open. For the five days a week that they were open, Ogata, the man who lived for the baths, waited for me so that he could retell stories of the coalmines. The schedule of the bath opening times had changed in the last week, and I had totally forgotten. Ogata would not be impressed.

The ultimate storyteller, more adept at chronicling stories than Oguchi, the *kami shibai* man, could ever be, Ogata has a range of tales that encompass everything from moral cautions to tales of personal violence, the war and the foreigners who lived in the area. A miner for more than 20 years with the H-san mine in Kawasaki, he moved to the M-san *tanjū* 23 years ago, when he was lucky enough to get a job at the coalface. A man who has suffered his share of pain and hardship, he has converted to Buddhism since he was hit on the head at a factory and declared clinically dead for an hour.

153

Although he is 63 years old, I first thought he was in his early 50s, so young and relaxed does he appear. In the baths he wears a small towel around his shaved head to keep the sweat from his eyes which twinkle constantly. Possessed of a wicked sense of humour, he merrily abuses and teases other miners and myself about our physical anomalies. Sasaki, his best friend, is exactly the same age, but quite thin, wiry even. Ogata always says that the reason Sasaki is so thin is that he is living in a *de facto* relationship with a woman who is 15 years younger than he is, and she 'keeps him going flat out in the saddle'. Sasaki is always embarrassed by this, and Ogata always plays the game out.

The baths are old. They were built in 1910, and the state of dilapidation is advanced. There is no paint left on the walls, and the concrete floor, which was once tiled, is now stained and cracked. The windows, which look out onto the *tanjū*, are broken, some are boarded up, and others are left as they are, the panes of glass miraculously defying gravity. Originally the pit-top baths for the miners, they have been left to decay by M-san in the almost 30 years since the mine closed down. Heated by a coal-fired boiler, with a mass of rusting pipes leading to a central boiler in the middle of an elliptical pool, the water is unbelievably hot. Just dipping the plastic bowl one takes to the bath into the water and pouring it over yourself can actually scald you. In fact, for more than a week I was not able to get into the bath, attempts to do so rendering my very white skin crimson in seconds after immersion. Gradually I got used to it, and was able to relax and enjoy it, but I could stand the heat for only five minutes or so at a time.

As a comparison, Japanese friends from Fukuoka, who ostensibly are quite accustomed to the heat of Japanese baths, were unable to enter the water at all. Ogata spends on average three hours a day immersed in the water. It has been suggested by some of the other men at the baths that this is why he has such flawless skin, although others have suggested that it is the reason for his perceived craziness.

Recording stories in a bath that was prohibitively hot, wet and steamy was to become one of my main problems. Unlike Ogata, I am not possessed of an eidetic memory for tales, and because I needed to record the information somehow, I had to try to overcome some logistic problems. In the end, I decided that I would compromise. I would get out of the bath and retire to the change-room, where, naked and sweating copiously, I would write his story in a notebook, trying to recapture the mood and the content of what he had told me. Then I would return to the baths, again facing the slow boiling torture, and listen either to the continuation of the old or to the start of a new story. I used to dream of a waterproofed Walkman, or at the least a waterproofed pen and paper, neither of which were available.

1

View of M-san Ita coal village (*tanjū*) looking down from the town hall in the first snow fall of the year (January 1988). The new five-storey apartments are clearly visible above the low roofs of the *shataku* (old housing), as is the flattened slag-heap (background, right). This is being cleared to make way for new housing.

2

Close up view of the author's accommodation on the day of arrival in the *tanjū* (1987). A gas cylinder for cooking had been thoughtfully placed outside the kitchen by the local gas agent, and an employee of the M-san Real Estate company placed plastic sheeting on the roof to prevent the house flooding. (The author's *kumi* was demolished to make way for the new apartments in 1991.)

3
The accommodation was less than luxurious, from bare light bulbs to dried mud walls, ferrets in the drains and rats under the floor boards. However, the *tatami* mats had been replaced by the local *tatami* man with second-hand but clean mats, and electricity was included in the rent of 4,000 yen a month.

4
Formerly the miners' baths at the coal pit entrance, the local baths were in a state of disrepair. Although well patronised, they lost money following the construction of the five-storey apartments with internal baths. Consequently they were closed down in 1992. During the author's stay in the *tanjū* the baths were open five nights a week; on the other nights a bath was not an option.

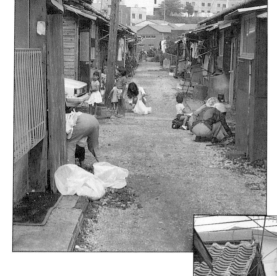

5
The annual *kusa tori* (grass or weed clearing) day. Women from each household in each *kumi* (block) are expected to remove any traces of greenery from the roadways to 'beautify' the *tanjū*. The town hall can be seen in the background.

6
The old housing contrasts starkly with the new.

7
Mt Asahi, Tagawa's landmark. The top of the mountain was bulldozed to extract lime for the M-san cement works, in the foreground. In front of the factory are vegetable gardens, leased to and tended by local residents who have to deal with the problem of acid rain.

8
Idegawa, museum curator,
women's activist, historian and
author.

9
One of the informants, a story-teller.

10
Two informants outside the author's *tanjū*.

11
The day of the annual traditional dance exhibition
(*odori kai*). Informants pose for a post-dance photograph.

12
The memorial at H-san mine, Kawasaki, for the 67 miners
killed in the flood.

13
The bridgehead which collapsed when the water level from the river (lower left) flowed over it and flooded the mineshaft.

14
The cemented H-san mine entrance, being shored up after subsidence following heavy monsoonal rain in July 1988.

15

The H-san 'improved' accommodation for miners and their families following the disaster. The future for M-san Ita?

16

Ishizaki and a friend in front of the Y-san memorial built by the widows of the 237 men killed in the 1965 gas explosion.

17
The *tanjū* in which the women of Y-san mine live. In the background is a *bota yama* (slag-heap). Other slag-heaps are visible behind this one.

18
The Kawasaki town annual *Bon Odori Taikai* (Festival of the Dead mass rally), 1988.

The following is an extract from my diary, dated 16 June 1988:

> Since I started this file, Ogata and I have become mates, and I think that I
> hear more about the history of the area from him than I do from anyone
> else. He knows a lot about the local customs, the history of the temples and
> shrines, the way that the coalmining developed in the region, who was killed
> in what gas explosions, the forms of education that were prevalent in the pre-
> war period, the different festivals held at different times of the year etc. All in
> all, he has become one of my best informants.
>
> This is all due to the fact that he likes two things in life better than all else
> — talking and bathing. It just happens that I am often in the right place at
> the right time. In fact, I often have difficulty escaping from the baths because
> he does like to talk! We have become a famous pair at the baths, and no one
> interrupts us when we are engrossed in conversation. I say nothing at all on
> most occasions, because I don't have a chance to get a word in edgewise. It is
> all good learning experience.

As a consummate storyteller, Ogata need not rely on the accurate
rendition of stories. However, as Walter Benjamin recognised in *The
Storyteller*, he tells his stories as more than stories. They are useful tales,
tales that have counsel 'woven into the fabric of real life' (Benjamin,
1977; p.87). They are full of wisdom and wit, and are the result of the
experience of a full life. He recognises this, as he recognises that there
are certain constraints incumbent on the anthropologist to render
people's accounts fairly:

> I want you to write about the real history of the place, not just some silly stuff
> that tells people about the good things about the coal industry. You have to
> tell them about the bad things as well, because if you don't, probably no one
> else will. The people who worked in the mines are dying off in this town, so
> you have to be quick.

Ogata was born in Kawasaki town, the youngest of three boys. He was
educated up to the fourth grade of primary school in Kawasaki. He left
school at eight years of age to work in the mines at Kawasaki H-san
mine. His parents were also miners, and when he was ten years old his
father was severely injured in a mining cave-in and was forced to give up
working, so the family relied on the efforts of the children to support
them.

As a child, he was a gifted artist, and spent a lot of time drawing
pictures of the miners as they came home from the mines. He also drew
many landscapes of the area, one of which I have in my possession. He
learnt to draw with charcoal, which is not surprising, given his
background, and then progressed to watercolours, the medium that he
chose to use for the rest of his life. While he was working in the mines,
he spent a lot of time after work in drawing and making sketches of the

workers and of the scenery. Eventually, after his parents died, he attempted to learn formally, but when a mining accident left him with one good eye, and with only partial sight in the other eye, he lost the will to continue. He decided that in order to eat it was necessary to work as a labourer, so he continued to work in the mines, moving to the M-san Ita mine in 1962. He has been there ever since.

Ogata's knowledge of local customs is quite profound, and he is regarded as the 'guardian of knowledge' by many of his ex-miner friends. He is an outspoken and often aggressive speaker.

Physically he is quite distinctive. He is short and stocky, weighing about 65 kilograms, with thick forearms and legs, and a shaved head. He shaves his head because of an accident that he had at work in 1970. He collapsed after a blow to the head and was declared dead by the doctor at the accident site. However, as the ambulance was taking him to the morgue, he miraculously recovered, apparently scaring the doctor badly. The near-death experience, during which, he says, he entered a tunnel with brilliant light on one side and a horrible cloister-ing darkness on the other, which smelt terrible, prompted him to convert seriously to Buddhism and to shave his head as a sign of his conversion. He went as far as to take a new first name in the Buddhist manner and went about changing his lifestyle in what could only be described as a radical manner: he gave up drinking.

At this point it must be said that for a miner to give up drinking there has to be a formidable reason, because there is tremendous social pressure incumbent on the miner to drink with his mates. In this there are some close parallels to the Australian notion of 'mateship'. That is, if a man does not drink with his mates, he is often regarded as not being a 'real' man. The social pressure that is brought to bear is exceptional. Particularly in this community, the ability to drink with your friends is the sign of a man who is a good man. That is, it is regarded by those both inside and outside the community as a 'typical' behaviour pattern within the mining community, part of the so-called *kawasuji kishitsu* (riverside character, the name used to describe the mining regions in Chikuho).

As a storyteller, Ogata's main strength is that he does not let the truth stand in the way of a good story. Further, he manages to load his stories with essential ingredients to keep his listeners interested: violence, prejudice, sex and racism. Like many miners, he reviles Koreans. They were lower than the *burakumin*, yet he feels that they, like the *burakumin*, have received substantially more than Japanese miners in the years after the coalmines closed.

Ogata tells stories of the bombs the Allies dropped on the region in their efforts to blow up the ammunition dump hidden in the mountains. 'They blew the fucking mountain apart,' he said. He talks about the invasion of the Americans. He says that they thought these men were really devils. Their skin was red, as was their hair, they were huge by Japanese standards, and they were rich beyond the dreams of the locals. The first time he ever tasted caramel or chocolate was when the Americans were there. But the overriding feeling was fear, a feeling of complete lack of control over their own environment, and a general sense of being completely outclassed by the enemy. He tells of how many locals felt obliged to give the Yankees presents as tokens of their esteem for them as fighters. He tells of the jealousy they felt that they were so well fed, compared with the Japanese who were starving after the war: the US forces had meat and rice and potatoes and other luxury items, which he could not have even imagined existed, and they got to eat three times a day.

Ogata tells of the fighting between the Japanese and the Chinese in Manchuria, the fighting between the Japanese and the Koreans in the Chikuho mines, and the fighting between Japanese in H-san. He remembers the violence, and wants others to know its extent, now that he can look back and see it in perspective. He tells stories of the politics of Japan: the need for politicians to lie and to cheat the people of Chikuho, while they get rich on taxes and money they steal from corporations such as Lockheed and Recruit.

A prejudiced, likeable, eccentric man with very outspoken views, Ogata's interpretations of Chikuho society were of immeasurable value to my research. He still keeps the idea of the storyteller alive in a different and more subtle way than the *kami shibai* man, complete with his props. His only prop is his memory, and that is quite spectacular.

His critical views of the history of coalmining in Chikuho correspond closely with those of Hayashi, my main informant in the next chapter. Although Ogata is a talented raconteur, he was never a political activist. Hayashi, by contrast, was instrumental in motivating the miners at the K-san mine to challenge the legitimacy of mine management methods. In order to emphasise the differences between the H-san case and the K-san case, I shall place the actions of the Hayashi union within the context of the oppression of human rights in Chikuho. This will allow the reader to appreciate the dedication necessary to challenge the strength of the ruling ideology of the coalfields. Hayashi's story highlights the difficulties and frustrations inherent in mounting a campaign to improve working conditions for miners.

CHAPTER 9

Labour Conflict:
The Case of the K-san Union Action

The working-class movement in Japan began when the JCP was established in 1922, after Japan had become a military force in East Asia, and following the Russian Revolution. The JCP was perceived as 'opposition' to the government, and all communist organisations were outlawed in the years leading up to the Second World War. In such oppressive conditions, union consciousness was poorly developed, and although labour organisations were in evidence in the 1920s, their power was severely compromised by the Police Regulation Law of 1923. This effectively destroyed the unions, based as they were on 'democratic and socialist' principles. Although some unions maintained their presence, industry-wide unions were eliminated from the political scenario. The working classes *en masse* did not unite and confront those people who held power in society, even though there were some conspicuous mass uprisings in the years immediately following the First World War.

The development of union consciousness is directly linked to Japan losing the war. That is, the Occupation, in compliance with its strategy to limit the power of the *zaibatsu*, sought to increase worker participation in unions. The inalienable right to democracy, the catchcry of the Occupation, underpinned the development of this policy. In actual fact the development of unions in compliance with the laws went ahead, but the running of the new unions was compromised, so that companies controlled the way the movement progressed to a large degree. Wages were controlled and the annual Spring Wage Offensive became little more than a conspicuous social outing, the protests of the Council of Trade Unions (*Sōhyō*) notwithstanding. Industry and government, after

158

consultations with employer and union representatives, dictated what sort of pay increases would be awarded.

The formal introduction of unionism into the mines, though, had a sweeping effect on the industry. For the first time there was talk of wage standardisation, restricted working hours, increased safety standards and improved accommodation for miners. However, notwithstanding the ideals, the companies moved as early as 1945 to increase their power over the workforce by creating unions of their own. These unions were company unions in every sense, often being organised by lower management or upwardly mobile workers to cause as little disruption to production as possible. In direct opposition to these enterprise unions' stance, *Tanrō* was formed in 1945 under the auspices of the JSP. *Tanrō* aimed to be the first union that would bring the workers together under a single banner, and to some extent it was successful.

Tanrō attempted to alleviate the oppressive working conditions in the mines through the network of affiliated unions they established in the early 1950s.[1] *Tanrō* had problems in that the structure of the mines in Japan did not allow for any central labour organisation, despite the new laws. Although they were well represented in the larger companies, the smaller companies, *asseiyama* (literally 'pressure mountains'), would not allow the formation of any union other than a company union.

In 1956, in response to a downturn in the economy, the companies strengthened their power base by introducing a number of co-ordinated moves, which were intended to disperse even further the already weakened power of the *Tanrō* affiliated unions, after the go-ahead for the TCRB) had been given. The measures included more vigilant supervision of the miners, increased quotas for individual miners, increased rent for company housing and the tacit agreement to ignore safety standards. The last position was taken as mine-owners attempted to invest in other industries the capital that had been set aside by the National Coal Board for safety equipment. The aim of the mine-owners was to maximise profits before the summary shutdown of the industry.

Anticipating trouble from *Tanrō* in response to this aggressive stance, the coal companies offered incentives to workers in many mines to leave *Tanrō*-affiliated unions and join company unions. These incentives included the pick of work at the face, improved housing, an increase in pay and guaranteed work in what was fast becoming an economically hostile working environment. The motive behind this move was obvious to many of the workers. The miners perceived that their legal right to join a union of their choice was compromised and that the companies were moving again towards total labour force control, which included automatic redundancies in the event of the predicted mass mine closures. These complaints were to become the centre of the industrial action that followed.

To illustrate some of the labour problems that occurred I shall draw on accounts of one labour confrontation that happened at K-san in 1957. The K-san strike action continued for a long time (101 days to be exact), and the miners were without support from *Tanrō* for 100 of those days. K-san was a small N-san subcontractor in Chikuho, and because of its insignificance it received almost no press coverage throughout the duration of the strike. The newspapers that picked up the story presented the miners as irresponsible law-breakers who were threatening both the economy of the mines and the national economy

The K-san case offers some insight into the processes behind union action in the smaller companies, and contrasts starkly with the situation in the bigger companies, and indeed with many small mines. The H-san mine, in particular, provides a strong contrast in terms of response to company pressures. Although the processes of fragmentation of unions and union infiltration by 'company men' were typically used by all mining companies, regardless of size, the small scale of the labour force at K-san (about 350) allowed the company to maintain its authority through the use of selective violence in a manner similar to H-san mine.

Union types

Before I attempt to look at these events in any detail, it is important to look at the structure of the unions that were operating in the coalfields in the post-war period in Japan. The internal structure of these unions is relevant to any attempt to analyse the events of 1957.

There were four types of unions. Firstly, there were the *chūō ōte*, which represented the big companies: that is, M-san, N-san, T-san, and F-san. These unions were officially organised under the *Tanrō* banner, but unofficially most operated on the premise that they were individual unions representing only the individual union members' interests, and that disputes were to be settled amicably with management. These were usually company unions.

Secondly, the *chūō ōte* represented the big, regionally powerful mines: for example, K-san and O-san. These unions were also mainly company unions and were also organised under *Tanrō* in much the same way that the bigger unions were organised, although they had considerably less bargaining power than the *chūō ōte* unions.

Thirdly, the *chūko chū*, which represented the interests of the medium-sized mines. These unions were company unions that operated independently from the larger unions, although in some cases they had ties with *Tanrō*. These were tied together under the Small–Medium Mines Labour Organisation, a politically conservative group that operated in co-operation with the small–medium mine-owners organisation.

Fourthly, the *chūko ko*, which represented the interests of the small companies: that is, mines employing less than 500 people. These unions were also tied in with the *chūko chū* and their respective alliances.

In summary, there was little cohesion within the union structure. If there was any form of consensus among the union leadership, it was that antagonising management would serve no positive purpose; that it would only make the workers sacrifice some of their wages for time out on strike and make life more difficult for them. This view was especially prevalent in the bigger companies, which had a reputation for employing the mining elite. Hence the miners at these companies tended to view the workers at the smaller mines with some distaste, calling them 'peasants and outcasts'.[2]

One informant who was a union representative with an M-san coal company union told me that 'of course' the unions operated in the interests of the workers, and suggestions that there was any sort of violence by the overseers in the big mines was untenable. However, when asked to comment on the extent of the violent sanctions imposed on Koreans and *burakumin* in particular in the smaller mines, he maintained that these miners were not really human in the first place, and the fact that they were employed was evidence of the magnanimity of the coal companies. The reason that emphasis is placed on violent and destructive episodes by a number of local historians and social commentators is that no one would be interested in the area if there were not a number of dramatic incidents with which to identify.[3]

. Locality was also a feature of the way that the miners viewed themselves and the people with whom they came into contact. In Hokkaido the labour movement never reached the violent climaxes that were typical of Chikuho labour relations, for instance. Another example of the problem of the legitimation of locality was made apparent after the mines had closed in the Chikuho region. A number of miners at the M-san Tagawa mine moved to Miike to find work with the same company, believing they would be looked after. However the miners in Miike regarded the miners from Tagawa with a certain amount of animosity, probably influenced by the commonly held belief that all outsiders were strangers, and that the Tagawa people were particularly unpleasant outsiders. This attitude was also apparent within the unions and within the coal towns themselves, and influenced labour relations and local union structure.

> We were considered to be strong but stupid by the other workers, but the fact
> of the matter is that we did only what we were told, and what's wrong with
> that? We also would not become union members because the company had
> told us that we had to join the no. 2 [company] union. We were just looking
> after our own interests, and we kept our heads down and worked the seam.
> Lots of the local men didn't like us because we didn't complain about the
> sort of work that we were doing. But we knew what it was like to be out of
> work, and the fact that the company had got us this work, even though it was
> a long way from Tagawa, meant that we had somewhere to live and enough to
> eat. We owed the company our loyalty, even though sometimes we didn't
> agree with what was asked of us.[4]

The surviving coal companies employed many compliant miners,
such as Hanatsuki, who came from out of town and were prepared to
work for them uncomplainingly. Bringing in men who were desperate
for work, and who had work experience in another town had the effect
of 'undermining' the solidarity of the unions. These workers were not
prepared to risk further unemployment by disobeying the orders of the
company. They were expendable and marginalised, as were the miners
who remained in the mines.

I shall rely on two main sources when dealing with the K-san strike.
The first source is a series of interviews with Hayashi, the leader of the
independent, non-company union at the mine during the strike, which
were recorded between January 1987 and November 1988. The second
source is the writing of Ueno Eishin, a sociologist who worked in the K-
san mine for one year as a miner. His work on the mining communities
in Chikuho is widely regarded by both academics and coalminers as
being the most authentic of all the studies conducted in the region. His
position as an authority on the coal communities was reinforced when,
at his funeral in 1988, eulogies were delivered both by academics from
prestigious institutions such as Kyoto University, where he had been a
professor, and by the leader of the Kyushu *Tanrō*.

Hayashi is currently the head of the Mining Relocation and Resettle-
ment Committee, which is responsible for the employment of ex-
coalminers and their families in the Chikuho region. It is also responsible for the development of policies that lead to legal action taken
against mining companies that have reneged on superannuation
payouts to workers.

The K-san mine was one of a number of small mines owned by
individuals who worked a seam and whose rights were derived from
leases from one of the big companies. In this case the seam was owned
by N-san Shinyu, one of the bigger mines in Chikuho in the post-war
period. Both the K-san mine and the N-san mine were situated in
Kurate, which lies to the north of Nogata, in the Chikuho region.

The following is Hayashi's story, told in his own words.

Company background

The managers of the company were also the managers of S-san (a notorious mine). I was an electrical worker.[5] When I was in Siberia I thought that unions were all communist in orientation and wasn't interested at all. When I got back, there was a ban on communism anyway. Actually, when I joined the company, independent unionism was banned, and because of that I decided that we needed a real union.

The more I worked at K-san, the more I realised that the company was run badly. It was an *asseiyama*, and the company heavies bullied the workers and beat up people who didn't follow the company line. In different mines the same sort of people existed, variously called *rōmu kakari*, *kinrō kakari*, etc. These people went around the *shataku* (company housing, equivalent to *tanjū*) forcing the men to go to work. If someone was sick, the *rōmu* wouldn't listen, and would tell him to get to work. If he still wouldn't, or couldn't, he was told to report to the *rōmu* office, where they used sticks on the workers to make them go down the pits. A lot of men were seriously injured in these exchanges, many with bleeding mouths and head wounds. After the damage had been done to them, the *rōmu* would say to them that even with these sorts of injuries they would have to work, and that it was a fair punishment for their slothfulness.

These sorts of criminal acts were by no means rare. The men were called into the office, punched in the head, and had ashtrays thrown at them. This was the way that the company ran the mine in actual fact.

In everyday life it was the *rōmu* who did this sort of work, but in reality it was the management who made them do what they did. The company president was the man who decided how to run the operation, and it was he who told the *rōmu* to use violence to 'encourage' the workers to go to work.

Up until 1956 the company was run by a local man who was not very successful. It was sold to the current owner in 1956. At that time the relationship with N-san was one of *kinsaki seido*.[6]

When I joined the company in 1949, there was already a union there. It was a union in name only. It couldn't strike or do anything at all. It was completely dominated by the company and the company policies. Because the union was so weak, I didn't think that it was worth joining at first. It really couldn't do anything that a union was supposed to do, you see.

After I had been there for a year, there was the annual union re-election. The election was to be held on a Sunday in 1950, because the company would allow the workers to hold meetings only on Sundays. At that time I didn't live in the *shataku* with the other workers. I lived about four or five kilometres from the mine, and thus walked to work everyday. Anyway it was my day off on that particular Sunday, so I didn't attend the meeting.

The next day, when I went to work, I was told that I had been elected the new union leader! When I joined the company I had said some things about the sort of pressure that the company was putting the workers under, saying that this was a worry, and so they voted me the leader in my absence.

I was the leader for a year. Just before the year's term was up, there was an incident in the spring. Near by, there was a coalminers' shrine called the *Yama no Kami Jinja*, but because the mine was small it had been a small and poor-looking *jinja*. It was where all the local people, the workers and those who were related to the workers went to pray and to hold festivals each year.

As that period was a boom period for the mines, and K-san had a relative amount of success, the number of workers had increased and the company had made a lot of money, the president rebuilt the *jinja*.

At the festival that year the office manager said to the assembled personages that the way the *jinja* had been rebuilt was cheap and shoddy, and that the money could have been used for better things. All of this was true. The son of the president was the vice-president, and he was present at the time. Hearing the implied slur on his family name, the vice-president attacked the office manager in front of the assembled crowd. The president was also there and, far from trying to stop his son, he joined in and started hitting the man with enthusiasm. A number of people had come to the festival, including the local police chief, and they were all gathered on the field below, watching the whole event. The president and his son got away scot-free and no action was taken to prevent them nor subsequently to prosecute them. Such was the influence of the family.[7]

Anyway, after this happened, we decided to start a democratic movement within the union. The man who was beaten up was not a union member, or even a miner, but seeing the man getting beaten up by the president and his son affected us all, and we decided that it was unforgivable. So we started the movement. This movement was designed to stop the sort of violence that had come to characterise the management style of the mine. The office workers didn't have a union of their own, but they approached us and we discussed how best to do this thing.[8]

We decided that the best way would be to look at how N-san forced the subcontractor to dig unrealistic amounts of coal as part of their agreement. First there was something called *sōgo hokken* (mutual insurance), which covered both the N-san Shinyu mine and K-san. Therefore, if N-san didn't put the pressure on K-san management to produce excessive quantities of coal, the insurance would cover both parties. By reducing this pressure, we felt that the need for the sort of violent management that we had come to see would be eliminated. We thought that if we made public the way that the K-san management was running the mine, it would hurt N-san. Our aim was for N-san to stop the president from running the mine in the way he had been, because we had enough of the violence, and knowing that it would hurt N-san if this became public we moved in this direction.[9]

To this end we approached the local police, the prefectural police, the courts and the Department of Judicial Affairs with the aim of securing our basic human rights under the law. We applied to the Department of Judicial Affairs to help us stop the violent way of running the company, as was our right. We asked the police and the courts to issue orders to arrest violent offenders. However, there were some big problems here for us, especially in relation to the police. You'll remember that the police chief was present when the company president and his son attacked the office manager at the festival. Not only did he not stop the violence as his duty required him to, but the main point of my complaint against him is that he treated with contempt our protests against his behaviour concerning the actions of the company president and his son. I felt complete contempt for the law at this stage.

As this movement gained momentum, we started to push for the democratic method of management, which was really our right. You see, throughout the post-war period, whenever a union threatened the status quo, the company moved in and put great pressure on its leaders to quit. Therefore we moved to oppose this trend. We didn't go as far as to say 'let's get rid of the president', but we did want the vice-president, who was in a nepotistic position, to get fired. So we presented the company with a list of demands.

At that time the K-san union was affiliated with *Fukutanrō*[10] the Fukuoka branch of Tanrō, which was really little more than a trade guild. While our movement was gaining ground, the *Fukutanrō* was nominally supportive of our position. Not surprisingly, *Fukutanrō* worked on the assumption that the company and the unions should be able to sort out any problems through discussion.

Anyway, after all the trouble we went to over the office manager, he was fired anyway. The president approached me and told me that he was not interested at all in the proposals that we had put to him. He threatened us by saying that if we wanted to continue to work in Kurate we had better do the right thing by the company and keep out of trouble. I remember this well. He said that if we continued in this way, there might just be an explosion in the mine that would accidentally kill us. We were very surprised at the open nature of the threat. I thought that there was nothing that we could do to change the man's mind at the time, so I said, 'That's all right with me, president. If you burn the slag to blow us up, you'll have to explain yourselves to N-san, and I don't think that you'd like to do that. N-san won't help you out.'

I went on to say to him that my union was not the sycophantic body he assumed it to be, that because we were associated with *Tanrō*, if there was a problem with the slag being burnt in an attempt on our lives, 280,000 workers would be around to help us out.

Anyway, after this exchange, we, the leaders of the union, the new head of the office, and the president all got together to discuss the problems that we were complaining about. There were some conciliatory attempts made by the company, which said that they would put money into the *Fukutanrō* to support the union movement. The president said that we should leave the matter of the firing of the vice-president for him to deal with, and that he would discipline the man. As to the issue of whether they would blow up the slag-heaps, this was left alone because we had reached a compromise in relation to the future of the vice-president. On top of this we were promised a democratic form of management from that time on.[11]

The Spring Offensive

In 1956 there was the annual Spring Wage Offensive. We presented a list of wage demands, and when they were not settled, we went on strike. At the beginning it was only a 24-hour strike, yet the company immediately proceeded to enforce a lockout. A massive amount of excess coal had been produced following the Korean War, and the company was happy not to pay wages, even if it was only for one day. Further, they approached the media to fight us. It wasn't as if we were on an unlimited strike. In fact it was the first time that we had ever gone on strike, and suddenly the company had imposed a lockout. That night at the union meeting, after considering the general state of affairs, we were surprised by the outrageous press reports roundly condemning us and supporting the stance of the company. The company continued the lockout for another 24 hours, and when we went back to work we accepted a compromise wage agreement.[12]

The no.2 union

It was then that the company decided it was time for a second union, which would support the company line without complaint, so the no. 2 union was formed, with the express aim of opposing the no. 1 union. I was beaten by the *rōmu* on that occasion because I had dared to speak out against the company, saying that the formation of another union within the company was an infringement of our democratic rights.

In short, the 24-hour strike occurred in 1956, and immediately after this the company formed the no. 2 union. This was contrary to the agreement that was reached in the discussions that we had in 1950, as described before. The no. 1 union was broken up, and of course we fought them about this, but the reality of the matter was that the management had not changed, and the violence was just starting all over again. In 1956 we got involved in more action. From September to October the mine became a battlefield. The Kyushu *Tanrō* was actively involved in the issue, and vehemently protested to the K-san management against the forming of the no. 2 union. The protests we started then were a portent of the trouble to come. The police took us down to the station and charged us with unlawful assembly. We were jostled and pushed around by the cops who wanted to show us that they were tough.[13]

Working conditions

To describe the work conditions with any degree of accuracy, you would have to say that the miners were working on a quota system. They weren't paid on a daily basis, but rather on the basis of how much the shift, as a group, dug out. However, the situation wasn't as simple as it appears. When the coal is dug out it is obviously unprocessed, and there is a lot of slag mixed with it. The dug-out coal was examined, and payment was awarded on the basis of its purity. For example, if a shift dug out one tonne, and it was determined to be 80 per cent pure, they got paid for 0.8 tonne of coal. In bad cases, the purity of the coal was as low as 60 per cent, so the workers received only the equivalent of digging 0.6 tonne.

Every day there was a work quota to be filled, which was based on one shift working eight hours. The quota was based on an agreement drawn up between the union and the company, and it ranged from two tonnes to three tonnes. Of course there were times when it was impossible to dig the quota. On those occasions we were forced to work until the quota was satisfied. To ensure this, the company sent the *rōmu* down the pits to make sure that no one left his workplace, even though there might be two or three hours' overtime involved.

What we wanted was not to get a different system of wages instituted, but to get paid for the extra hours that we were forced to work in the mines if something untoward prevented the quota being filled. But K-san would not pay any money for work done in this manner: no overtime or even pay normal hourly rates for all the extra hours we were asked to work. When you consider all the problems of that year, it was not just one thing that caused the trouble that was to come, but a series of events.[14]

The 101-day strike and intra-union conflict

Thus we moved into 1957. That year the same sorts of wages problems developed. The same problems plus a new one: the no. 2 union had been formed in the interim. As far as the company was concerned the no. 2 union was now the official union, and we (the no.1) had ceased to exist in relation to the Spring Wage Offensive. We discussed the Wage Offensive with the leaders of the no. 2 union, but they chose to accept a company offer of a 50 yen a day wage increase, which we felt was too little. So we ended up fighting with the no. 2 union, and splitting from them completely.

We were told by the no. 2 union and by the company that a wage agreement had been reached with the complete co-operation of the union and the company, and that our opinions were no longer considered germane. They said that there was no way that they would make allowances for our claims that the wage increases were too small. So at that stage our union decided to go on strike. The strike got gradually longer and longer and eventually continued for 101 days.

The following is an extract from Ueno Eishin's book *Moyashitsukusu Hibi*. It describes Ueno coming back to the mine after an absence of three months.

I got off the bus at K-san. There were the barricades. To the north of the narrow bus road was the mining complex, to the south the home of Yasunaga, the president. A coal cart emerged from the mine mouth and dumped its load onto a conveyor-belt, which took the coal to the sorters at the north. Around each of the buildings at the dark northern end were high fences, and in the middle of the compound was a barbed-wire fence, which stretched across the width of the land, separating the dirty workers' section from the president's home.

In the rain I walked to the Labour Control Office and through the windows I could see the bustling activity inside. A heavy barricade surrounded the building, and to one side of this barricade the coal and the slag sorting was going on. All this activity was because of the no. 2 union. It depressed me and made me want to howl like a dog.

A little farther to the north was the no. 1 union office, but around here the mud had settled. No one had been here for some time. I could find no sign of life. No union members, no leaders. Deserted. There was one sign which hung at a strange angle from a wall of one of the *tanjū*, the red ink faded on the waste paper. It read:

Do your best, fathers.
We, the wives, will do our best
To bring peace to our households and
To bring about an open and democratic mine.
(Signed: The K-san Women's Co-operative)[15]

Hayashi returns to his story.

One big problem was that although we were on strike, we needed to be able to eat. The *Fujinkai* (Women's Association) and *Tanrō* helped us out by giving us *nigiri* (rice balls) and rice as part of the strike aid fund, but we were not able to survive on just that. Everyone started to do part-time work to support themselves. We all got some sort of labouring work outside the mine. But the no. 2 union leader approached the bosses where we were working and told them not to employ us, and said that they would sabotage the operations if we were allowed to continue to work. They went all over the place threatening the labouring companies with disruption if we were employed. We could not physically attack the no. 2 union, so we decided to hold a meeting with the leaders of the no. 2 union outside the union shrine in the field nearby in order to try to resolve the problem.

'Why are you doing this? We're all workers and the fact that you are disrupting our means of living is unforgivable,' we said. Eating was important to us, and if we were on strike, it was not adversely affecting those in the no. 2 union, so why were they out to get us, we wanted to know? Rather than a meeting, this was really a protest. The protest ended up taking a long time, but it certainly wasn't getting anywhere. As the meeting was breaking up, I said that the threat of disruption to our lifestyles was intolerable, and we ended up by calling for a demonstration. That is, we were joined by the *Fujinkai* in the demo against the no. 2 union and the way that they were trying to starve us.

If the whole affair had ended there, it would have been good, I think, but tempers were up and the no. 2 union leader was attacked by some of our members, knocked over and kicked and punched. He didn't get up. This became another problem for us. After this, the company accused us of being violent, something that was used as a rationale to prevent any attempt at conciliation. As a result of this affair I was prosecuted by the police for the assault, and for causing a riot. There were five of us who faced these charges. Eventually the case got to court where I was found to be the responsible party for the assault. This happened during the 101-day strike.[16]

The company used this affair as an excuse to dismiss me from work while I was on strike (all five of us were fired). However, I took a civil suit out against them, because when I was dismissed the charges were still pending, and nothing had been decided by the courts. The substance of my suit was that I was dismissed on unreasonable grounds. I won this case.[17]

Ueno wrote the strike up in some detail, but this sort of incident was not written up. During the 101-day strike there were many sorts of problems.

Gangster violence and union friction

While I was leader of the no.1 union I was very aware of the gangsters who were employed by the company, and made a lot of comments about them at the time. Therefore I personally was in danger from these hoodlums. I was threatened on many occasions, and of course I was chosen as the big troublemaker and was picked on often.

On one occasion I was called by the boss of the company and asked to attend a meeting to try to settle the strike. He told me to come with just the other leaders of our union and said that we would be able to resolve the situation somehow together. Well, when we got there (there were three of us), we were met by eight or nine of the *yakuza* who worked for N-san, and no company president. We realised that we were in big trouble, but we smiled and said that we would wait for the president, who was due to come at any moment. My young lieutenant said that he had to go to the toilet, and he slipped out the window and went for help. Unfortunately, by the time the rest of the union members had been contacted and had come over, the *yakuza* had already beaten us severely. I was hospitalised for two months. You see they broke my hands and some of my ribs. But I didn't let that slow me down at all. As soon as I was out of hospital I was back into it again.

During the 101-day strike there was torrential rain and the houses flooded and the roofs leaked. Although it was the company's duty to repair the houses, and to make sure the roofs didn't leak, when anyone from the no. 1 union went to the office to ask about repairs, they were refused point blank. They were told to 'fuck off home', by the office workers. Much of the friction was generated by the no. 2 union leader who hated us with passion, and used his influence where he could to make things hard for us, with the aim of breaking us up.

Of course, there were also a number of quarrels with the no. 2 union members directly, too, and in some cases the wives of the different unions also took to quarrelling with each other. Within the *tanjū* this caused big problems for everyone, because the places were so tightly packed together. They were telling each other to fuck off, and to stuff themselves. The situation was really getting pretty grim.

Sometimes the company supplied the no. 2 union officials with free drinks after work at the company store. When this happened, the no. 2 union members got drunk and smashed the windows in the no. 1 union office on a number of occasions. If any worker had any sort of connection with the no. 1 union, they were often beaten up.

The company sent the gangsters around to our houses to tell us to get out. But that wasn't all. They would come around the *shataku* with clubs in hand and beat the people who were supporting our stance. Although no one was killed in these exchanges, they were violent, and people were hurt and frightened. After the gangsters had been around, the leader of the no. 2 union would then come to the *tanjū* and tell us that if we stayed with the no. 1 union these incidents would continue to happen. However, if we joined the no. 2 union there would be no more of this sort of thing, and our houses would soon be repaired, because he would talk to the company and convince them to do this. This was all prearranged, as the timing of the no. 2 union leader was always exact.

Within our ranks there were some weak people who had had enough by this time and joined the no. 2 union. Their houses were soon cleaned up. There was a vacant lot near the *tanjū*, and here, using the company's money, the no. 2 union built some new houses. This was done to help break the no. 1 union. That is, we could see what sort of benefits the no. 2 union was enjoying, while our members were starving and living in hovels. There were quite a lot of people from the no. 2 union living in the new housing. This problem came out in the last meeting of the two unions and the company. That is, the company said, 'Such and such is paying this amount for rent on his new place'. In the last instance I protested strongly about this. When you think about this, it's pretty obvious that the company was doing this for special reasons: that is, to let the no. 1 union members see how the other people were having all these benefits, with the aim of disrupting our unity.

There were people within the no. 1 union who were affected by the way the no. 2 union was getting these advantages, but, in the end, everyone within our union said that although you can buy things with money, you can't buy someone's loyalty.

As Ueno said, seeing all this luxury in front of our eyes was sorely tempting, but the men who remained were the ones who were the real workers, the ones who would not compromise their principles. The men who eventually joined the no. 2 union were predominantly those who weren't skilled at their jobs and had no confidence in the cause that they were fighting for. I think that the men who switched sides were these types, don't you? Those of us who remained were the ones who were secure in the knowledge that we were skilled at different aspects of mining work, and we had confidence in our ability to win the battle. At the time I thought that, and even now I have no reason to change my beliefs on this score. Those who had confidence in their skills and pride in their work could endure the temptations while those who didn't were left in the position that they had to switch sides. The ones left in the no. 1 union were mainly this type of serious miner. I think that it was because of this the union did not break up.

Production was affected at the beginning of the strike: that is, it fell off. But after the company created the new, no. 2 union and built new *tanjū* for the new workers they brought in, production increased again, as the no. 2 union increased its numbers. The numbers increased to such an extent that the no. 2 union was soon larger than us. This was part of the strategy to ignore our union's existence.[18]

However no one from the no. 1 union was fired. As we went off to our part-time jobs in the mornings, we saw the results of the no. 2 union's efforts reflected in the coal being sorted outside the pit entrance, and the coal being moved along the conveyor-belt. We were very worried that we had become quite redundant at the time, to be honest. The no. 2 union was not really a union, and they had not won any wage increases in the time we were on strike. The wages stayed the same, at the levels that the company dictated, and the union's worth was absolutely zero. Whatever the company said, the union followed, you see. As far as we were concerned, we would fight for our rights even if it took a year or more, because that was the only way to do things, but the no. 2 union would not fight. We were angry with the no. 2 union, and our anger had nothing to do with the wages battle. It had become a matter of protecting the right to have an organisation that was free. While this was the main issue, there were other issues tied up with this, namely that the company's method of management had to be opposed at all costs, and a form of democratic management had to be instigated.

Breaking the strike

After the strike had reached the 100-day mark, *Tanrō* called a national 24-hour strike to pressure the company to stop bullying us. Before it got to that stage, the Kyushu Small–Medium Mines Labour Organisation had called a two-hour strike to protest the actions of the company, which affected all Kyushu small to medium-sized mines. This was a temporary strike in sympathy for our cause. Even after this the company waited things out, and weren't prepared to settle the affair. When we reached the 100th day, all mines nationally went on strike for 24 hours in sympathy. After this occurred, the *Kōgyō Renmei* (Industry Association) convened and held discussions with *Tanrō*. Eventually, the strike was settled.[19]

As you'll remember, the official reason for the strike was that the no. 2 union had accepted the company offer of 50 yen a day pay increase, which we had opposed as being too little. Well, as a result of the strike we eventually received a settlement of 52 yen a day pay increase. After all that trouble there was only a two yen a day gain!

But as I said before, the reason we were on strike was not really because of an increase in wages, but to oppose the way management ran the company, to give us democracy in the workplace, and to protect our right to a free union. So even a two-yen wage increase was a victory of sorts. That was how the strike ended.

During the strike a large number of men from the no. 1 union joined the no. 2 union, as I mentioned earlier. On the other hand, there were a lot of defections from the no. 2 union to our union after we won. These men were often new recruits who had seen what the management style was like, were surprised by it, and left the company union, because they thought that the no. 1 union was right in fighting against these violent management practices. These people often joined our union to look for a certain amount of freedom, which they didn't have in the no. 2 union. Particularly after the members of the no. 2 union saw the results of the strike with their own eyes, they gradually came over to our ranks, in twos and threes.

After these mass defections to our union in 1958, the company formed the no. 3 union! The aim of this union also was to destroy us, because of what we stood for. This union existed purely for the purpose of allowing the company to interfere with the workforce. We realised the nature of this very early and called a meeting with the management to present a case to them, that if they continued with this union we would take them to court and sue them for breach of the labour laws. So the person responsible for the labour control at the mine was fired, because the company had no other choices in the matter. They maintained that the president didn't know about the affair at all, and the labour manager was sacrificed. And with him being fired the no. 3 union was officially disbanded.[20]

From that time on the labour force was organised on the basis of the no. 1 and no. 2 unions, and in 1959 there were discussions about the new bonus schemes, which had been introduced that year. Anyway we went on strike over this in 1959. The wage strike that we went on continued for 101 days, as you know, but this one went on for 114 days! This one has never been written about.

After all this, a new office manager came to the company. He was responsible for the labour force in general. He was a man named Hashimoto who hailed from the *Kōgyō Renmei*. He said that the method of labour control being used at K-san was no good. He didn't say this to us directly, but he did make these comments within management circles. In response to this responsible attitude the two unions united in 1960. At that time there was talk about the *Zentankō* (the right-wing National Coalminers' Union) and the *Tanrō* affiliations of the respective unions, and eventually it was decided that *Zentankō* was doing nothing at all, and that therefore there was no reason to have any affiliation with it. The no. 2 union joined the no. 1 union unconditionally. Shortly after, in 1962, the mine was closed.

We united the two unions around the same time that the Miike striking workers split into two unions. After we had joined together, the Miike miners' two union movements started, for sure. I probably can't be trusted to remember properly, but the Hopper Incident at Miike was in May 1960. I'm pretty sure that the date's right.

Before the mine closed down there were incidents like the management problem I talked about, and of course there was the problem of strikes too, but when the mine actually closed down the idea that we were there to stay as a union had been accepted by the company to a large extent. Because of this, when we made demands as to what we expected after the mine closed a final agreement was reached between the company and the union.

Management and labour policies

Hayashi's story highlights some repressive practices used by management in dealing with workers. These are still employed by the more hardline companies within Japan, according to some of my informants. Yet in the 1950s and 1960s the use of violence to manipulate unions and control the workforce was widespread, particularly within the mining companies. Often, perhaps due to their isolation and their disproportionate share of political power, small mining companies tended to be more violent and less democratic than large companies, although it has to be said that the larger companies were in a position to employ only men they were confident would not join one of the radical leftist unions.

From the company's view, in order to deal with the problem of worker power, the first and most important step was to establish which people were involved in the unions, and which people were leading them. The next step was to attempt to isolate these men by creating an alternative that offered financial incentives in the short term, as with the establishment of a no. 2 union. The third step was to apply conspicuously violent sanctions to members of the old union in order to convince the members that not only did the new union offer more financial rewards than the old one, but also that members who joined the new union were to be given favourable treatment. The fourth step was to enlist the aid of 'officials' to deter the public from sympathising with the strikers. The police and the mass media were involved, and through this alliance the newspapers published accounts of the irresponsibility of the miners and of their wanton destructive rampages, which the police had documented at the company's instigation.

Lockouts became the method of dealing with demonstrations against the company, and the police were mobilised to deal with the miners. The courts were geared to make the miners pay for any disruption to production caused by industrial action. But the main problem for the miners was the defection of miners from the old union to the new one, in the face of protests from within the union. The workers who defected generally maintained that they had to eat, which is why they wanted to continue working, against the advice of the union leadership.

Surprisingly, the concept of 'scabs' was not really evident in any of the miners' actions at K-san, and picket lines were not organised. Resentment that the other miners were not prepared to support their fellow workers existed, but there seems to have been a certain amount of sympathy towards their position.

> Yeah, they went back to work and left us in the lurch. But most of these guys had families to support and had a lot of debts, so we understood why they went back to work. In the end it was a simple matter of choosing between eating and starvation for some, I suppose.[21]

From a historical perspective, it has often been said that one of the main reasons that Japan's unions have never held very much power is that there is little or no solidarity within the rank and file. Yada went as far as to say that the unions existed only to support the companies.[22] The concept of a unified union under an independent leadership was anathema to the Japan of the post-war economic boom. The economy was moving in many directions as it made inroads into international markets, labour was constantly undervalued domestically, and publicly the unions were seen as a hindrance to the development of the economy. The ruling LDP continued to govern well in the electorate's eyes because the standard of living had markedly improved after the war. Socialism was seen as a form of anti-capitalism, and thus anti-development. Hence the unions were portrayed as a 'disruptive and violent group' who were attempting to blackmail the country through their heinous actions.[23]

The companies were able to break down whatever solidarity existed within the unions by introducing new labourers in times when work was scarce. These labourers were employed on the condition that they joined the company union. Generally, the members, and where possible the leaders, of the troublesome union, were temporarily made redundant to make room for the new workers, as in the K-san case. It is sufficient to note here that there are a number of significant factors involved concerning socialisation and the development of a form of political numbness that have come to be representative of many Japanese people's attitudes towards government in Japan.

From an outsider's perspective, it may seem extraordinary that the K-san miners had not taken any form of action before the time of the strike, especially considering the violent labour control techniques used by management. Apart from the labour control that was enforced in the mine itself, the company was able to control the miners' financial, residential, social, religious and, in some cases, family lives. This was made possible first through the control of the miners' place of residence, the *tanjū*. The mine-owners were under an obligation to supply housing for the miners, and managed to turn this to their own advantage in many cases by supplying controlled institutions throughout the *tanjū*. Shops, entertainment areas, religious festivals, currency, schools and banks were all controlled by the mine. A monopoly had been firmly established, which extended to miners' lives. Not only was their labour bought and sold as a commodity, but the commodities that the miners traded in were also owned by the company. The practical situation for many miners was that they were totally dependent on the mines, not only for their livelihoods, but also for their social, political and religious activities. Strong feelings of local identity developed, fuelled by the twin concepts of the company as common foe and as necessary evil. These feelings were exacerbated by the way that the miners were viewed by outsiders. That is they were seen as 'an overpaid, militant, selfish group, which acted always purely in their own interests'.[24]

Ishizaki, a person who has written a considerable amount on the history of Chikuho and the coalmines, said:

> They were regarded by non-miners as separate from the rest of the com- munity, a hard-headed bunch who drank and gambled too much, and who had no idea of social obligations. In short, they were regarded with fear, and with a certain amount of respect for the dirty, hard and dangerous work that they did.[25]

The way they were seen by the outside world reinforced the position the miners allotted for themselves in the scheme of things.[26] This, in turn, had a powerful influence on the way the miners dealt with labour problems. For many miners, mining was the only work they knew, and because of the way they lived and worked, they felt that they could not do work outside the industry. Consequently, the attitude of many men was similar to that of Ogata, who worked in the infamous H-san Mine in Kawasaki-machi:

> If the working conditions were too bad, you simply quit the job and went to look for work at some other mine. That was if you were allowed to quit. Sometimes the management would put pressure on you to stay by sending the *rōmu* around to tell you what would happen if you left the mine. Usually these threats were quite serious, so when you left one of the small companies, you had to be careful that you used a different name in your new job, and often people ended up leaving their families in order to escape.[27]

In a society where, according to many eminent Japanese social psychologists, sociologists and behaviourists, the group is the centre of all social activities,[28] the lack of cohesion within the labour movement stands out. Simply put, the company, through its monopoly of not only the means of production, but also of the environment in which the workers lived, was able to enforce the concept of the company group over worker solidarity. This was achieved through the use of violence and intimidation on the one hand, and coercion on the other. However, this situation changed when the demand for coal, and the resultant demand for labour, dropped sharply in the wake of the Energy Revolution. Certain elements in the labour force realised the tenuous nature of their own job security and, the threats of violent sanctions from the company notwithstanding, formed groups to protect their jobs by protesting the impending closures. This issue became the rallying cry for the labour protests of the 1960s, which were arguably the most powerful expression of worker dissatisfaction in Japan's industrial history.

The K-san case was exceptional in that there was a strong, independent labour movement, which acted in the workers' interests despite pressure from management. Mines that had relatively strong non-company unions were regarded by other miners as the 'good' mines: that is, where the working conditions were fair, the incidence of violent and repressive management techniques was limited, safety equipment and training was properly catered for, and as a result few men were killed at the pit face. Mines where the development of labour consciousness was retarded were seen as being dangerous.[29] The statistics of mining accidents bear out the assumption that the more repressive mines were the scene of the most mine deaths, both at the workplace and at home, the latter applying to violent deaths, officially unexplained.

One estimate of the total number of deaths in the Chikuho area alone, which does not include the very small *tanuki bori* 'badger holes', for the period from 1922 to 1965 is over 11,000.[30] This figure is exceptionally high, especially when compared with figures for similar enterprises outside Japan. It is in fact more than 20 times the accident death total for the same period in Britain where the mining workforce was 40 times greater than in Chikuho, according to Dennis, Henriques and Slaughter.[31] Yet union action such as the K-san incidents notwithstanding, labour consciousness did not really become active until the mines were threatened with closure in the late 1950s and early 1960s, and the unions were able to organise themselves into a powerful political lobby. Although *Tanrō* was the agency responsible for this consciousness developing, it is noteworthy that the larger companies were the only participants in the action of the 1960s, M-san Miike mine being the focus of attention. The smaller companies, although subject to the same rationalisation pressures, were often not affiliated with *Tanrō*, because these companies had seen to the establishment of company unions at the expense of independent unions. Subsequently, smaller companies were not involved in the action initiated by *Tanrō*. This seriously weakened the solidarity and the effectiveness of the movement when the TCRB came into effect and demonstrations and strikes were called for on a national level.

It is axiomatic that in times of adversity labour unions develop solidarity to protect their positions. In the Japanese coalfields it is noticeable that the unions did not develop any form of consciousness until a huge number of jobs were threatened. It was only in response to this pressure that the unions were able to break away from the oppressive environment of the company. One of the major problems was that the unions, even the 'independent' ones, were inherently conservative, and the concepts of strikes and industrial action were poorly developed within the mining industry. Partly this was a response to management methods: violence was used routinely on individual workers, while any hint of action was even more harshly dealt with. But partly it was a reaction to market forces, which had effectively increased the number of available miners considerably following the decline of the industry.

The TCRB and the unemployment that was to be generated by the introduction of this policy proved to be the catalysts in the development of the miners' union unrest. Shortly following this action by the K-san union, the M-san Miike miners went on strike for one full year in a violent and famous offensive. The Miike action, which has been well documented in Japanese, had at its roots the issue of survival in the face of the serious redundancies the miners faced rather than the more 'principled' reasons of the K-san case. Yet the companies' responses to both actions were remarkably similar: the fragmentation of the offending union, 'compromise' deals with the 'enlightened' new union leaders, and promises of long-term changes and worker security. None of the promised benefits were implemented.

One of the ironies of the K-san case was that after the sacrifices the workers made, and within a couple of years of the resolution of the strike, and within 12 months of the reconciliation of the unions, the mine was closed. By this stage the union had had enough direct conflict, and management, under the new direction of Hashimoto, was much more reasonable about redundancy packages for the men. However, notwithstanding the softer line that the company eventually took, the workers from the K-san union won few concessions in the longer term.

The K-san case should be seen as the first of a number of union actions that moved towards establishing better working conditions for workers. It was also the only case in the Chikuho mining industry where industrial action was initiated and carried through by local workers alone. The motivation for the K-san action was fairly narrow, and the development of a working-class consciousness was not on the union's political agenda, as evidenced by, among other factors, its relaxed attitude towards non-unionists. Rather it was concerned with establishing a more equitable system of management than the system in operation. The type of management the union opposed could be seen as a hangover from the war, where violence and coercion were standard practices. Given the United States' Occupation decrees that unions were to be 'democratised', and that every worker had the right to join a union, theirs was a response aimed at simply improving the quality of their daily lives.

The K-san case was a landmark in Japanese industrial relations for a number of reasons. The first is that the union acted on its own behalf, with no real outside support, though admittedly with the tacit approval of *Tanrō*, which had been very quiet politically up to this time. Secondly, Hayashi, as leader of the union, was not prepared to compromise, even in the face of the extreme pressure exerted by the company. This strength of leadership should not be underestimated, nor the fact that he and the members of the no. 1 union were prepared to be stood down on a matter of principle. Thirdly, although the legal framework existed to support the stance of unions against employers, it had not been tested until Hayashi successfully sued the K-san management to protest his unlawful dismissal, following the incident outside the company office. Finally, the power that *Tanrō* was able to wield was demonstrated decisively when they finally did enter and solve the dispute.

The Miike industrial action that followed on the heels of the K-san action was seen as a catalyst for the development of union consciousness in Japan. The student protests, protests against industrial pollution, consumer movements, anti-war and anti-nuclear power movements, to name just a few, all seemed to gain momentum after the dramatic events of the confrontation between miners and police at Miike. But before the Miike action the actions of a small group of principled miners in Kurate established the perception that union protest was viable in a society where the union movement had been largely cauterised. It is conceivable that the industrial actions precipitated by the K-san union and the unprecedented, if tardy, response from *Tanrō* in coming out in support of this small union were responsible for the development of the more militant and conspicuous labour conflicts of the 1960s.

Interestingly, there are no other cases of successful industrial action in the mining industry recorded until the Miike strike in 1960, although there were many miners in a similar position to the K-san workers. It seems almost as though, as soon as the K-san case was resolved, it was forgotten by local people, or at best dismissed as being a single, unprecedented instance of an individual leader's power to influence others. The Miike strike, on the other hand, attracted widespread interest nationally, presumably because of its scale and the publicity it engendered, and also because of the developing conscious-ness of miners that their jobs were in danger following the formalisa-tion of the new energy policy. They could no longer afford to be apathetic about labour issues. In the Miike case and in subsequent labour actions the miners were helped considerably by the new wave of Marxism that was sweeping the country. Outsiders acted positively to support the miners, and the consciousness that flowed from outsiders who came to the coalfields was one of the great strengths of the new, rather short-lived labour movement.

The following chapters, which concentrate on the gradual, but temporary, empowerment of the miners through the activities and organisation of sophisticated, experienced outsiders, illustrate the importance of a broader philosophy in appealing to the miners as a distinct, socially repressed group. The decline of the industry, and the hurried and graceless departure from the region by many coal companies contributed strongly to the dissatisfaction of miners. This eventually manifested itself in first the industrial action, and then the legal action that I describe on the following pages.

NOTES TO CHAPTER 9

1 *Tagawa Shishi*, 1979, p.426.
2 Sasaki, interview, 1988.
3 Kubota, interview, 1988.
4 Hanatsuki, interview, 1988.
5 Because he was an electrician he had been sent to work in a supervisory capacity in Siberian coalmines during the war.
6 Mining right lease agreement. The company had the right to work N-san's land if they sold the coal they produced through N-san, with the N-san trademark attached, at a price that N-san fixed. They were also required to pay a levy on each tonne they dug up.
7 The police chief, a former K-san manager, who was in the crowd when the assault took place, eventually filed a report that Hayashi and his union members had incited the office manager to physically attack the president, and that the vice-president had acted only to save his father's honour. This record was obtained by Takazaki, then head of the local court.
8 It is doubtful whether Hayashi's union movement was really based on this event, given the rather different accounts of other men who worked in the mine. Rather it seemed as though this instance of violence, which was perpetrated at the highest level on what

was regarded as sacred ground (the shrine) was the last straw. It gave focus to the widespread feelings of resentment directed at the management for allowing the mine to be run in a repressive and violent manner.

9 It should be noted that the union seriously underestimated the extent of N-san's interests, thinking, as they did, that the company would be damaged by adverse publicity. The problem for the union was that no newspapers would publish information that could be considered damaging to N-san.

10 *Fukuoka Tankō Rōdōkumiai* (Fukuoka Coalminers' Union).

11 The company's sudden change of tactics here is hard to understand, given Kurata's account of their uncompromising attitude towards the union. In a discussion with Idegawa about the interview afterwards, she said that this form of diplomacy was *tatemae*, and meant only to pacify the miners while the company developed a more sophisticated strategy to deal with the miners. It served to keep production going, reduce management–worker conflict and give the company 'breathing space'. (Personal communication, 1988.)

12 The militancy displayed by the union in this case (actually going on strike) was highly unusual in 1956 in Japan. The company's response to the union's action, though, was to become a standard within the industry for dealing with formalised worker unrest. Hayashi understates his role in the action here. According to other labour union sources, he was the prime agitator in the strike, basing his stance on the success of overseas trade union movements. In particular, the success of the British coalminers' actions in the mid-1950s, which were reported in the JCP newspaper *Akahata* (Red Flag), influenced him in deciding to take action. Although the action was ultimately unsuccessful, it enhanced the solidarity of the union members.

13 Ueno wrote in his book, *Moyashitsukusu Hibi* (1985e) that the action the union precipitated against the company was the first such labour action in the coalfields. The animosity of the union was supported by *Tanrō*, which sent 50 men to help the miners physically fight the company *rōmu* and the police. More than 20 men were hospitalised, and it is a source of some pride for the miners that 15 of these were police. The violence continued for more than a month in a series of running battles, with the miners torching company property, until the police requested reinforcement from the prefectural government, which effectively broke up the demonstration. No miners were prosecuted individually by the company or police on this occasion.

14 Ueno wrote about his experience with the mine, corroborating the story of Hayashi: 'K-san was seen as the most repressive and violent mine in the region. The company used to take the law into its own hands to force production up ... Miners often had to work 12 to 13 hours to fulfil the company quota per shift. If we didn't manage to make the quota, the difference was taken from our pay. The overseers (*rōmu*) never saw the inside of a pit in most cases, yet they blithely raised the production quota to unrealistic levels. Sometimes those who could not make the quota and whose work was not seen to be satisfactory were attacked with pick handles after work by the *rōmu*. But because this was officially just "keeping the work force in line" and because no one would come forward to challenge the company, or supply the law with evidence to prosecute these people, the villains who beat and sometimes killed miners escaped scot-free.' (1985a, p.14).

15 Ibid. pp.9–10.

16 The demonstration that Hayashi refers to was a major riot. The police were called in to try to calm the warring groups, who had attacked each other ferociously, according to witnesses (Otani, Suzuki, interviews, 1988). By the time the police arrived, the miners from the no. 1 union had succeeded in bashing a number of *rōmu* and members from the no. 2 union. Equally, a number of men from the no. 1 union were seriously beaten by the police and by the *rōmu*, who were armed with iron bars and lumps of wood.

17 This was a landmark case for the unions, and Hayashi was the first person to take legal action successfully against a coal company, according to Takazaki (interview, 1988).

18 These miners were recruited from the ranks of farmers and locals who had little or no experience in the coal industry, but who were happy to work for the (relatively) good pay and housing.

19 The settlement was made after a week-long series of meetings between management and *Tanrō* officials and representatives of both unions.
20 The no. 3 union was formed because the other unions had, by this stage, reconciled many of their differences. Although they were not officially united under the *Tanrō* banner until 1960, they expressed similar aims. The company was apparently under the impression that the same methods employed in breaking the solidarity of the workers in the first instance would work again, hence the move to form a third union.
21 Hayashi, interview, 1988.
22 Yada, 1975, p.143.
23 See for example, the *Asahi Shinbun*, 14 January 1961, editorial on the miners' strike at Miike.
24 Nakayama (local doctor) interview, 1988.
25 Ishizaki, interview, 1989.
26 Metcalfe has noted that miners in Maitland saw themselves as entering hell when they descended into the pit (1988).
27 Ogata, interview, 1989.
28 See Nakane (1970), Lebra (1984), Vogel (1980), for example.
29 Sasaki, interview, 1988; Ogata, interview, 1988.
30 Onishi, *Gisei no Tō*, (The Tower of Sacrifice) 1975, p.2.
31 Dennis, Henriques and Slaughter, 1956, p.132.

CHAPTER 10

D-san and the Students

In the 1960s the national student movement was active over a wide range of issues, but the common theme of these actions was the fight against capitalism. The students viewed miners as an especially oppressed group, not only because of the intrinsically oppressive nature of their work, but also because of the violence that traditionally had been associated with the mines in Chikuho. After the miners' actions were given widespread press coverage following the labour protests in the late 1950s and 1960s, some of the students were motivated to come to Chikuho to support the workers by volunteering to work with the unions, often in the union offices.

The students thought that with some organisational help, the miners who were being abused under the present system would be able to stand up to the power-holders. They took upon themselves the role of the educated, concerned, altruistic Marxists, determined to win for the miners the rights the miners themselves could not win under the oppressive conditions of the legal system. Given the ignorance of labour dispute strategy within miners' ranks, often because of the isolation of the profession, it has been said that the students were the catalyst in bringing about concerted action against the mine-owners.[1] Mizuno, a man who came from the Tokyo students' group to work in the office at D-san, saw the students' role as primarily a teaching and supportive one in the fight against the violent and unfair practices of a large number of mines in the region.

An examination of the circumstances surrounding the strike at D-san in 1962 offers insights into the nature of labour relations and into the apparent equanimity with which miners viewed the extreme working conditions.

181

Management and *yakuza* relations

In 1962 there was a major strike at D-san mine. D-san was a big coal-mine, employing over 1800 miners in a number of pits. Not all the workers struck, but those who did seriously disrupted the company's operations. It was the first instance in the mining industry where workers occupied the premises in a sit-in. The strike was a response to the pressure to which management had subjected the miners over a long period. According to Mizuno, the sight of the Miike workers striking for a year in 1960–61 provided an incentive for the D-san miners to stand up for their democratic rights.

In relation to daily violence, this was one of the more notorious, large mines, mainly because of the mine-owner's close association with the head of the local *yakuza* organisation. The implications of this relationship were that many of the labour overseers were employed from the ranks of local *yakuza*. This was not totally a bad thing, Mizuno says, because generally they were men who were known to the miners, and as such were not considered 'evil'. Misguided bullies, perhaps, but not evil.

Within Chikuho there is an awareness about some things which is quite different to other areas. For example, the *yakuza* are held with contempt by most people living in 'normal' society; they're seen as being below contempt actually — the *yakuza, bōryokudan, uyoku*, etc. However, for many young people, when the area was being destroyed (the coalmines being closed down) the *yakuza* had an alluring image. To become a *yakuza* was to do the ideal work. The kids would say: 'If I do well, I'll become a fantastic *yakuza*, or a great and famous criminal.' So young men learnt how to fight, extort and gamble rather than learn how to pass exams. Being a *yakuza* was about all they could look forward to, these coal kids.

That is an example of the way the Chikuho people used their own culture to assimilate and reinterpret outside information in a quite localised manner. They simply did the opposite of what was expected of them.[2]

Many informants told of the sympathy they felt towards the *yakuza*, particularly the young ones, who, being unemployed and ineligible for welfare, turned to crime in order to survive. Despite their violent acts, they were regarded generally as victims of their environment.[3] However, the strength of the miners' resolve to save their jobs, their income and their dignity was to create a situation in which the sympathy felt towards the *yakuza* was outweighed by more immediate considerations of survival. In short, conflict between the miners and the *yakuza* was certain to erupt, if the miners were pushed hard enough with little reward for their efforts.

This situation did in fact emerge. The company suspended wage payments because of the recession in the industry, and the *yakuza* were ordered to maintain the peace. This was a recipe for confrontation, and in 1962 violence erupted on a scale not seen before in D-san.

There was a single company union in D-san within which two violently opposed factions had developed by 1960.[4] One faction was controlled by those miners sympathetic with the Tokyo students and the actions of the Miike miners in going out on strike. The other faction was controlled by men who were worried that any form of labour action would deny them the opportunity to work in the mine. Although the option of opposing the company through the agency of an independent union did not exist, as there was in K-san mine, the polarisation of the labour force was clear-cut. The latter faction was supported by the company which, although it had made plans for closing down in 1963, had decided to extract the coal that was left as cheaply as possible.

The rumblings of revolution that were started in Miike were soon felt in D-san, and by early 1961 the socialist faction of the union was trying to get some guarantees about safety standards, wage increases and redundancy packages from management. The company employed some tough young men from a *yakuza gumi*, run by a man named Ito from Kita Kyushu, to ensure the socialist faction did not become too troublesome.

Mizuno elaborates the point:

> When compared with other mines (of the same parent company), the D-san workers were subjected to pressures not evident elsewhere. Family pressure was brought to bear on individuals to conform to the management concept of what a 'good union man' should be.
>
> Mr Ito's *yakuza gumi* were the ones responsible for running the labour control section. These guys infiltrated our union organisation from the bottom up, gradually assuming responsibility at the top of the hierarchy. If this had been in the past, they would have been thrown out, but as it was, within a short time they had assumed control of some of the major positions of power within the union.
>
> There were a number of young men within this faction who were known as the *tankō-kai* (coalmine *yakuza* gang), because of their naturally violent tendencies. They were really just *yakuza*, and you could see this in their dealings with those within the coalfields: walking around bullying the workers who would not join the company union. However, they were not connected with the company officially. Rather they were responsible to the labour overseer, and thus were employed by him personally, but paid out of company funds.
>
> I suppose you could say these guys were the strong arm of management, and they were certainly 'in' with each other. They were often bought drinks after work by management.
>
> They existed solely to bully us, to try to put us in our places. In the end we couldn't stand up to the pressures that we were subjected to. We were picked on, beaten up, excluded from the union, and our wives were raped and bashed. This pressure was put on us to make us modify our views about wanting a more democratic union!

Anyway, these guys would stand around looking tough, drinking at work, but doing nothing. They were the parasites, not us. We wanted to be paid a fair rate for the work we did. They did little, and yet got well paid. If one of us was severely beaten, or involved in a disturbance with these men off the premises, the police were called in and the fighting parties were taken to the cells and locked up. But while the *tankō-kai* men were bailed out by the *yakuza* boss, *we* had to bail out our members, or else wait until the court case was heard.

Although this sort of thing happened dozens of times, the police were never called in to sort out the trouble at the mine itself. Rather the company waited until the *rōmu* had decided who were the guilty parties, and only then did they contact the police, who hauled both sides off to the police station. The *rōmu* themselves were never arrested by the police, because they were regarded as the unofficial police deputies in the coalmine precinct. It was the combination of the pressure that was placed on us to conform, the violence that was tightly controlled by the *yakuza* and the company *rōmu*, and the police absence in internal conflicts which made the system work in this mine.[5]

Mizuno says that the miners were always regarded as the aggressors in the eyes of the law. Like many other towns within the coalfields, the town's mayor and the head of police had a strong relationship with the mine-owners, which tended to influence the way the miners were treated by both the police and the judiciary. It was not until the major court case, finally settled in 1975, that the D-san miners had any decisions made in their favour within the legal system, and that decision followed a widespread publicity campaign that the miners had initiated.

As I have briefly remarked, Chikuho was regarded by outsiders as one of the wildest places in Japan: untamed and dangerous for 'normal' people. This image was perpetuated by the media, and by the actions of the miners themselves in disputes. Accounts of miners attacking riot police, and *yakuza* attacking the miners in turn, led to the reputation of the area as violent and unsafe. In a country where the system of *on* and *giri* (obligation and reciprocal obligation, in simple terms) is regarded as an essential part of the social order, and there is a general requirement that people constrain and control themselves for the sake of the country,[6] the miners appeared to be an atypically violent group. Mizuno maintains that desperation drove the men to the extremes of behaviour they exhibited during the D-san strike. The miners' desperation was brought on by a combination of the immediate threat to their incomes by the company's inability to remain solvent and the ever-present and escalating incidences of violence. In the end the miners themselves had recourse to violence, as it had become the currency of everyday dealings they had with those who held power over them.

The 1962 strike

The strike was over the company refusing to pay the miners for work they had done, and their refusal to pay retrenched miners severance and retirement pay (the mine was already slowing production and sacking workers as the demand for coal slackened). Yet, regardless of the seriousness of the claims, only the Mizuno faction took the decision to strike; that was about half the miners. The faction attached to the company was seduced by company promises to pay the men the wages that were owing. Moreover, the company faction was too intimidated by the company to consider joining the action at first, and they continued working for more than a week while the Mizuno faction occupied the no. 2 shaft in a sit-in.

In response to threats of industrial disruption, the Mizuno men were locked out of the mine, in what had become a standard tactic for mine-owners dealing with industrial unrest. However, a group of 20 unionists had overcome this minor problem in a rather imaginative fashion, sneaking into the mine and eventually halting production. Mizuno describes one incident during the strike, which played a key role in the development of a more unified union consciousness:

You see, at first we took over and held the entrance to the no. 2 shaft. According to the injunction taken out against us by the company, we were trespassing on company property. A group of 20 men didn't care about the legality of their actions, and had sneaked into the mine, hiding under the trucks in the space where the gasmasks and breathing apparatus were stored. They then got off the trucks at the bottom of the railway, near the end of the Endless Windlass, and sabotaged the railway by sticking the carriage pins into the tracks and machinery. One man picked up a truck and physically derailed it by himself.

It was on about the tenth day that the company made an appearance. They didn't know what was going on in the mine, but they certainly did know that the miners had stopped production. So, in order to compel the men to give up, they decided to send the riot police down the mine to where the men were holed up. Even using a guide, the riot police weren't sure exactly where the men were down there, so they were not confident of immediate success.

We on the surface and the men down the pit all knew that the guys holed up in the mine were committing a felony, so they went all the way and placed dynamite strategically throughout the tunnels. They reckoned that if anyone tried to get in there to get them out, there would be an explosion, and the police, the miners and the mine would all be blown up. When the police realised this, they quickly retreated. At about the same time, our group entered the mine to stop the police from removing the miners down the pit. We were ready to fight, but then we found out about the dynamite as well, and we headed for the surface as fast as we could.

The guys in the mine wouldn't come out, no matter what sort of persuasion was attempted. The fact that they were able to defeat the riot police was pretty tough, I think, and admirable. Those on the surface decided to help those underground, regardless of whether they were in the same union faction or not, and it was through this action that we were able to close down all company production.[7]

Although the union had been seriously factionalised following the infiltration of the pro-company men, the concept of community united the union in the face of threats of *rōmu* and *yakuza* violence. When the men associated with the Mizuno faction staged the sit-in, the Ito faction continued to come to work, but they brought *sake* and food for the opposing faction members.

The company was really angry about this, and many of the Ito faction workers were beaten by the *rōmu* for their actions. Still, they helped the striking workers, even though they weren't in their faction. These guys kept the assistance up right to the end. Although the union was divided at leadership level, the men themselves didn't separate really. There was no hatred between the men of different factions. Rather, there was a growth of sympathy and camaraderie as the strike progressed. This is because both sides slowly changed their stances. We became less dogmatic, and the Ito faction members came to challenge both their own leaders and company policy as the strike continued and they saw the level of violence directed against their workmates.

Up till then a large number of men thought that the strike would only endanger their livelihoods, and that they wouldn't be able to survive, so they removed themselves from the action. But when they excluded themselves, they were forced to become independent and accept company policies, which included a condition that they receive half-pay, because the company couldn't afford to pay them proper wages. As they watched one person, and then another join the battle with the company, the majority of these men switched sides.[8]

When the miners emerged after more than two weeks underground, they were given a heroes' welcome by the other miners. However the company immediately started court proceedings against the union for halting production, trespassing and jeopardising mine safety, and injunctions were also taken out against prominent individual union members.

You know those long, rubber, riot batons? The company said that we had threatened their men not only with these batons, but also with knives and of course the dynamite, while the sit-in was going on. And that we had shouted 'Let's kill them!' and then charged at the police and the *yakuza*.

It was a futile effort by the company. We had a good lawyer, who convinced the court that expressions such as 'I'll kill you!' and 'I'll beat you up!' were normal daily expressions within the mining community, and that they carried little literal weight. If it was a city society, perhaps we would have been indicted for these verbal threats, but because it was a coal town there were no problems for us. You see, people talked like this in their own homes, couples arguing, parents and children talking, etc. Threatening people was just a part of daily life within the coal communities, so this charge was basically dropped. The judge handed down a suspended sentence.[9]

Following legal action taken by the union against the company over the non-payment of back wages and severance benefits, which came in the wake of the industrial action, the company was forced to make a commitment to pay the miners money owed. However, the company said that they did not have the money at the time and offered to settle the dispute by paying the men back their money in 30,000 yen monthly instalments over a period of ten months.

But after everyone got their first 30,000 yen the company decided that it didn't want to pay out any more, and after that no one got even 1,000 yen. When you consider that, it stands to reason that the company would try to degrade our position in court, to protect their reputation and turn the proceedings away from the wages issue.[10]

It is revealing that the mine-owners closed down the mine within three months of the action, claiming insolvency. This declaration legally exonerated management from having to pay the agreed severance pay and back wages, because it was expected that the government would assume responsibility for all company debts when they bought the mine out under the terms of the TCRB. When it was revealed that the company had been declared bankrupt, and that there was no work available for the miners, a new union strategy was developed, which concentrated on the concept of worker-ownership of the mine.

The miners went as far afield as Fukuoka with their protests, actively targeting the mining company's creditors, the Fukuoka Bank. By foreclosing on the company, it effectively put the miners out of work. Thus their response, instigated by Mizuno, was to talk to the bank president to try to get him to either change his mind about the foreclosure, or to support a plan for the workers to buy the mine from the company, using the superannuation funds that the company had deposited in the bank on the miners' behalf. However, the president would not see their deputation, publicly declaring that any money the company had deposited in the bank, whether it be on the miners' behalf or not, was the property of the bank. He went on to say that he would not support a charity such as the coalminers, who were not to be trusted.

In response, the miners decided to start a process of civil disobedience and disruption. They marched the 50 kilometres to Fukuoka, painted slogans on the walls of the bank, held rallies outside the banks, disrupted customers and finally closed the main thoroughfares in their attempts to get a fair hearing for their case. Many miners were arrested and subsequently imprisoned and fined for their part in 'disrupting the peace'. Much of the sensation was reported in the press, both locally and nationally. The miners were criticised by the media for being lawless and irresponsible.[11] When Mizuno was fined 30,000 yen for breaching the public peace, the press crowed that 'justice had been done'.[12] The company went into receivership, and the mine was closed. Eventually (in 1975!) a compromise was reached between the now-unified union and the government, where the government agreed to supply the miners with enough company land so that they could build their own homes. Although the miners received only a pittance in cash, the land was a major concession, and they finally won a moral victory.

Violence as legal defence

The methods of protest employed by Mizuno and the union were quite unlike any labour action seen within the mining community before. Certainly the Mizuno faction was influenced by the conspicuous Miike strike the year before, although the miners in that case met with little success. The union campaign was much more sophisticated than previous actions, employing both confrontationist and litigation-related tactics to combat the company's attempt to force them to back down.

Aware of the dangers of a union that displayed solidarity, the company had employed men from the local yakuza gumi to infiltrate and disrupt the union. Although perhaps half the miners were convinced that the only way to be paid for work already performed and simultaneously keep their jobs was to conform to management demands, after the success of the sit-in they actively supported the Mizuno faction. An all-in confrontation with an outside yakuza gumi, brought in by the head of the rōmu, occurred in a last-ditch effort to break the union when the men emerged from the mine, defiant and successful. But the union, flushed from its new-found solidarity was effective in physically repelling the attack. In fact, the miners forced the yakuza to retreat to their Fukuoka city headquarters where they surrounded the building threatening to 'kill the bastards'.[13]

When the company took out an injunction against the union for trespass, assault and threats of violence, the union hired the best lawyers they could find and took the unprecedented step of placing the violence and the threats of violence they made within the overall context of the coalmines. They contended that expressions of violence were normal miners' terms in their everyday lives, and that the miners themselves lived under threat of violence at the hands of gangsters. Therefore expressions of violence and the reaction of the miners in physically defending their position were justifiable. In suspending the sentence, the courts supported their position, implicitly agreeing that violence and the threat of violence was a way of life for the miners. The court case was a landmark decision in coalmining labour litigation, and affected the Y-san incident litigation which occurred some ten years later (see chapter 12).

The union correctly identified company shortcomings when they took further, unprecedented action against the company's creditors when the mine was put into receivership. Their actions were not supported by *Tanrō*, which, after the resounding defeat at Miike, had been seriously weakened and had moved farther right politically. However, the miners were so conspicuous in their public protest that the government was forced to make a compromise arrangement with them. After legal action, taken this time by the union against the government, as the company's agents, the government agreed to supply the miners with land and building materials, formerly owned by D-san, with which to construct a new community. The miners were also paid some of the money they were owed by the company from the government's TCRB fund. The union's tenacity and the ability to analyse the legal and financial restraints won them the opportunity to at least rebuild their lifestyles.

The Mizuno union's sophisticated understanding of their legal position established an important precedent in the development of labour-related conflict in the coalfields. The union was aware of its members' rights under the law, and of its ability to defend them successfully against unjust litigation. While it is probably true that desperation drove the union to take action in the first place, the subsequent development of a unified consciousness was important in establishing the grounds on which it could act. The relative success the miners had repelling both the police and the *yakuza* on a number of occasions was instrumental in establishing the necessary confidence to pursue other, litigation-related courses of action.

The action against the bank in Fukuoka, while partially conducted outside the law, was calculated to cause such disruption that the government would eventually have to settle with the union. The union displayed solidarity in the face of extreme provocation by the company and the law, and were able, with a relative degree of success, to resolve the dispute in their favour.

One of the main reasons for the miners' success was the presence of Mizuno, who brought with him a sophisticated understanding of the economic and legal structures of society. But the miners' developing consciousness of their own legal rights and of their ability to challenge repressive, often violent management techniques employed by the company in keeping them complacent, were critical factors that cannot be underestimated. Although the consciousness they developed was not really an archetypal class-consciousness *per se*, their views on their own position in the world were considerably modified by the influence of the Miike strike, and by Mizuno's arrival at the union office.

Unlike the K-san action, the D-san action was predicated on the threat of non-payment of back wages and the threat to the job security of all the miners. The tactical success of the miners' union in instigating effective action at the mine itself through the sit-in, and through resisting the physical threat of the gangsters and the police, led to unanimous support for the union from the workers. This step, where support was galvanised for the union, was virtually unprecedented in Japan's mining industrial relations. The threat to their livelihoods was so intense that workers were able to stand firm in the face of *yakuza* pressure and also be able to withstand the legal challenges made by the company to force them back to work.

The development of litigation-consciousness undoubtedly marked a milestone in the evolution of union strategy challenging the legitimacy of the mine-owners' proscriptive and repressive management practices. By forcing the company to pay the back wages, and by the arrangement whereby the company workers were able to purchase the land from the company on which they eventually constructed their own homes, the union used the legal system in a manner which no union, including the Miike union, had been able to before. The union was able to win for the miners a victory that was in stark contrast to the conditions of their working lives, where arguably they were perennial losers.

The township is still settled by the miners and their families. The union started a registered construction company, which is now one of the more successful companies in the region, with funds that the miners received from the government in lieu of the back pay and severance awards. Other miners were able to develop small secondary and service-related businesses in town, and whereas many other towns in Chikuho are economically depressed, this town is quite solvent financially.

NOTES TO CHAPTER 10

1 See Ueno, 1985a, pp.118–126.
2 Mizuno, interview, 1989.
3 Idegawa, interview, 1988; Ishizaki, interview, 1988; Oguchi, interview, 1988.
4 In 1958 the company had moved to eliminate the possibility of starting a union that opposed the company-controlled union. Miners who belonged to *Tanrō* were not employed by the company.
5 Mizuno, interview, 1989.
6 See Nakane, 1971, for example; and Benedict, 1946.
7 Mizuno, interview, 1989.
8 Mizuno, interview, 1989.
9 Mizuno, interview, 1989.
10 Mizuno, interview, 1989.
11 See, for example, *Asahi Shinbun*, 11 October 1962, p.3.
12 See *Nishi Nihon Shinbun*, 25 November 1962, p.2, for example.
13 Mizuno, interview, 1989.

CHAPTER 11

Mizuno

The role of Mizuno in the D-san action was critical, so it is worth considering his involvement in a little detail in order to understand the influence that intellectual agitators have in the process of the development of labour-consciousness.

He was at Miike in 1959, and he first joined the union when he heard about the violence at D-san. He went to the office of the 'Old' union to help organise resistance to split the union into two factions, which was just starting. As a member of the *Zengakuren*'s more moderate JCP-affiliated faction, he thought that he would be able to do more for the union by helping to organise staff within the office than by joining the protest lines. He was studying economics at Tokyo University at the time, majoring in labour relations, and his studies led him to an understanding of the nature of political resistance in Great Britain and the United States. He became one of a number of advisers for the union. In particular, he was interested in the politics of resistance, and the Marxist–Leninist philosophy of workers' rights.

At the end of 1959 a friend who worked in the D-san mine contacted Mizuno and explained the situation there. He told Mizuno that the union was corrupt, and that the miners were being abused by the system of piecework contracts that the company had implemented in an attempt to defray some labour costs. He was afraid that the union would capitulate to demands by the company to accept further decreases in wages. Violence was pervasive in the mine, and the leader of the *rōmu* was known to be connected with the local *yakuza*. These were good reasons why the workforce might be compromised.

Mizuno went to the office of the union in 1960, where he worked as a clerk for six months or so, before entering the pit. He was elected leader of the union in April of that year, but because of his JCP background he was against the idea of any one individual holding the leadership of any group, and so convened a committee to examine any proposals put forward by the membership. This committee published newsletters, distributed union propaganda to the miners and the public, and attempted to bail its members out of gaol when they were in trouble.

Mizuno was the force behind the move to employ legal assistance for the union when it was in trouble, a decision arising from the experience of other mines' labour actions, which had generally been conducted without official legal advice. In 1962 Mizuno gathered an experienced team of politically astute activists from outside the area around him, and together they were able to develop the strategy for taking on the company in both legal and civil arenas.

As an individual Mizuno generates great power, both physical and psychological. In 1988 he was a broad-shouldered, fit-looking 45-year-old. He has a ready laugh, and an impish sense of humour, obviously taking great pleasure in regaling me with stories of the miners' outrageous victories against the *yakuza*, a group of people whom he regards as being socially and mentally retarded. He thoroughly enjoyed discussing the miners' sit-in in the mine, holed up with their sticks of dynamite, merrily threatening the riot police and the gangsters, two of the most feared organisations in the country.

Modest to the point of being self-denigrating, Mizuno is still completely open, seemingly unaffected by the esteem in which he is held by the local community. He is highly educated, eventually finishing his economics degree, and then studying medicine, acupuncture and *shiatsu* (acupressure). Although his education is apparent when he speaks, he seems to make a point of conducting conversation on the level of the person with whom he is talking, without sounding patronising.

Very confident and generating charisma, it is easy to see how this man was able to instil within the miners the need for taking concerted action against the company. He is now well known for his acupuncture and alternative-healing skills, and he has a reputation for performing miracles for his patients. He lives, with his wife and many chickens, in the converted union office of the D-san mine.

Like Kuroyama, Oguchi, Hayashi and Takahashi, Mizuno is still actively involved in the community he helped to maintain. Through the medium of stories that he tells to his patients and trainees (he teaches *shiatsu*), he is able to relate past experiences of coalmining to local people, and to the new generation, who did not experience the coal era. His audience is limited, but, as he says, he has their undivided attention when he is applying the sometimes quite painful *shiatsu* techniques.

Power, and its corollary powerlessness, were at stake in the attempts to lead a dignified existence in the wake of a tumultuous past. The incidents following 1962, and the capacity of Mizuno and other outsiders at the mine to organise and challenge the status quo can be seen as attempts to empower miners with the knowledge and motivation to forestall their marginalisation on the periphery of the labour force. Unlike the K-san case, or even the Miike case, where miners were effectively reduced to peripheral political and economic status, the benefits of the actions of the D-san union are still apparent.

CHAPTER 12

The Y-san Disaster

In 1965 a methane-gas explosion ripped through the no. 2 shaft of the Y-san mine, killing 237 miners and seriously injuring another 150 men. This disaster was Japan's second worst post-war accident, and was remarkable for the number of errors that occurred before and after the explosion. Although an internal company inquiry found that the management of the day was correct in its actions, an independent inquiry conducted by the Fukuoka Mine Safety Commission found that there were 'suspicions of improper behaviour' on the part of management, but that these suspicions could not be proved beyond all doubt.[1]

The families of the dead and injured men took the unprecedented step of filing a civil suit against the Y-san company, suing them for compensation. This case was started even though the company and the union put considerable pressure on the widows and families of the dead and the injured miners to give up the case and take a small settlement. It was a landmark case for a number of reasons, not the least of which was that the courts found that M-san, the parent company, was negligent, the first time a mining company had been put in this position. This decision established a precedent that affected the outcome of other civil suits within the Japanese legal system over recent years.

The involvement of outsiders in this case once more ensured that the widows of the men killed in the disaster had the opportunity to pursue a relatively comfortable existence. This was achieved by mounting a sustained and comprehensive offensive against the Y-san company, and through the group of widows maintaining solidarity in the face of strong-arm tactics used by the company to convince them to accept a smaller settlement.

The legal success of the miners rang the death knell for the industry in Chikuho. Mining companies were placed in the unenviable position of not being able to afford appropriate safety measures, and not being able to afford compensation payments, should the inadequate safety measures fail.

From the perspective of the families of the dead, the successes in court became almost irrelevant. Many had died or moved out of the area in the 11 years that it took to settle the case.[2] Although the activities of the outside intellectual agitators certainly allowed them to taste the power of self-determination under the law, in many respects it was a matter of too little, too late.

However, before I look at the outcome of the case in depth, it is worth investigating in some detail the circumstances surrounding the disaster and the subsequent events.

Historical background

Since the 1940s M-san had owned the colliery in the town of Y-san, which is situated in Kago-gun, in Chikuho. A large mine that in its heyday employed more than 1,000 men, it was an archetypal big Japanese colliery in that all other industry in the town revolved around the mine. When the TCRB was introduced in the early 1960s, the company decided to sell the mine to the government under the terms of the Bill, because it had been operating at a loss for some years. This was announced to the local population, which reacted with some consternation.

According to the *Chikuhō Nōto*, a number of cases occurred where a major mining company publicly declared that it could no longer remain operational because of escalating labour, equipment and maintenance costs, and because of the low market price of coal. When public despair at this turn of events reached a peak, the company stepped in with a compromise arrangement by which the company would be 'sold' to a subsidiary company with lower running costs and higher production, with the aim of making the company solvent again. By this stage local workers were so desperate for work that they were prepared to accept the compromise package and work for reduced wages in more demanding, and often more dangerous, conditions. This process of debt-selling and subcontracting occurred not only in Y-san, but in Hokkaido's H-san coalmine, in the N-san Takashima coalmine, and in the Aichi Prefecture shipbuilding industry.[3]

In Y-san, when the company declared its intention of closing the mine, the miners' union, apparently unaware of the company strategy, called a meeting of the local townspeople with the aim of discussing their future job prospects. The township decided to plead with the company to show compassion, and to continue their operations in the town. The company was firm from the outset, and there seemed to be no chance of any agreement being reached. Five months after the company's initial announcement that the mine would close, M-san responded to the town committee, saying that the possibility of a second company taking over the running of the mine was not out of the question. However, the workers would have to be prepared for a decrease in wages, and for an increase in working hours, with the additional rider that the overall production of the mine would have to increase. The union fully supported the move to second company status and encouraged the miners to accept the terms of the agreement.

In short, because of the highly competitive coal market, the company wanted to justify cutting wages and costs, while maintaining and even increasing production. The 'takeover' by a second company (a company wholly owned by M-san) was the answer. When the second company was operating in the black, and while there were few problems within the labour force, the new ownership was quite effective in increasing productivity and profitability, but as the subsequent legal case showed, when problems developed within the second company, the ultimate responsibility was found to rest with M-san.

One Chikuho revivalist had the following to say about the process described above:

> At the meeting of the townspeople, the people begged M-san to continue the operations. M-san probably really had intended to continue the operations all along, but from the very beginning it had released a load of bullshit saying that it was closing the place down. In reality it was just waiting for the town and the union to say, 'The no. 2 company would be fine. Please do it for our sakes.' So M-san said that for the sake of the workers they would just have to sell out to the no. 2 company, because it couldn't be helped. And by doing this M-san was able to lower wages and increase the working hours with no obstruction. The union was not prepared to fight the company. They were afraid that if they argued with the company, the company would take steps to close the mine down. Therefore they tended to agree with them.[4]

Another informant further described the situation:

> The president of the old company became the president of the new company. The mine was backed with capital from M-san. They owned the lease and were paid off by the Y-san company. The company changed names, but in actual fact was being run by M-san from start to finish. Nothing had changed, except that the company was able to make money thanks to the tighter labour rules and work conditions — and looser safety standards. The mechanism of the mine was economically the sole responsibility of M-san, and they ran the company.[5]

Although the townspeople had desperately wanted the company to continue operations, the reality of the no. 2 company was difficult for many of the miners to deal with. Wages dropped to 75 per cent of the original M-san wages, working hours increased on average to 14-hour shifts, and production demands increased by 250 per cent. Safety standards were allowed to slip, and, combined with the nature of the work and the long hours, the accident rate climbed dramatically in the first year after the 'takeover'. A number of men who had worked many years for M-san under the original company quit the new company and looked for work elsewhere. Only 18 per cent of the original workers remained. A chronic labour shortage resulted. This in turn led to the situation where the mine was forced to advertise for miners, offering to train them and house them in the emptying *tanju*.[6] Because of the depressed state of the local economy in the early 1960s and the contraction of the rural economy, many young farmers who had never worked in mines came to join the company's new subcontractors, attracted by the prospect of a reasonable wage (compared with farming), free housing and secure employment with a big company.

Thus only a small percentage of the miners had long-term mining experience. This was to become a pivotal point in the case that followed the disaster.

Working conditions in Y-san mine

The facilities within the mine were allowed to remain in poor condition. None of the safety, digging or coal-moving equipment was updated after the new ownership occurred. Much of the digging at the face was done by hand, and then manually passed on to the conveyor belt, a situation that had been unchanged since the 1950s. The miners were expected to work long hours in excessive heat for poor wages. Moreover, little or no training in the use of the available safety equipment was given to the men, especially the new recruits. This proved to be a major contributing factor to the high death-toll after the explosion. The Y-san mine had 'safety tunnels', like all the mines, but, as it transpired, the new miners were unfortunately not aware of the location of these emergency exits.

A critical view of the mine operations

Sono, an informant whom I would classify as a member of the Chikuho revivalists, was forthcoming in his criticism of the running of the Y-san mine, and of the handling of the accident. As a radical socialist, he was a vocal and often active political agitator for the rights of the people he regarded as oppressed by the 'bonds of monopoly capitalism'. The miners were his archetypal proletariat. When Sono first came to the region in 1964, he, like Mizuno from the D-san union, was a member of the Tokyo Students' Movement. Embracing the Communist Manifesto, he took his message around the coalmines in the 1960s, with the aim of recruiting unions to the cause. In 1960 he went to China for three years to undergo training courses. Soon after he returned, the disaster at Y-san occurred.

The disaster was, as he says, 'like a personal attack on [his] values', and subsequently he was determined to investigate the circumstances surrounding the deaths of so many men. He and his group were deeply involved in motivating the Y-san Widows' Movement to take legal action against the company after they had publicised the nature of the accident through their leftist press contacts. Sono said that the cause of the accident was traceable to the way the company ran the mine. That is, the safety of the miners was a secondary consideration, listed well below consideration of profitability for the company.

> It was definitely mining safety that was the issue. As far as human lives were concerned, no matter how many hundred metres the mine was below the surface there were really no standards of safety enforced. It was the cost of the mine that was the determining factor in these cases, to make the dig as cheap as possible was the only factor that counted. The company just thought that it was the only way to do business. When an accident occurred, the company directors just nodded their heads and made placatory noises.
>
> In the case of Y-san Tanko, for example, there were on average 240 workers on every shift, and the company knew that methane-gas build-up was a problem with this dig. However there were only 190 gasmasks placed in the mine in case of emergency! So, even if a person knew that there had been a gas explosion in the mine, there was nothing that some of the people could do about it.[7]

The company effectively was able to neglect safety standards and training. This is indicative of the nature of the company's influence over the union and, through the union, over the men. It also highlights the power the company had to ignore the recommendations of the seemingly powerless, but officious, FMSC.

Some miners referred to the union as the 'dogs of the company', saying that the union's position undermined any attempts by the miners to have independent representation. The union's response to workers' requests to the company to improve wages and safety and working conditions was that if they didn't like the situation they could 'get out, because there was always someone else ready to come to work in their place'.[8] As in the H-san case, the union had a strong pro-company stance, which severely compromised the human rights of miners and, in the longer term, those of miners' families.

Mine management was under pressure from M-san head office to increase production and to make the mine profitable. This was achieved through employing semi-skilled, cheap subcontractors, and through ignoring the expensive demands of the FMSC to monitor and improve safety standards. In order to meet the new production requirements, working conditions were made more demanding and wages were cut. According to Sono:

> To get away with this, the company employed 'temporary workers', who were basically inexperienced in the mines, as subcontractors. They had nothing to compare the work with and therefore were fairly easily manipulated. The number of these men increased dramatically, and as a result of these policies the company was able to move out of the red.[9]

The above-ground staff numbers were also cut, so that, among other staff reductions, the engineering section (which was responsible for monitoring gas build-ups, mine construction projects and the general excavation of coal) was operating with barely a skeleton staff. Certainly staff and wage cuts had a powerful influence on the company's economic performance. The mine's improved production figures in 1965, compared with 1963, produced a huge leap in profitability.[10] They moved from operating at a large deficit to operating at a considerable profit. However, as the 1965 accident illustrated, this was achieved at an enormous cost, measured in human lives.

> In relation to the safety issue, because it would cost a lot of money to train the men in the correct safety procedures, management decided not to do it. So as far as the company was concerned, it was prepared to send workers into these dangerous conditions without any training. It was the maximum production at the lowest cost ethic. In Y-san's case, the above statements were made publicly and became the crux of the subsequent court action against the company.[11]

One widow said about the conditions in which her husband worked:

> My husband left home every morning before 7 a.m. and more often than not didn't get home until after 10 p.m., when he completed work. This was because he was forced to work two shifts in a row. The heat was appalling in the mine: for 99 per cent of the time it was more than 40 degrees [110 degrees Fahrenheit]. Because they had to go to work 26 or 27 times a month, sometimes doing two or even three shifts in a row at a time, the men had to be extremely strong. If they had to work only 15 shifts straight before they got a day off they were called 'lucky' by their workmates.[12]

The opinion of the woman above as to the conditions in the mine was verified by an informant who worked in the mine, both before and after the new company 'takeover'. The following extract refers to conditions with the new company.

> The mine was stinking hot. In fact there were no places on earth that were hotter than where I worked, I think. Just walking to the face from the elevator was exhausting, and by the time we finished shifts, which went on for up to 20 hours, we were so tired we could hardly see. If we were slow in digging, or if we were caught resting, I heard of many cases where the *rōmu* beat the men with those big wooden batons.[13]

As in many other mines, management employed overseers to maintain production. The union at this mine, like the union in H-san, was a company or enterprise union, and as such was not concerned whether its members were overworked or mistreated by the *rōmu*. It was as committed to keeping up with production as management, especially given the tenuous circumstances of their employment in the mine.[14]

The accident

On 1 June 1965 the explosion rocked Y-san. Methane-gas levels had increased to five times the safe limit over a period of a couple of hours within the no. 2 shaft at a depth of approximately 780 metres. The damage to equipment was so extensive that the actual cause of ignition is difficult to determine, but it is thought that a spark from one of the old conveyor-belts started the explosion. The concussion from the blast was felt 20 kilometres away by residents of a small farming village, and the pall of black smoke was visible from as far away as Iizuka, 30 kilometres to the south-east, according to reports in the *Asahi Shinbun*.[15]

One man who was working in the mine on the day of the explosion described what happened. He was 17 years old at the time, and had little mining experience, like the majority of the men in the shaft he was in.

> I didn't hear the explosion, you know. The first thing that I knew of the accident was when the lights and the electricity went out. I was down the no. 1 shaft, so I was quite a way from where the accident occurred. The tunnels didn't connect, you see, so there was no way that I could have known what was going on. Anyway, because the lights had gone out, I thought that it would be a good idea to get to the elevator shaft and to make my way to the surface to see what had happened. When I got there, the union representative told me that there was no need for panic, that we should all go back to our work and use our cap lamps until the lighting was restored.
> We all worked until the shift finished, you know — for perhaps five hours after the explosion. Anyway, when we got out of the mine, we went into the baths, and I noticed that the men from the other shaft weren't there, so I assumed that they had been forced to work overtime again — this happened

all the time. As we were all leaving the gates, I noticed the smoke in the air (it was heavier than usual) and I asked one of the security men what was going on. He told me that the company had said that it was nothing to worry about, and that we should all go home.

I went home, and my mother told me that there had been a huge 'bang' from the mine, and she asked me did I know what it was. I didn't. I suppose that it was about three hours after this that I was rung up at home by the *romu* at the mine, and asked to come to work to help clear up the mess that a 'minor accident' had caused. When I arrived back at work, there were fire engines, ambulances and police crawling all over the place. It was crazy. The *romu* boss asked me to go down the shaft with the rescue crew to help the men who were stuck down the mine.

After that day I never felt the same about mining again. Down in the shaft there was torn and broken machinery, which was buckled and twisted. Dust was everywhere, so you could hardly see in front of your own eyes. And because the pumps had been turned off, the water was up to our waists. And the smell! It was like a terrible fart. I could smell it through the gasmask. When we got out of the elevator, I stumbled in the water and fell. When I got up, I was holding a human hand. It was terrible. There were dismembered bodies everywhere. Farther down the tunnel, away from the site of the explosion, the mine looked like it had always looked. There was no obvious damage to the machinery or the roof, although there was water everywhere. It was in the tunnels at the bottom of the mine that we discovered the first of the miners who had died of methane poisoning. Their bodies were lying all over the place, but none had gasmasks on, and their faces were twisted in pain. I was so frightened I had to get out.[16]

Inoue's story highlights the lack of communication with the workers in the no. 1 shaft, something emphasised in the legal proceedings. However, the extent of the company's negligence went far beyond this. When the build-up of methane-gas had first been detected in the no. 2 shaft, the chief of operations within the mine had tried to contact the surface engineering section to tell them to turn off all the electricity. This was standard practice in cases where there was a sudden build-up in gas levels, because a spark from any of the machinery could have started an explosion. Unfortunately for the miners, there was no one at the engineers' office at the time, management having decided that it was not necessary to have safety staff on call throughout the shifts. The miners then contacted management head office and notified them that the gas levels had exceeded the safe levels by a factor of four, and that they needed to have the electricity turned off.

Management suggested to the miners that their instruments were wrong, that they should check the gas levels, and then get back to them about it. In the meantime, the management would get someone over to the engineering section to check the gas from there. Fifteen minutes later the explosion occurred.[17]

The company didn't let the miners in the other shaft know what was going on (that an explosion had taken place), because they didn't want to lose production from a premature shutdown.[18]

Even after the explosion, management continued to act irresponsibly. A junior member of the office staff immediately called the emergency services, notifying them of the explosion and asking for assistance. Management was informed, and it quickly overturned this decision to get help from outside. It rang the emergency services and told them that the situation was under control and that outside help would not be necessary. Miners in the no. 1 shaft, rather than being contacted to help with the rescue operation, were left undisturbed to finish their shift. The inquiry found that these actions, presumably performed to save 'face' and to keep production running, were negligent.[19]

Of all the miners killed in the explosion, only about 20 workers died as a direct result of the explosion. The others died as a result of gas poisoning as the gas circulated after the explosion. The men that survived were the ones with considerable experience. They knew right away that the gas was around and tried to make their way to the surface as quickly as possible.

Of the miners who were on that shift, 70 per cent were employed with the subcontractors, working for low wages because they didn't have any direct mining experience. This was because it was the no. 2 company. These were the inexperienced temporary workers who had entered the mines for the first time and didn't know much about the mines at all. The company was required to teach these people about mine safety, but they didn't. So the majority of these people had no idea where the gasmasks were kept nor how to escape from the mine. The people who got out were generally the veterans, who knew where the exits were.[20]

The accident site was a long way underground, so even if luck had been with them, the quickest time possible to get to the surface from that site was about 40 minutes. And the gasmasks had only enough air in them for 30 minutes. While the masks conformed to the letter of the safety regulations, the specifications that the FMSC had enforced were really not very useful at all.[21] Not only were the numbers of gasmasks insufficient and the air in them inadequate for the trip to the surface in case of emergency, but also few of the miners knew where the masks were kept or how to use them. This was because company policy had dictated that safety training was not an essential part of their function, particularly in the case of subcontractors.[22]

The delays in turning the electricity off, by making the miners and the engineers recheck the gas levels, and the delay in calling the emergency services doubtless contributed to the extremely high death-toll, but on top of these immediate problems the safety issue and the relative inexperience and lack of training of the young subcontractors were significant factors.

A cynical perspective would be that the company was determined not to lose production, and that it would go to any lengths to achieve this end. The reluctance to call in the emergency authorities for fear of a public investigation that would result in the mine being closed for an indefinite period is relevant here. The delay in calling in the emergency services probably cost many miners their lives: in the five-hour delay, most of the men suffocated. Those who survived managed to do so by escaping into tunnels least affected by the gas and waiting for the rescuers. By not having anyone stationed at the engineering section for emergencies, especially given the pre-existing problems that the mine had with methane-gas build-up, the company also contributed to the disaster.

The accident has to be seen in the economic context in which it occurred. The mid 1960s were the most severe years for coalmining Japan had seen. Under the terms of the TCRB, Chikuho mines were being closed at a tremendous rate, the market was being 'undermined' by cheap, high-quality coal imports from Australia, the USA and Canada, and domestic sales had shrunk to a fraction of the 1950s' levels as oil and petroleum products competed directly, and successfully, with coal for a large section of the domestic energy market. Unemployment was becoming an even more serious problem in the coal areas than it had been, and work opportunities in the Chikuho region in particular were extremely limited. Coal companies were no longer seen as the 'shining light of industry', and few could offer the so-called 'lifetime employment' that so pervasively characterises foreign perceptions of Japanese business. Given these circumstances, and notwithstanding the safety issue, it is not beyond comprehension why the Y-san mine management would consider carefully whether they could afford to slow production for the sake of what was, after all only a 'little bit of gas'.[23]

The process of litigation and offers from the company

After the accident the company offered to pay the families of the dead men an individual settlement of 400,000 yen each. This was equivalent to about three months' wages. Moreover, the families of the sub-contractors who lived in the *tanjū* were required either to pay rent and other expenses from the date of the settlement or to get out of the *tanjū*. Other families were allowed to stay in the *tanjū* for up to twelve months after the accident, and were then moved to a rundown section of the company housing. The company said that it could not afford to support the women and their families any longer. The widows were not happy with this arrangement, because they had to continue to feed, house and clothe their children, and they felt that this was not possible on the amount of money they were offered. Also, they wanted the company to erect a monument to the dead, so that they would have something to be proud of, to show their children, when they grew up, what their fathers had done. On top of this, the families of the dead wanted the company to acknowledge its responsibility for the accident, removing the responsibility from the dead miners.

Initially the union was adamantly against any further compensation or money to build a monument to the dead. The union leaders believed that the only hope the men who were left working in the pit had of keeping their jobs was for the company to relinquish any further responsibility for the families of the dead men. By doing this the company would save money and be able to continue operating. The attitude of the union was one of pure economic rationalism, an attitude that ignored the legal requirement of the company to look after the interests of its employees. One of the widows commented on this attitude.

> The union leaders said to us, after we had gathered together to complain about the company's treatment of us, 'Even though you are widows, it is foolish to think that the company, or that we, will look after you for ever. Neither the union nor the company can afford to look after you, you know. Sooner or later you're going to have to stand up for yourselves, and learn to look after your families. We are not the welfare agency.' The fact of the matter is that we were the first widows to have got any money out of the company, even though there had been many deaths in the mine in the year and a half since the new company took over.[24]

Notwithstanding the pressure from both the company and the union to take the settlement, some of the families of the dead men were determined to win concessions from the company. But factions had appeared within the women's group. Some women thought that they would be successful in agitating for some further compensation, but the majority thought that by themselves they could never call the company to account and that they should be satisfied with the offer.

> We are just ignorant women, the wives of ignorant men. What chance have we of winning against the powerful company? They can throw us out of the *tanjū* the moment we cause trouble. We need someone who knows about these things, and whom we can trust.[25]

Another problem was that the money was to be paid into the union funds, because the union was seen by the company to be the representative of the men who were killed. The union decided that although the arrangement was for the widows to be paid from this fund, union expenses, legal fees and a large percentage of the money to be used for the building of a monument to the dead would be withheld. As a result, the widows individually were to receive 230,000 yen.

A year after the accident, the widows had been moved into the 'new slum', the dilapidated section of the *tanjū* that the subcontractors had formerly occupied. The wives and families of many subcontractors had moved to other towns and cities, so that only about 60 per cent of the women remained within the *tanju* .

The stocking company ploy

At this stage, the company decided that the women who remained were becoming a problem. Although the no. 2 company did not pretend to honour the 'lifetime employment' practices of many of the larger companies, management decided to attempt to ameliorate the conditions in which the women found themselves. To placate the women, they donated a section of unused company land and a shed to a local stocking manufacturer, so that this company could establish a factory for the women to work in. This was because the company had said that it could not afford to pay the women all the compensation money up front, and that the pay would have to be in monthly instalments. The establishment of the factory would deflect responsibility from the company to look after the women, and be relatively inexpensive to set up. The average monthly pay for the workers in the factory was 11,000 yen, less than a quarter of the official poverty cut-off line. Although the pay was poor, compared with most small to medium-sized mines, where average compensation for miners killed in accidents was between 30,000 and 50,000 yen, the Y-san deal of an average of 230,000 yen *and* employment, albeit poorly paid, was exceptional for Chikuho.[26] Within twelve months, though, the factory had gone bankrupt and the women once more were without income, a situation that was exacerbated by the company's reluctance to pay the monthly stipend to the widows, citing cash-flow problems among other reasons for not complying with the law.

In 1967 the Criminal Investigation Committee found that the company was guilty of negligence in regard to the accident. Four men from the company, including the mine manager, were put on trial, found guilty of negligence of safety standards and of incompetence in dealing promptly with the accident, and were sacked by M-san.[27]

Outsiders' involvement

The result of the criminal prosecution had a profound effect on the Sonos, who decided that the case was worth serious investigation. Sono and his wife, who at this stage were living in the vicinity of the mine, volunteered to help organise the bereaved families into a political group, with the aim of taking legal action against the company. The case that followed was a protracted and bitter legal struggle, which resulted in the 1978 decision by the district court to award damages of five million yen to each of the plaintiffs, a decision that was hotly contested by the company. However, the decision stood, and the company was forced to pay. Again the company cited cash-flow problems and suggested payments be made to the families on a monthly basis, again through the union, which was now defunct (the mine closed in 1973). Once more the Y-san Widows' Movement (YWM) had trouble getting any money from either the company or the union, even though they had won the case.

Fragmentation of the group's interests and members was perhaps the most difficult problem to overcome in the short term. By the time the case was heard by the courts, some ten years after the original legal action had been started, many of the women from the YWM had moved to other, more hospitable climes, some had died, and others had lost interest in the outcome of the case. In 1977, when the case first reached the district courts, there were 178 members of the YWM left, of whom some wanted to pursue the case to its bitter end, while others were content to let the matter drop, maintaining that it had taken so long up to that point that it was unlikely they would receive anything from the courts, and anyway their lives had become so hard that they were used to poverty.[28] There were many reasons cited at an impromptu meeting held in the *tanjū* just before the case was scheduled to start, as to why they should continue with the struggle. Some of these were:

> To be able to hold a memorial service for the dead miners, who had not been exonerated legally for the accident; to display their anger and resentment over the way the company had treated them over all these years; to apologise to the dead for allowing the company to treat them as fools; to be able to explain to their children that their fathers were not evil and wasteful men, and that they had died doing their duty; to expose the discrimination that existed against Chikuho people, and miners in particular; and to expose the nature of the company and the union, those agencies that had tried to prevent the women seeking justice under the law.[29]

The formalisation of these aims followed the involvement of Sono and his political faction. After the 1967 court decision that the company was criminally negligent, the Sonos used legal and press connections to ensure that the case had some publicity, even though this publicity was generally confined to the radical press. Launching an action against the company was not a real problem, but the divergent aims and attitudes of the bereaved widows made collective action almost impossible. To unify the group and to formalise its structure, the name was changed from the Y-san Bereaved Families' Group to the Y-san Widows' Movement (YWM), and an agenda was set up. This allowed the group to focus on what it thought the families were entitled to receive under the law. Lawyers associated with the JCP were employed on a commission basis to handle the case, acting on instructions issued by the YWM.

Other well-known Chikuho people took an interest in the case, including Ueno, Idegawa, Mizuno, Takazaki, Oguchi and Ishizaki. A series of meetings was arranged, with guest speakers from other coalmines who had similar experiences, litigation experts, coal history and economic experts all taking part. On the basis of these discussions it was decided that the YWM would take legal action against the company, because for the first time they had a case whereby the company had been convicted of a criminal charge. According to the lawyers, this meant that the YWM had the opportunity to cash in on this unusual decision of the criminal courts and win concessions from the company on a level never before seen within the industry.

Publicity for the plight of the women had been a problem from the day of the accident. Although journalists from the major newspapers came to the mine to cover the explosion, it received front-page treatment only for a short time, and then was all but forgotten by the media. The committee of experts (the Chikuho revivalists) was aware of this, so publicity about the YWM was arranged, first through leftist press connections, and then through the writings of Ueno, Idegawa and Ishizaki, published within academic journals and collections of local histories. The Sono group started a privately funded and produced a journal called *Chikuhō Tsūshin*, which was concerned with the inequalities found in Chikuho. Of course the Y-san case was frequently discussed within this monthly magazine, and court updates were published monthly, as were two columns concerning the case, one by Sono, and the other by the leader of the YWM. The distribution of these journals was limited at first, but because there were so many people in the Chikuho region who were classified as 'disadvantaged', and because the journal used language accessible to the poorly educated, using simple *kanji* and grammar, its circulation increased to such an extent that by 1970 four full-time staff were required to handle its publication.

Support for the women came from as far away as Hokkaido, where mining was undergoing a severe rationalisation process at the hands of

M-san, N-san and H-san, for all these companies closed mines during the 1960s, 1970s, and 1980s. However, particularly effusive support was received from the families of the miners killed in the M-san Miike disaster of 1963, where more than 460 men lost their lives. The company had never admitted liability for causing the accident, and the investigation into that disaster had exonerated the company from any responsibility. As a result, the families of the men killed had been offered a similar settlement to that originally offered to the Y-san women. Because no criminal conviction had occurred in this case, and because the women were inconsistent in their demands from the company, no serious challenge to the settlement was ever issued. Consequently the Miike people were hopeful that if a precedent could be established in the Y-san case, they too would have the opportunity to redress what they considered a miscarriage of justice.

Settlement

In 1978, after an eleven-year campaign, the YWM agreed to an out-of-court settlement on the advice of their lawyers. They would each receive five million yen compensation for the deaths of their husbands. Accommodation within the *tanjū* would remain as it was, the women continuing to live in the segregated and dilapidated houses. The company, although it had been convicted of negligence, refused to make a public admission to that effect, and also refused to supply additional finances for the building of a memorial. A further stipulation of the agreement was that the company continue to pay the women on a monthly instalment basis over 20 years, and that the money would be paid through an independent body — the old company union. The first instalments would cover the building of a memorial, which the company would erect on land that the YWM was required to buy. After legal fees had been subtracted from the sum, which totalled approximately 2.5 million yen, individuals were to receive approximately 120,000 yen a month for 20 years, and be liable for all living expenses incurred in the *tanju* in which they lived. This was approximately the same amount as the average monthly wage for a miner in 1965. For the purpose of comparison, a miner's average earnings in 1978 were about 250,000 yen a month.

Considering the length of time the case had taken to get to court, the terms of the agreement and the restrictions imposed by the company, the settlement was not generous, but compared with other mining accident settlements, it was exceptionally good. The families of the miners killed at H-san mine had been forced to agree to a *total* settlement of 500,000 yen.[30] What, then, was the difference between these two cases? How was it that the Y-san women, given their disparate aims and poor self-image were able to take successful, unprecedented legal action against the might of M-san?

H-san and Y-san compared

At H-san mine the overt nature of violence and coercion that the *rōmu* had used so freely over a long period and the intimidation and forced adoption of company values and ideology that this punitive system brought about within the miners' community prevented the families of the dead even considering taking action against the company. Not only were the usual physical threats of violence employed, but also economic and isolationist policies were instituted to deal with potential trouble-makers. The women were told that if they wanted more money from the company, they would be on their own. Their right to company housing and subsequently to the new state-sponsored Coal Villages Restoration Scheme Housing apartments would be waived, and they would have to find their own accommodation and incomes. Given the ignorance of these women about their legal rights and their appalling self-image as 'dumb coalminers' wives', the choice between improbable compensation from the company and a guaranteed place to live in was no choice at all.

The size and structure of the respective companies were also relevant. In the smaller, more cloistered environment that typified the H-san mine, all the miners and their families were known to the *rōmu* and the union. The union played a vital role in reinforcing the company's policy after the accident, as they did in Y-san, but within H-san it was a role that was made more powerful by the lack of opposition. As I have discussed in earlier chapters, opposition to company policy was suppressed through the use of the *rōmu* and, where necessary, outside intervention. The economic circumstances within which the miners and their families found themselves, and the lack of alternative employment within the industry during the 'Scrap and Build' era forced many miners, at least on the face of it, to conform to company demands. On top of this was the threat of economic sanctions, especially the threat to remove them from their housing. This was a powerful weapon, which the company, through the union, sought to exploit.

Whereas the local media kept the story of the trapped H-san miners running in the newspapers for more than two weeks, editorials about the accident were limited to technical matters concerning the rescue efforts, and the occasional comment about responsibility for the accident. The miners and their families were, for the most part, ignored. Reports about the widows were restricted to local newspapers, and these reports dealt with the 'unfortunate circumstances' into which the widows had fallen, and how 'courageously these strong women stood up to the unfairness of life'.[31] Because reports were restricted to the local area, and because within Chikuho the reputation of the mine as a violent and uncompromising place was well understood, insiders were loath to act to help the women. The president had publicly and conspicuously said that the mine would look after the families of the dead, and it was assumed by most that this would happen.

Not only the ideological isolation, but also the physical isolation, of the community had a profound effect on the lack of resistance. The H-san people's contacts generally were restricted to the *tanjū* and to other small mining communities, and within these communities miners and their families had a profound understanding of mining company compensation policies, so disasters were trivialised. Although there was a great deal of bitterness about these policies, the overwhelming sentiment expressed was *shiyō ga nai* (it can't be helped). As Ogata said:

> Miners were always sympathetic towards each others' tales about how they had been hard done by, but they had heard it all before. Nothing that they could do would affect the outcome and make the mine management treat miners like human beings, after all. Basically we were all concerned with keeping our heads above water, and so miners, as a whole, really were only concerned with what was directly in front of their own eyes. It's hard to believe, but even in that period we were all too scared to stand up to the company. I mean, we all had to eat. And the union was corrupt. There was nowhere to turn. The company had all of us in their pocket. If we tried to resist we were beaten or worse, thrown out of the company with nothing.[32]

Because of the small size of the company, management was able to take measures to prevent powerful or charismatic workers from taking a stand against the company, weeding out the leaders and making examples of them. The threat of violence was constantly present, and although the miners were inured to the violence to a large extent, they knew the rules and how to play the game accordingly. There was no protest. Because the president never acknowledged the company's responsibility for the accident, and because, for whatever reasons, legal action was not taken against the company by the FMSC, as it was in Y-san, criminal liability was never established against H-san mine.

Another important factor was the timing of the accident. Whereas the community was devastated by the accident, it was neither the first nor the largest accident in the region. It occurred in 1960, the year in which the students' movement came into its own, politically, but this was before the students and the leftist activists became heavily involved in the region. In many ways the disaster at H-san provided a strong incentive for those concerned about the abuse of human rights in the coalmines to become involved in Chikuho. Following the disaster, many students (such as Mizuno and Oguchi) drifted into the area with the intention of assisting the miners to challenge the power of the coalmines and to secure fundamental human rights for the people of the coalfields.

Overall, isolation, intimidation and coercion, in the short term, and the memory of violence meted out by the company as reprisals for non-conformity, over the long term, helped to maintain the status quo within H-san. Although many miners were disillusioned with the mine, and certainly disillusioned with the paltry compensation offered by the company as a result of the inevitable closure of the mine following the disaster, they were not able to develop a collective and powerful enough counter-consciousness to challenge the ideology of the company. The same argument could be applied to the widows of the disaster. Because management had acted to narrow the widows' choices, through controlling their physical and ideological environment, they were able to make a deal with the women that did not severely compromise the company. This was reinforced by the support of the union, by the lack of opposition to the scheme and by the financial position of the company after the accident.

In the first instance, the Y-san women were in a similar position structurally: they were not conscious of alternatives to the amount of compensation the company offered, and were certainly ignorant of the possibility of litigation against the company. Outsiders, however, helped them realise that, first, there had been a miscarriage of justice in that their husbands' lives had been too cheaply valued, and, second, that without a collective understanding and approach to solving the problem they would be incapable of changing that state of affairs. Perhaps even more importantly, the knowledge that there were steps that could be taken to redress the situation, in light of the criminal charges brought against the company, allowed the widows to develop a strong and initially uncompromising stance. It is in regard to this that the Sonos and the Chikuho revivalists strongly influenced the outcome of the situation.

The Y-san community was as isolated as the H-san community in almost every respect, the union was as severely compromised, violent sanctions had been imposed on recalcitrant workers, and company pressure had been brought to bear on the widows after the accident to accept what was, for the coal industry, a reasonable compensation deal. The major differences were that the Y-san mine was still operating after the event, it was supported by a large infusion of capital from M-san, and it was successfully prosecuted by the FMSC for negligence.

Sono's group initially, and other prominent Chikuho people sub-sequently, through hard work and often radical tactics were able to persuade both the courts and the company to alter their stances with regard to both the accident and the widows. The Sono faction was actively involved from the beginning in organising the widows into a political group with a common cause. Given company pressure to force the women to accept the compensation offered by the company, it is indicative of the solidarity of the women that they were not distracted from the original purpose of their action. The motivation for continuing with the case was powerful enough for them to endure slanderous attacks on their character by the union, physical attacks on their families and friends, and a malicious strategy that attempted to ostracise them from the remainder of the *tanjū*, the so-called '*burakumin* treatment'.[33] However, this solidarity was made possible only by the intervention and support of the group of outsiders.

The process of making the case public over the long period before it was heard by the courts was instrumental in maintaining morale within the group. The publicity that the activists generated reached a wider audience than any efforts of the women alone would have done. In this sense, some Chikuho teachers who were involved with the case were also able to influence their students as to what had taken place at the mine after the accident. One 11-year-old schoolboy who was interested in Y-san wrote the following in an article published in a left-wing magazine:

> When I went to Y-san for the first time it was because I was interested in finding out what happened to all the people at the mine. The reason that the explosion happened was because there was lots of gas in the mine and something like a spark ignited it, and it blew up and 237 miners were killed ... But the company was concerned only with making money and they didn't care that there were all those people down there. The people doing the hardest work were the ones who got killed, not the ones in the office. And then the company said that the miners' families were allowed to get only a small amount of money from the company to live on.
>
> They couldn't live on the money that the company gave them, and all those other kids who are about my age are in real trouble these days — they can hardly afford to eat. But when the YWM complains that they don't have enough food and that their houses are falling down, the company just says, 'It's become a habit, all this complaining, and it's getting really irritating'. That's discrimination, isn't it?[34]

Rumours spread about the new pressures that were being applied to the women, whether they were still holding on, how much money they would likely receive, and why they bothered with taking the company to court in the first place. Oguchi, in particular, was a source of information, because Y-san *tanjū* was one of his regular stops. He would gather the rumours from threads of conversation and pass his own interpretation of what was transpiring on to people in other coal villages on his route. Idegawa, Ueno and the Sonos, who discussed the issues with their diverse connections, were instrumental in keeping the case alive in the minds of local people. Ironically, the only group to oppose the action, apart from the company, was the remainder of the workers at the mine, who were afraid that the company would be forced to close on account of the hefty claims that the women were making. However, the downturn in the economic fortunes of the coal industry in the early 1970s was enough to force the mine to close well before the case was heard in 1978, making the objections to the case from local residents difficult.

One other point worth mentioning is that the YWM gained considerable support from other socially disadvantaged groups who perceived their case as the watershed it was to become, notably the *Buraku Kaihō Undō* (Buraku Liberation Movement), and the *Kyōsei Renkō* (Korean Forced Workers' Organisation). Many women activists were conspicuously supportive of the action, sending in letters of encouragement over the years leading up to the case, and sharing in their somewhat muted joy when the women agreed upon the out-of-court settlement in 1978.

Analysis

The contrast with the H-san case is enlightening because it illustrates quite clearly how the mechanisms of power can be overturned if there is enough *outside, informed help* available for seriously disadvantaged groups. This is consistent with the approach of Gramsci (Hoare, 1972), who maintained that it was up to the 'intellectuals' from the Party to act on behalf of the masses who were ideologically still children, and therefore incapable of dealing with the subtle and manipulative pressures brought to bear on them by a cynical and self-centred power elite.

From another perspective, Stephen Lukes' theory that the powerful act to prevent potentially explosive matters becoming issues is illustrated clearly by the dichotomy above. In the H-san case, the powerful controlled not only the means of production and the environment in which the people lived, they were also able to exert sociological and economic pressure on the individuals who may have caused trouble to accept the arrangement they promulgated. Above and beyond this, the company had the tacit backing of the system of litigation, which was made more pervasive by the declaration of financial insolvency that followed the accident, thereby eliminating even the potential for the miners' families to claim further compensation under the law. The company remained immune from FMSC or government prosecution, even though its record of violence and irresponsibility was well established in folklore. In turn this worked to prevent the families of the dead men instituting legal action of their own.

Isolation at H-san, both physical and ideological, reinforced the notion that the miners and their families were totally dependent on the company, which had the effect of restricting the range of political, legal and economic alternatives they had at their disposal. This was reinforced by the role of the union as the company's watchdogs, employed to maintain the status quo, and to encourage the miners to keep out of 'trouble'. The feared *yakuza*-like *rōmu* were also employed in this capacity, their actions totally unhindered by any outside interference. The police never interfered in internal 'disputes', a position never questioned by either the miners or the police, the latter preferring to leave any problems to the mine to handle.

Although the Y-san women had to contend with this type of prejudice and segregation, they were able to change the pattern, as it were, through the influence of outsiders who came to know about the case. Through the efforts of people such as Oguchi, the *kami shibai* man, the Sonos, Ueno, Idegawa and Mizuno, others who were concerned about the problems which coalminers and their families faced were able to act together in a spontaneous display of solidarity and support for the women. The sheer number of publications produced to support the women, and the number of organisations that offered both financial and moral support doubtless had a powerful effect in influencing the company's lawyers to do a deal with the women.

Perhaps the glimmer of hope that the case offered for other abused groups was reason enough to excite the gossip that was so widespread at the time. Years of physical and economic oppression, with little hope of financial freedom, had taken its toll on the miners and their families. The impending collapse of the industry, the bleak future ahead and the even more sobering thought that they had lived through the 'good days' were reasons in themselves to see the Y-san case as a positive sign that there was change in the air.

Society had changed in the years since the H-san disaster. Politically Japan was still conservative, the students were still active, and the JSP was still in political opposition with just enough support to block constitutional amendments in the Upper House. But the political *climate* had changed considerably. Japan had moved from being a second-rate developing economy to a first-rate developing economy. By the mid-1960s Japan was the third largest economy in the non-communist world. There was more money in the country, and the trend of consumerism was starting to gain ground. Television had come to the *tanjū* and with it came the widening of people's outlooks. No longer were they restricted by the area in which they lived. They had the opportunity to experience a new range of activities, and to see on television representations of a new range of cultures besides their own. According to Oguchi, the introduction of this one consumable changed the whole perspective of the mining communities overnight.[35]

The older miners were generally illiterate, and therefore the introduction of television had a profound influence on the amount of information they were able to receive. Although radio had been around for years, Chikuho's geographical situation in a 'basin' made it difficult to get reasonable reception. Chikara, another informant, said that after television came the mining communities went from being ignorant places, where some people had not even crossed over the nearest mountain range, to communities where people were able to discuss national political and economic events with a surprising degree of sophistication. In other words, the miners started to realise that they did in fact inhabit a world where events that did not directly concern them still affected them, such as the changeover from coal to oil. People were becoming better educated generally. The level of literacy had increased to such an extent that within the post-war generations the literacy rate among children was almost 100 per cent; therefore they could read, something the majority of the older miners and their wives could not. In the early 1960s there was an information boom, and it eventually reached Chikuho.

Because the Y-san company was larger and more open than H-san, and because the town in which it was situated was larger and more cosmopolitan than H-san, information concerning the mine could not be so effectively concealed by the old-boy network. The leaking of information about the disaster and the widespread, if somewhat leftist, publications and groups that supported the widows were relevant in gaining a reasonable hearing in the courts. One of the reasons that many of the Chikuho revivalists got behind the widows was that they felt that it was a symbolic case, which could change the perceptions of local people about litigation, which in turn could help to alleviate the 'dark image' of the Chikuho people. If this case was seen to be successful, and other cases could be brought to the attention of the courts, then it seemed likely that the 'official' versions of history, which had labelled the miners an unruly, untruthful, violent, slothful group of human beings with no pride in themselves, could be turned around, and the slow process of re-educating the population not only of Chikuho, but also of Japan, could begin.

More than anything, according to Idegawa, there was a need to explain *why* the people of Chikuho had become so dependent on welfare (that it was related to companies such as M-san discarding the miners and their families 'as if they were old stockings'), as in the Y-san case.[36] Furthermore, the companies refused to supply any aid to the areas they had stripped of the resources to build their international empires. This 'injustice' and the lack of respect the companies showed the people who laboured all their lives for them are in one sense truly Japanese, according to Ogata.

> The powerful in Japan can always walk over the powerless. It has happened since the days of the earliest samurai, and is still happening. While things are going well, the companies are happy to encourage the workers to do their best for the company, but at the first sign of trouble, it is those who have dedicated their lives to an industry who will be the first to be made redundant.[37]

Idegawa supports this view and added that the thing most people had difficulty accepting about this was that the companies refused to acknowledge two fundamental principles of Japanese society: *on* and *giri*. The satisfaction of proving the company wrong was the women's driving force. Only through successful action were the people able to rest, because the *giri* had been returned, the husbands of the widows set to rest, and the gates opened for further action by the relatively powerless against the powerful in society. As Takashima said, 'The truth had to come out in the end. The companies couldn't keep lying and getting away with it for ever. I was glad that I saw it, because it made my heart sing.'[38]

The Y-san case and the development of local consciousness

This protracted incident, which from the time of the disaster to the time the women received compensation took more than 13 years, was notable for reasons other than the success of the litigation and the opening of the way for future litigation. The group of people I have described as the Chikuho revivalists first came together around this issue. Sono's wife, Eiko, was working at the office of the mine when the disaster occurred. Through her efforts they were able to collect a large amount of information about the running of the company and then present it to the widows to use as evidence in any action they might like to take against the company.

The public manner in which the Sonos attacked the case, producing newsletters that were given away to local people, and then starting the publication of the *Chikuhō Tsūshin* magazine, which paid for itself for more than 12 years, attracted attention from other minority groups within the region. There was an emotive response to the claim for justice in this case. Perhaps because M-san was such a big company, the pressure it placed on a small group of women who seemed defenceless was widely regarded among Chikuho society as unreasonable. Moreover, the fact that the company had been charged and prosecuted over the incident seemed ample reason for them to adopt a conciliatory approach. Yet they continued to bully the women.

As a result of M-san's actions, the individuals who made their expertise available to the women were motivated by a number of personal reasons, but overall by the sense that a fundamental injustice needed to be redressed. The minority groups that contributed to the newspapers and magazines had their own political positions, which they wanted to express, but underlying these positions was the thread that certain injustices needed to be set right. It was a moral campaign, concerned with changing the widows' present circumstances, offering them support, while promoting their own perceptions of society, and its problems.

This collection of individuals, all with a history of radicalism, exchanged similar ideas, although they were often couched within different political paradigms. From the desire to change the present circumstances of the women in the YWM, this informal collection of intellectuals and radicals realised that to change commonly held perceptions of contemporary society it was necessary also to change the perceptions of the past. To dismiss the coalmining industry as a necessary evil and to denigrate accordingly the value of the labour of the miners or alternatively to deify the industry as the 'backbone' of the region would uphold a false consciousness, which would disguise the true nature of Chikuho society. Although this position was not formally taken, the trend of the articles in the *Chikuhō Tsūshin* moved monthly more towards this end.

During the case, Oguchi relayed not only the rumours of the current litigation, but also the rumours of past violent episodes. Idegawa began her research on the coalmining women, starting with the *burakumin* who worked in the 'badger holes'. Ueno concentrated his efforts on producing the definitive series of Marxist critique of the coal industry in Chikuho. Sono continued to edit *Chikuhō Tsūshin* and to hold classes on revolutionary ideology for disenchanted radicals. Ishizaki decided that she would have to publish her book on the hardships of being a *burakumin* in Japan's repressive society. The groundswell movement that was directed at implementing social change in Chikuho was under way, although its power was to be limited. The current welfare situation is evidence of how the long-term penetration of the radical ideas of the revivalists has yet to be assimilated.

NOTES TO CHAPTER 12

1 FMSC Report, 1974.
2 The case began in 1967, two years after the accident, and was concluded in 1978.
3 See *Chikuhō Nōto*, June 1978, pp.41–54.
4 Ikeda, interview, 1989.
5 Sono, interview, 1989.
6 Sono, interview, 1989.
7 Sono, interview, 1989.
8 Oguchi, interview, 1989.
9 Sono, interview, 1989.
10 The figures rose 59 per cent in 18 months, according to Yada at the Fukuoka coal Research Centre at Kyushu University in 1988.
11 Sono, interview, 1989.
12 Ikeijiri, interview; quoted in *Chitei: Gasu Daibakuhatsu*, 1978, p.27.
13 Saito, interview, quoted in *Chikuhō Tsūshin*, March 1978, p.34.
14 The union perceived that miners were able to work in the mine because of, firstly, the goodwill of management and, secondly, the company's continued profitability. The latter depended on the efforts of the workers. The union was not prepared to compromise its position by making demands on the company about working or wage conditions.
15 See *Asahi Shinbun*, 2 June 1965, front page.
16 Inoue, interview, 1988.
17 Matsumoto, interview, 1988.
18 Sono, interview, 1989.
19 FMSC Report, 1966, p.3.
20 *Chikuhō Tsūshin*, July 1978, pp.36–7.
21 Sono, interview, 1988.
22 Inoue, interview, 1988.
23 Kurashige, the operations manager, quoted as saying this in his own defence at the first trial, in *Chikuhō Tsūshin*, February 1979, p.116.
24 *Chikuhō Tsūshin*, March 1978, p.33.
25 Ibid. p.36.
26 Idegawa, interview, 1987.
27 Although officially sacked, the men were re-employed by other M-san-associated companies according to local revivalists.
28 Idegawa, interview, 1987.
29 Notes from the meeting, September 1977, courtesy of Sono.
30 Ishizaki, interview, 1988.
31 *Nishi Nihon Shinbun*, Chikuho section, 28 June 1960.
32 Ogata, interview, 1988.
33 Oguchi quoted this phrase, meaning that they were treated as total outcasts (interview: 1988).
34 'U'-kun, in *Chikuhō Nōto*, June 1978, p.51.
35 Personal communication, 1989.
36 Idegawa, personal communication, 1988.
37 Ogata, interview, 1988.
38 Takashima, interview, 1988.

CHAPTER 13

Sono

In 1964, Sono, one of the more powerful influences behind the success of the YWM, first came to Chikuho. His impressions of the region were very strong:

> When I first came to the area and drove around the place, the strongest impression that I got was of a stratified society. At the top were the residences of the presidents of the coal companies, and spread out below were the company houses of the office workers. And below them on the plains were the houses of the miners. And below them, in the least convenient places, in houses that looked like they shouldn't have even been standing, were the workers in the subcontracting mines. The structure was easily understood just by looking at the height of the respective housing. It was a stratified society that you could see before your eyes.[1]

As a Tokyo student activist involved in civil rights movements, Sono was passionately interested in attempting to alleviate the repression he perceived in the coalfields of Chikuho. He was influenced by reports from leftist activists of the M-san Miike disaster in the same year, which described how the victims' families were awarded almost no compensation following the accident. According to the reports, the company was not prepared to take responsibility for the accident, which killed more than 460 miners, nor were the authorities prepared to take action against the company on behalf of the victims' families. This situation seemed a classic case of the extremely disproportionate power of Japanese industries to exploit and abuse workers.

With this orientation, Sono was concerned that the miners were not able to represent themselves effectively. This was because the threat of violence in their everyday existence precluded the consciousness necessary to challenge the status quo. In particular he concentrated on the involvement of the *yakuza* in the industry, and in the area in general. He describes the way he perceived the situation when he arrived in Chikuho:

> When I came here, there was a movie called the *Yama no Kai*, which was about the Saian (a slum in Tokyo). It concentrated on the workers' union that was being formed at the time and which was being persecuted by the *yakuza*. The first person who made a film about the town had been killed by the *yakuza*. So the people who had commissioned the first film got another director, and he also was killed by the *yakuza*, after one year. Both of them were killed. So the making of that film was terrible. However, before he died, the second person to be involved with that film also came to Chikuho to record events on film. According to him, the *rōmu* management was visible here in the coalfields of Japan, just like in Saian.[2]

Sono maintained that, particularly in the smaller mines, incidents of violence and union repression were high. However, in the larger companies, the power of management over labour was immediately apparent. He supports this view with evidence used at the trial of the manager of the Y-san mine.

> This man was always totally in support of M-san, and only ever said good things about the company. However, in court he talked about the behind-the-scenes way that M-san was run. He talked about the M-san *rōmu* a lot. He related how after a few drinks the M-san *rōmu* said at a meeting with *rōmu* from other companies, 'Today there was a cave-in and someone's arm or leg was cut off.' One of the *rōmu* from another company said, apparently as a joke, 'Your company kills people, fuck you. If this was at our company and one person was killed the company would be finished.' 'Ha. Ha. Ha.' They all laughed. 'That's the reason that the *rōmu* exist. The workers are totally expendable at our company,' the M-san *rōmu* explained. Or so this man said in court.[3]

It was the culture of violence and the powerlessness of the miners that fascinated Sono in the early days of his involvement with Y-san. An outsider with strong political views, he wanted to help redress some of the problems that he identified; in particular, the poorly developed collective consciousness of miners and their families was worth pursuing and, where possible, changing. Moreover, the continual abuse of human rights, which was tightly linked with his understanding of the practice of monopoly capitalism, and the co-operation of government with business, worked strongly to prevent the enlightenment of the miners.

The relations of power were most clearly identifiable in mining accidents. In only one case to the present has the management of a mining company been prosecuted for negligence in the event of an accident. Sono maintains that the compensation awarded to victims' families has been so poor that in many cases it amounted to virtually nothing. This is because miners' civil rights are poorly developed.

> On that day in Y-san 237 men died. If, for example, a plane crashed and 237 people were killed, it would be impossible to even consider such a small settlement being paid by the company concerned to the families of the victims, even at that time. Impossible. Whatever company a person works at, whatever sort of factory there is, if an explosion or an accident occurs, the families of the dead are generally looked after to a certain extent.
>
> But as far as the mines were concerned, if an accident occurred, the usual way of looking at it was that it couldn't be helped, and that it was all part of the job. This is a form of prejudice. So you can also say that the company always wins in these situations.
>
> In any number of terrible accidents that have occurred in the mines in Japan, the company was absolutely responsible for what went on, for killing the workers. But rather than demanding that the company admit liability, the people generally asked the company to please allow them to continue to work for them![4]

The Y-san case became a personal crusade, largely through a couple of coincidences. Sono's wife was employed as a clerk at the offices of Y-san. While she was there, she observed the acrimonious relations between the widows of the disaster, on one hand, and management and the union, on the other. When the case went ahead, it was a perfect opportunity for the Sonos to become involved in definitive action. In 1967 they had started a local newsletter, which concentrated on civil rights issues, and which expressed their views on issues that concerned Chikuho people. The precedent established by the courts encouraged the Sonos to help organise the widows into a cohesive movement to challenge the hegemony of the company.

The fundamental reason for Sono's involvement still revolved around redressing what he perceived as a basic miscarriage of justice. The mining companies, in his view, had a disproportionate influence, not only on the lives of their workers, but also through manipulation of the bureaucracy and police, over the miners' legal status and their rights as human beings.

> In the case of police prosecutions, the persons who are arrested have certain rights, because they are the weaker party, and as such they have the basic human right to claim that they are innocent and to be treated as such. In the mining cases however, the powerful people — in this case the company — have *all* the rights, and the injured miners and the families of the dead miners have no rights at all under the law.
>
> A good example is the Miike explosion. Of course there was an explosion — over 400 men were killed — but if you listened to what M-san had to say at the inquiry you would think that there had never even been a serious

accident in the first place. The families of the dead miners made representations about the event in court and to the official inquiry, but M-san
assembled a team of lawyers and scholars to attempt to show that if there was
blame to be placed on any group, it was on the miners. The mine was safe,
after all. All these scholars had been called upon to give evidence on M-san's
behalf with the aim of proving that the company was not responsible for
causing the accident. They went through the evidence very thoroughly,
discrediting key witnesses for the prosecution, and in the end the scholars
decided that there really hadn't been an accident in which M-san was the
responsible party. This was the scientific investigation into the accident.

What happened was that the police said that the account of the accident as
relayed by the dead miners' families and the injured miners was a fabrica-
tion, and that the truth of the matter was that M-san was not responsible for
the accident in any way, therefore no culpability could be attached to the
company. So the judge decided that there was a large enough element of
doubt and the representation of the company was taken as being the correct
account of events. That was the way the case was set up. It was really very
strange, and I was angered by this.[5]

As a compelling and authoritative storyteller, Sono still discusses the
stories of the Y-san case and other mining incidents with those who are
interested, and no doubt influences many through his articulate
rhetoric.

Sono now lives on a commune in the hills behind Kawasaki, growing
organic food and teaching groups of young unemployed people how to
survive in a non-urban environment. In particular, he and his wife are
concerned with preparing younger generations for an uncertain future.
In this way he continues with the philanthropic philosophy he followed
when he first came to Chikuho. The issue of the welfare-based society
which Chikuho has become now drives the Sonos in their attempts to
redress social inequality.

CHAPTER 14

Welfare

If the coalmining industry was representative of Chikuho in the period until the 1960s, then welfare has come to be equated with the region since then. This section looks at welfare, its history and the impact it has had on Chikuho since the coal industry went into decline. It is arguably the ascendant 'industry' in Chikuho in the 1990s.

Until the Second World War, welfare had never been an integral part of the Japanese politico-economic scenario. It took the Occupation forces' intervention to instigate changes within local mandates concerning welfare. Once the groundwork for a welfare system had been established, the Japanese government made the system idiosyncratically Japanese in content. Japanese cultural standards were introduced into the legislation, which sought to make the family unit, rather than the individual, the basic component of the welfare system. This trend has continued to the present day, although it has become more cynical as the need for welfare cuts has been rationalised at all government levels, and the financial responsibility for the maintenance of welfare programs has been transferred in large part to the families of those who are incapable of supporting themselves.

Legislation introduced since the Second World War in theory has had to conform to, among other clauses, two basic premises written into the Constitution of Japan. Article 25 says, 'All people shall have the right to maintain minimum standards of wholesome and cultured living'. Another clause states that 'The State must make every effort to promote and expand social welfare, social security and public health services to cover every aspect of the life of the people.'

This discussion centres on these premises, with the aim of discerning

224

to what extent the pledges have been upheld, on both a macro and a micro level. To understand the nature of the macro perspective it is necessary to look at the evolution of the welfare process in Japan over the years, and to isolate the key cultural, economic and political issues that have been closely associated with the passage of welfare legislation. Without delving too deeply into the legislation *per se*, I think it is worth digging out some of the more momentous welfare-related decisions, and airing them within the context of the current political economic climate.

The micro perspective, while in some ways less comprehensive than the macro view, allows a depth of insight into the ways that the passing of laws have affected individuals living within the system. In chapter 15 I shall concentrate on one case, to illustrate how the changes in the law and the attitudes of the community and welfare personnel have affected one young family. Particularly within the coalfields, where there is a high level of unemployment and many people appear to be living in poverty, an analysis of the circumstances within which this family has found itself is revealing. This view will challenge the official wisdom of politicians, who blithely assure the local population that the government has their best interests at heart when reducing welfare payments, including child allowances and old-age pensions.

A brief history of welfare

Before 1945, Japanese politicians were reluctant to introduce legislation that provided adequate welfare for the population of Japan. The Poor Relief Law of 1932 was the first law passed by the government since the 1874 Indigent Person Relief Regulation. The Poor Relief Law sought to introduce aid, such as livelihood assistance, medical care and maternal and childcare assistance. This period in Japan's history was marked by its aggressive overseas military activities, which led to the Pacific War. With Japan's involvement in the Pacific War, all social welfare programs came under the jurisdiction of the military, and the reforms of the early 1930s were lost as welfare funding was cut. This situation continued until the end of the war.

In 1946 the Occupation Army included in its many legislative reforms welfare measures to support a devastated economy. The guidelines of 1946 included a wide-ranging and comprehensive system of welfare modelled on the US system, but it was not long before the Japanese government was able to manipulate the legislation under the guise of 'cultural esoterism'.

The guidelines established by the Supreme Command of Allied Powers (SCAP) were:

1 National relief should be carried out on an equal basis without discrimination.
2 The protection of those who are poor and in need of daily necessities should be assisted by the nation.
3 The responsibility for welfare should be placed not on others, but on the nation.
4 The amount of the budget for assistance should be sufficient for the protection of the poor and should not be limited.[1]

Although the structure was established by these guidelines, for a number of reasons the state was reluctant to assume full financial responsibility for welfare. The scale of assistance necessary in the post-war period was so large that private institutions were soon set up to fill the gaps in the official welfare system. Article 89 of the Constitution of Japan states that public money or other public property should not be used for 'charitable, educational or benevolent enterprises not under the control of the public authority'.[2] This legislation was introduced to prevent the Japanese government establishing and funding elitist educational institutions that would enable a revival of the nationalist fervour that had led to the aggressive militarism of the 1930s and early 1940s. However, assistance from the government was a necessary step for the establishment of private welfare associations, and the government sidestepped the limitations of the legislation by establishing 'semi-government' bodies, which were officially under government control, but in practice were able to act autonomously with the help of government grants-in-aid.

The Social Welfare Service Law of 1951 established the structure within which the current welfare laws are situated. Welfare offices were set up as agencies for social welfare administration and private welfare agencies, and the so-called 'social welfare corporations' were also established. As Japan became more economically solvent in the early 1960s, welfare legislation changed, and the emphasis was placed on private superannuation schemes, pension plans, medical care and child-minding facilities, which were all partially supported by national funds. Large companies in particular helped to fund these plans, and many smaller companies also took part in the superannuation schemes. In areas where unemployment and poverty were prevalent, these funds and the private bodies that controlled them had little influence. The financial responsibility for maintaining programs designed to employ and/or support these people rested with national, prefectural and local governments. Government expenditure, which was concentrated within the poorer areas, had started to became a major liability for the governments at all levels by the mid-1960s.

Unemployment became a major problem within the coalfields as a result of the government's plan to phase out coalmining. More state funds were diverted to maintain the special programs that Tokyo had introduced to handle the situation. These special programs were public works projects, employing ex-coalminers to work in the construction of Chikuho infrastructure. Nowhere in Japan was the program more widespread than in Chikuho. The wide, smooth arterial roads that were built as part of the initiative during the 1960s are still testimony to the scale of the projects.

The public works programs in which the coalminers took part were originally funded by the nation under the terms of the TCRB, but as the time and scale of the programs increased, the national government was less than happy to continue its unconditional support. Consequently a large part of the burden of the special measures legislated by the central government to support the out-of-work coalminers was passed on to both prefectural and local governments. This was consistent with welfare legislation amended in the mid-1960s to force local governments to shoulder a larger part of the economic responsibility for their own welfare programs.

This shifting of responsibility for funding welfare systems from national to local and prefectural governments has continued until the present. The percentage of funding welfare that is the national government's responsibility is constantly under review by the Temporary Administrative Research Council and the Temporary Administrative Reform Committee. Since 1986, for example, 50 per cent of the funding of care for the physically and mentally disabled has been supplied by the national government, while the remaining 50 per cent comes from local government. In the case of public assistance (that is, living expenses for the infirm and unemployable) 70 per cent is funded by national government coffers, while the remaining 30 per cent comes from local funds. However, this is presently under review, and it has been proposed that the cost of maintaining this program should be shared equally by both local and national governments.[3]

Moving some of the financial responsibility from the national to the local and prefectural levels has had a profound effect on the nature of welfare spending. Local governments are unable to support official welfare agencies to the extent that they would like, and there has been a trend over recent years to privatise the welfare industry, particularly in relation to childcare centres and old people's homes. On top of this, the call for volunteers to supply not only their own time to maintain certain welfare programs, but also to provide amenities for welfare recipients, has been vociferous. In 1988, for example, 60 per cent of the people involved in the welfare industry were 'volunteers', some of whom received token allowances from government sub-agencies, but the majority of whom worked gratis.[4]

In the early 1970s, welfare in Japan was reformed quite radically. Child allowance was introduced and the National Health Insurance was reformed, so that medical care became free for all people over 70 years of age. On top of this, the system of old-age pensions that had been introduced in 1961 was revised so that all Japanese were covered either by the superannuation scheme or by the 'people's pension plan'. Revision of the system was due in large part to agitation by radical elements in local government, which had promised their constituents that they would be looked after.

The system of government in Japan, as in many other nations, allows local, prefectural and national governments to be of different political persuasions. For example, in 1988, in Tagawa City the local government and the mayor belonged to the JSP, the Fukuoka Prefectural government was also JSP, whereas the national government was LDP. This conflict of political interests has had the effect of forcing change from the bottom up, as it were, not necessarily from the national government level down. If local governments decide to liberalise local welfare conditions, then the prefectural and national governments are forced to follow suit, eventually.

A somewhat-neglected piece of legislation introduced in 1975 was the Employment Insurance Act, which replaced the Unemployment Allowance Act. This Act separated two types of unemployment benefit: the Employment Insurance and the Public Assistance Allowance. The former was to be given to those insured with companies, the latter to those who were not insured or whose insurance benefits had lapsed. The Employment Insurance Act, which is still law, categorises individuals in arbitrary age-groups and considers the duration that the individual contributes to the insurance fund. On the basis of these criteria, a benefit is paid over a period of time determined by the age of the individual. It is partially (20 per cent) funded by the Ministry of Health and Welfare, but is in large part self-funding. The Public Assistance Allowance is a standard welfare allowance, which the government pays: 70 per cent by the national government and 15 per cent each by the local and prefectural governments. I shall discuss this in more detail below.

In 1983, after economic growth had slowed somewhat, the government decided that it was subsidising too many welfare costs, and health insurance for the aged was introduced, whereby all Japanese over 65 years of age were required to pay insurance premiums and a percentage of the medical fee for services used. Consequently, even for the aged, a patient charge was introduced. In 1986 the pension system was overhauled again, this time reducing in real terms the amount that an old-age pensioner who had no other source of income would receive.

Decline of welfare

Although welfare spending has increased significantly over the past four or five years, welfare for the aged has, as a percentage of national welfare expenditure, actually decreased.[5] This is in spite of a rapidly ageing population and a low birth rate. Government initiatives to lower welfare spending have come about as a result of financial analyses of national government expenditure on pension programs, which were commissioned by the Ministry of Finance. These analyses showed that the surpluses generated from the current pension plans were not adequate to take the pension schemes into the twenty-first century, and that individual contributions to the schemes would have to rise to unacceptable levels to maintain the program. In large part this was because of the high rate of contribution by the population to the government-subsidised pension programs, on the one hand, and because the population was ageing very rapidly, on the other.[6] Moreover, the demand for welfare has increased from other sectors of the population, not least from working couples, single mothers and the unemployed.

Excessive reliance on welfare is anathema to the government's ideal of a sophisticated and cosmopolitan culture, an image the government has tried to foster over the years. An increase in welfare payouts was noticed with some alarm in the early 1980s. This brought about the rationalisation of the welfare system so that the government could take the country into the twenty-first century.

The national government's subsequent commitment to lowering welfare spending spawned the 123 Legislation, an attempt to reinstate a major Japanese cultural tradition (the extended family) and, in the process, reduce welfare expenditure. Simply put, the 123 Legislation dictates that the social welfare worker must request that all members of a welfare applicant's family support the applicant where possible. The applicant then receives the difference between the sum pledged by the family members and the lowest acceptable standard of living (LASL) allowance for the area classification in which the applicant lives, which is covered by the Welfare Act. For example, in Tagawa the LASL allowance is 48,000 yen a month. If the welfare office can get pledges of 30,000 yen a month from an applicant's relatives, the welfare office pays the applicant 18,000 yen a month to bring the allowance into line with the figure required to sustain life. In other words, the system works to reify the role of the extended two- or three-generation family, and by so doing cuts government welfare expenditure considerably for a number of reasons, which I will look at later in the chapter.

According to Takashima, publications that substantiate official government claims that the standard of living in Japan is now as good as anywhere, that education levels are the highest in the world, that adequate measures are taken within traditional cultural structures to care for the rapidly ageing population, and that there is no need for welfare in today's Japan are perpetuating a fiction.[7] The system of lifelong employment that still pervasively underlies social consciousness, the strong Japanese work ethic, co-operation between labour and management within the corporation and the notion that the company takes care of its own are often raised by sympathetic analysts to demonstrate the point that Japan is a culturally discrete, benevolent and economically successful culture. Some statistics on Japan released by the government support this view. Low unemployment, low demand for welfare and an ironclad social security system are evidence of the highly efficient way the country is governed. However, it is arguable that the statistical picture presented to information- and figure-hungry domestic and foreign analysts does not accurately represent the many faces of Japanese society.

In contemporary Japan there are still many impoverished and discriminated-against people. Many of those subject to discrimination are Koreans and *burakumin*, but as the Japanese government continues vigorously to pursue economically oriented goals, economic discrimination is becoming a more subtle, but common, problem. It is socially stigmatising to be classified as a 'welfare recipient', and the widespread knowledge that it is demeaning to have to live off the government has had the effect of gradually reducing the number of successful applications for welfare support, even in cases when there has been a real need. This has been achieved through a number of methods, including the application of the 123 Legislation, the introduction of tougher interpretations of the welfare laws by caseworkers and the very detailed investigation to which applicants and their property are subjected as a matter of course.

In addition to the 123 Legislation, other policies introduced since 1984 have attempted to bring pressure to bear on groups and individuals to reduce welfare expenditure through the policy of 'administrative reform', local governments have been asked to reduce local welfare spending by turning present welfare facilities into institutions run by third parties, thus effectively transforming them into 'user pays' bodies. The privatisation of welfare corporations (retirement homes, home helpers, childcare centres, education groups, handicapped groups' helpers) has led to many people not getting the care they need, and which was provided for in the original welfare legislation. In particular, people at the bottom of the social hierarchy are most at risk within this system. Company employees more often than not contribute to company superannuation schemes, public servants are covered by a special government superannuation scheme, and farmers, fishermen and other self-employed people are covered by their own schemes. However, casual and part-time workers, the majority of them women, are not entitled to either superannuation benefits or childcare facilities at the workplace, because regardless of the work that they are doing, they are officially seen as 'non-permanent' staff, and thus their company privileges are limited.

Privatising rest homes for the elderly has had a devastating effect on the aged population. The government old-age pension scheme (*kokumin nenkin*), which has been supported by the state since the 1960s, has changed so that since 1986 an assets test is applied to potential recipients. The poor payments awarded under the pension scheme are evidenced by the fact that more Japanese over 65 are currently seeking work than any other age-group.[8] In simple economic terms, this is because people cannot live on the low allowances they receive from the government alone, and are forced to seek employment to boost their incomes. Notwithstanding this, the gradual decrease in real welfare expenditure is used by the government to imply that Japan has dealt with its welfare so effectively that the government can concentrate on more important issues.

Takashima sums up one attitude that is becoming prevalent as public welfare groups become more organised within Japan:

> You might think that high economic growth would increase people's income and solve social welfare needs. The reverse is, in fact, the case. High economic growth created many sorts of new needs and made social services an indispensable commodity, not just to low-income groups, but to working families as well. This is because economic growth has seriously weakened family and community ties. Adequate social services are required not only for the poor within the community, but also for the working family who are not able to rely on the traditional family structure because of their work commitments. We cannot allow the government to take us back to the dark days before the Second World War, when there was no welfare for anyone.[9]

Takashima's comments are quite appropriate, considering the introduction of the 123 Legislation, which has as its core the cultural principle that the family is the centre of society. While this is consistent with many people's interpretations of traditional Japanese society, it is difficult to reconcile in contemporary Japan. The job and education markets are such that, more often than not, university graduates and high school leavers leave the area they grew up in so as to search for work. As distances between cities are reduced by improved communication and transport facilities, more people feel comfortable about leaving their birthplaces and travelling to areas where there are better work opportunities. Particularly within the rural areas, traditionally the bastion of conservative Japan, there is an ever-increasing trend for young people to leave home and migrate to the big cities. Old people recognise that the countryside and the land and work that goes with it no longer appeal to many younger people, who are attracted by the pace, excitement and financial potential of the cities. In short, the traditional family unit, still said to be the cornerstone of Japanese society by official government sources and a number of sociologists, is no longer the force it used to be.

Stresses are being placed on the welfare structure not only in the cities, as country people migrate in large numbers, but also in the rural regions, as human resources dwindle and investment declines. In Chikuho there is a much higher than average concentration of people over 65 years of age. This is due in large part to the lack of vocational opportunities in local towns and cities, which has pushed the young out and left only the old. Unless there is an industrial revival in the region over the next few years, the need for welfare will continue to increase until the coalminers and their families start dying off. Whether they will be replaced by another generation of people dependent on welfare depends to a great extent on the actions of government, and on whether or not it will squarely face up to the issue.

Welfare dependence is symptomatic of an alternative work-related ideology, which is becoming prevalent in economically depressed areas such as Chikuho. It cannot be made a non-issue by slowly reducing funding and ignoring the social and economic consequences, nor can the burden for this 'non problem' be passed on to local government and the private sector. In Chikuho, where high unemployment and high welfare rates have continued for more than 30 years, cutting funding to needy people does not solve the problem: it deflects it. There is a need to review the reasons for the development of the so-called welfare mentality of the region, and to consider ways in which the economic health of the region can be restored.

For the people of the Chikuho region, the dependence on the coal industry has been replaced, in many cases, by a new dependence on welfare. This is precisely because the structure of the industry was so monolithic that at present there are only limited opportunities available to the population, now that the major source of employment and revenue has moved on. Whereas the far-sighted planning approach to enterprise is widely recognised as one of the keys to understanding Japan's economic success, the myopic attempts to deal with the ripple effects created by the closure of the coal industry in Chikuho stand out as a blatant contradiction.

NOTES TO CHAPTER 14

1 Notice to Japanese Government — SCAPIN 775, 1946, quoted in Takashima, 1988.
2 Dazai, 1986, p.9.
3 Ibid. p.14.
4 Takashima, 1988, p.43.
5 Ibid. p.12.
6 Noguchi, 1986, pp.174–7.
7 Takashima, 1988, p.8.
8 Takashima, 1989, p.12.
9 Ibid. p.8.

CHAPTER 15

Welfare in Chikuho

The Chikuho region has the highest per capita welfare recipience rate in Japan, and in response to this statistic, the authorities have made strenuous efforts over the years to reduce this to levels more in line with the rest of Japan. Nationally, welfare statistics show that Japan has one of the lowest per capita dependence rates in the world, less than two per cent in 1989. The extremely high dependence rate in Chikuho has become anathema for the authorities, for it contradicts the prevailing image of Japanese industriousness and efficiency.

Tagawa-gun informants blame the coal industry for the extent of poverty and welfare dependence in the area.[1] The withdrawal of the coal industry from the area left the local people with few directions to move economically or socially. It was tantamount to an economic death sentence, particularly within the smaller towns and cities whose socio-economic infrastructures were undeveloped. Tertiary or service sectors were poorly developed and poorly funded, locals being dependent on the coal companies for economic, political, social and religious direction. This dependence on the coal companies for most of the basics of daily life was an integral part of the management techniques employed by the companies to keep workers complacent and malleable. However, as the small monopolies folded, or withdrew in line with the so-called Energy Revolution policies introduced at the macro-economic level, Chikuho people transferred their dependence from the coal companies to the government, and especially to the welfare agencies.

That welfare dependence in Chikuho is endemic is unarguable: there are masses of statistics that support this position.[2] What *is* contestable

234

is how the welfare is distributed, to whom it is distributed, and how the people to whom it is distributed use it to survive in contemporary Japan. As I have described in chapter 14, the 123 Legislation has had a profound influence on welfare distribution in Japan. Even in Chikuho, where the welfare dependence rate is still extremely high, the introduction of this policy has reduced the potential number of welfare recipients considerably.

It is my intention to examine in more detail the implications of this policy, although in this chapter, rather than focusing on the macro perspective, I will focus on the micro. I shall thus attempt to situate the discussion within the context of everyday social interaction, examining in some detail the day-to-day existence of a couple of informants who are dependent on welfare. I shall contrast this with accounts from a prominent and active senior social worker. He works in Tagawa, and is a section head of the prefectural welfare office.

Distribution of welfare

It is necessary to introduce briefly the political context in which the distribution of welfare is carried out. Structurally, welfare is distributed on two levels: the prefectural level and the city level. The prefectural welfare office is responsible for the distribution of welfare to towns and villages in their prefectures that are not classified as cities; that is, to the towns and villages that are not large enough to have developed the bureaucratic institutions that cities possess. Because these towns do not have their own welfare offices, applications for welfare can be made at the local town hall (or post office, if there is no town hall). The applications are then passed on to the relevant prefectural welfare office, normally situated in the region's major city, within the prefectural government building. Although the funds made available for welfare in these cases come from the national government and the prefectural government, the *gun* system of local government control is used to determine which area is responsible for what towns and villages.

In Fukuoka Prefecture 28 towns and their associated villages come under the control of the prefectural welfare office. Seven *gun* welfare offices handle the applications for and distribution of welfare to the people within these towns. Tagawa-gun, for instance, is responsible for the distribution of welfare to nine towns and their associated villages. In contrast, the city welfare offices have a clear and unambiguous charter, which provides for the distribution of welfare only to those who are registered inhabitants of the city.

Logistically the prefectural welfare offices are under a great deal more strain than the city offices, because applications are made from a geographically diverse area. Sending welfare officers to the towns to investigate individual cases is made more difficult by the distances involved, because the welfare workers have to make the central welfare office their base. This means that cases are considered with sometimes only sketchy knowledge of an applicant, and without due regard for the social and economic circumstances in which the applicant lives. The local *minseiin* (volunteer town welfare investigation officers) attempt to investigate the welfare applications before the welfare workers conduct their investigations, but their reports are recommendations only. Since the introduction of the 123 Legislation the government has moved to reduce the number of welfare workers, and these reductions are being felt within the prefectural welfare offices in particular, as demands are made of the welfare workers to reduce the number of successful welfare applications. The fact that by successfully implementing the 123 directive the welfare workers are in danger of making themselves redundant is not emphasised.

The city welfare offices have less pressure to conform to the letter of the 123 Legislation, although within certain cities with unacceptably high levels of welfare dependence there has been a strong movement in this direction. Generally, the level of welfare dependence in the cities is considerably lower than in the towns, which come under the umbrella of the prefectural welfare offices. This reflects the relative wealth of the respective societies. It also indicates the type of history that has brought about the present circumstances: that is, those areas that, since the Second World War, have been able to develop relatively complex and diversified economies have low levels of welfare dependence, while those societies with poorly developed economic infrastructures tend to have high ratios. In the case of Chikuho, towns such as Nogata, which developed alternative industries to coal were able to ride out the post-coal depression with relative ease, whereas towns such as Kawasaki, which were almost totally dependent on coal, suffered considerably, and even today reflect the past in their extraordinary welfare dependence rates, high crime rates and pervasive social problems.

The problem areas

Before the coal companies came, Kawasaki was a small agricultural town of about 1,500 people who grew rice and produced *sake*. A tight-knit community, isolated in a remote part of the Chikuho Basin, it was separated from the outside world by a ring of mountains. The discovery of coal brought with it a huge influx of people from other parts of Kyushu seeking the relatively well-paid work in the mines. The proliferation of small mining communities in the Kawasaki region, although often self-encapsulated entities, brought about the development of a fairly sizeable entertainment sector in the town itself. Bars, brothels and gambling houses appeared soon after the first coalmines opened. The coal companies' presence also allowed for the development of a railway system, which is now defunct, and improved communications between Kawasaki and other towns and cities.

As coal interests withdrew from the region, it became apparent that the remaining commercial infrastructure, which had been developed to enhance the economic performance of the coal industries, was unable to cope with the growing number of unemployed miners and their families. Many farmers had been forced to sell their land to the mining companies as their fields started to subside owing to undermining. Agricultural production all but ceased on a commercial scale. In short, the agricultural, social and economic infrastructures were unable to deal with the demands that were placed on them by the people following the exodus of the mining concerns.

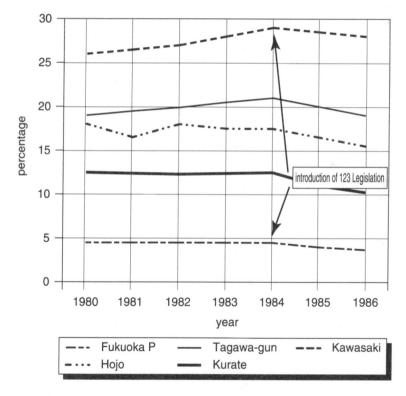

Figure 17: Fukuoka Prefecture Welfare

Contemporary Kawasaki still suffers from a poorly organised commercial centre, poorly developed public facilities (though in recent years a new public hall has been erected) and, by Japanese standards, astronomical welfare dependence (see Figure 17). Within Japan, Kawasaki is famous for three things: the H-san mine and its violent reputation; crime, and in particular the *yakuza* involvement in the region's business interests; and poverty, with its accompanying welfare dependence. The welfare situation, in particular, has attracted the interest of a diverse group of commentators over the years. The Japan University of Welfare Studies, for example, has conducted annual economic and sociological studies in the region over a number of years. These studies have attempted to measure any changes in welfare dependence, the economic climate and the high crime rate, using sociological data gathering and analysis techniques. Professor Otoma, who heads the group of academics investigating the situation, has identified the following issues as worthy of further study:

1 The nature of second- and third-generation welfare dependence, particularly in the under-20-year-olds bracket.
2 The need to overhaul the welfare system to cope with chronic, perennially depressed areas such as Chikuho.[3]

Attitudes towards welfare recipients vary according to observers' position in society. Professional people, government employees, many welfare officers and industry tend to view them as a group of people for whom there is no hope, and they have no sympathy for the people's predicament. This opinion is based on the perception that welfare payments are responsible for the government budget deficit, which in turn has resulted in increased state and prefectural charges and taxes. The make-up of the welfare recipients (in particular, the high percentage of elderly people) is ignored. A Tagawa doctor summed up the feeling among many of those opposed to welfare as a principle, saying that people on welfare are 'users, and lazy. They use our taxes to support their gambling and drug habits. Many of them are Koreans or *burakumin*, you know. It's a disgrace that we support their worthless lives.'[4]

Local governments, too, while acknowledging the role that the Energy Revolution had in the destruction of Chikuho's economy, are roundly critical of 'excessively generous welfare benefits',[5] and support the move to restrict payments. This support is rationalised in purely economic terms. Governments maintain that if welfare recipience is reduced, business investment from outside will increase, because there would be greater confidence in the local workforce. This in turn would greatly enhance the area's future economic potential, alleviating the need for welfare. It is a circular argument, but one that is becoming more prominent within Chikuho. The race for investment orders from outside the area is on, and the development of a viable communications and commercial infrastructure is now incumbent on any would-be participants. The prevalent government attitude in areas where there is chronic welfare dependence is that money spent on welfare could better be spent on building roads and housing, developing factory sites, and beautifying the environment in attempts to lure industrial investment.

From the perspective of many ex-miners, this talk of 'developing a new economic infrastructure and creating new business' is simply rhetoric. People say that the only money that Kawasaki or Chikuho will ever attract is *yakuza* money, and that the only sort of work that would come into town would be gambling, drug running or prostitution, which are traditional Kawasaki work niches. Ogata, a 65-year-old ex-coalminer, said:

> Politicians say that they're going to do something about the region — they've been saying this for years. But what have they done? Nothing! When they build a new factory or do something to get new businesses into the area, it's women who get the jobs because the factory wants to employ only part-timers. The only people who actually benefit from this sort of investment are the politicians who try to win votes, and the companies who make profits by employing cheap women labour. The rest of us get nothing. They don't care what happens to the area. It's *tatemae*.[6]

This attitude is prevalent within low income groups in Chikuho, although often it is not articulated so clearly. Within Tagawa-gun, as the elderly population increases at a rapid rate, more people are becoming dependent, at least in part, on welfare. Already the majority of those welfare recipients over 65 years of age take part-time or casual work as labourers so that they can afford luxuries.[7] Cuts to welfare proposed by the government, if introduced, will have resounding repercussions within this group of people who are predominantly former coalminers and coalminers' families. Already financially stretched, the cuts will debilitate their efforts to maintain a relatively independent lifestyle.

Kazuko, a woman who worked for more than 25 years in the M-san coalmines, and who lives in Tagawa's M-san Ita *tanjū*, said that welfare is not a privilege (*yakutoku*). It is a right (*kenri*). Like many others who are subsisting on welfare, she had given most of her working life to the coal industry, and when the mines closed she was left with nothing except her superannuation. The super benefits she is entitled to pay only for her basic living expenses. She receives 65,000 yen a month from the superannuation and is entitled to work in the community employment program for the aged, sometimes earning a further 10,000 to 20,000 a month, which supplements this income. However, she states that she is

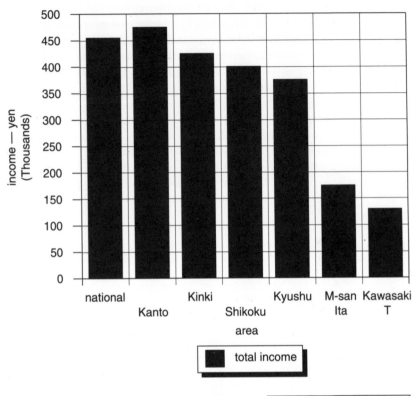

Source: National Survey by National Statistics Bureau (1986)

figs for M-san Ita from survey Sept 1988

Figure 18: Average Monthly Household Income

considerably more comfortable than the miners from the smaller mines, such as the Kawasaki industry. Statistics I obtained about general income levels support this position (see Figure 18).

There is a strong feeling among many older ex-miners that they deserve welfare support, given that they laboured for so long within the industry that was the backbone of Japan's post-war economic recovery. Moreover, because of the conditions they endured, the sacrifices they made and the violent and inhospitable nature of the industry in general, there is a commonly held belief that the government should recognise the extent of their efforts and reward them. A number of bureaucratic and attitudinal obstacles make this recognition highly unlikely. Some of these obstacles originate at governmental levels, but others are quite apparent at other levels of society. The issue of second-

and third-generation welfare dependence raised by Otoma, the illegal pooling of welfare within single households, and the series of scams perpetrated against the welfare office, often by *yakuza*, are examples of obstacles that the authorities believe exist. These present powerful rationales for the development of a policy that actively seeks to decrease, rather than increase, the size of the benefit and the range of people who are eligible to receive it.

In the following pages I shall present parts of two interviews I conducted in the early part of 1989. The people I spoke to in the interviews did not know each other, but the subjects and themes discussed converged as the respective informants described their views on controversial issues.

Suzuki

Suzuki is a supervisor for caseworkers at the Tagawa-gun welfare office and is responsible for the distribution of welfare benefits to applicants from, among other areas, Kawasaki town. He has worked in the welfare system for more than 20 years, and although critical of the current system of welfare distribution and especially the 123 Legislation, he continues to work under the guidelines established by the government, imposing his own interpretations of the relevant laws in cases where he sees fit. He has a comprehensive knowledge of the welfare system, and is forthcoming in explaining some of the contradictions inherent in the current policies. However, like many other welfare workers I spoke with, his personal feelings are balanced with both a sense of duty and a sense of self-preservation, which in effect means that although privately critical of policy decisions taken at a higher level, he feels obliged to follow the welfare laws in practice.

Suzuki has taken his personal feelings further than most in that he has become an active campaigner within welfare worker ranks, agitating for reform of the system. He has gone so far as to publish in local union publications articles and supporting statistics showing that the government's position on welfare is cynical and unjustified. His opposition to welfare policies notwithstanding, his views on the distribution system are sometimes at odds with the views expressed by the informants in the other interview.

The Hari family

Hari is a 30-year-old man who lives near Kawasaki. He is married and has a two-year-old daughter. He worked at a dry-cleaners after he left school. During this time of employment he fell down the stairs at home and injured his back. He was hospitalised for one month, and when he left hospital he was told to stay in bed for two more months. He has been unemployed for 11 months officially, but he personally has had no income for more than 18 months since he hurt his back. Because his wife, Tazuko, was not working, the family had no income apart from the unemployment insurance to which he had contributed for more than ten years. This insurance gave him 70 per cent of his basic wage for a period of six months, after which, when he had not found a new, less physically demanding job, he was forced to apply for unemployment welfare (*seikatsu hōgo*).

In the time since he applied for and received the *seikatsu hōgo*, he has had a number of jobs, in none of which has he been able to continue for any length of time. He has been hospitalised on 12 occasions with lower back pain, for periods of up to six weeks. His wife's and his own views on the welfare process offer some insights into the effects of the 123 Legislation on a small family in Kawasaki.

The Hari family lives in a housing estate built for ex-coalminers and their families near Kawasaki. Standing out like an isthmus in an ocean of rice paddies, the *tanjū* is visible as you drive out of town towards the southern mountain range. A small general store, a potter's shop and the requisite *sake* store, with the ever-present automatic drink-machines, the back-lit red-and-white Coca-Cola sign smashed and flickering fitfully, do little to inspire confidence as you approach the village along a narrow causeway raised a metre or so above the paddies. The Hari house is white painted stucco concrete of a design identical with all the other houses on the street, with a small garden, which in this case is showing some signs of neglect. It has two bedrooms, a small living area, an internal bathroom and kitchen, an external laundry, and a *genkan* (entrance-way).

When a typhoon devastated the old *tanjū* in 1980, the residents were entitled to government compensation. With the funds they decided to build a series of two-storey semi-detached homes, so that both the older and younger generations would be able to live in the same vicinity without encroaching too much on each other's privacy. That is, the elderly parents would live in one half of the semi, and the children would live in the other half, the latter thus being able to keep an eye on the elderly. Of course, in cases where there were no second or third generations, the semis were considered stand-alone dwellings, and people who didn't know each other well lived in them. The residents of the housing estate consider themselves very lucky for having suffered the typhoon, for without it they would not have been able to build such comparatively comfortable housing.

The Hari family was able to move into the housing estate because Tazuko's mother and father both worked in the local mines and they had lived in the *tanjū* for more than 40 years. By proxy, the children of miners are entitled to take first option on vacant housing when it becomes available. As the local mine closed in 1963, most of the people who worked there are getting quite old, and as they die a new generation of their children and young relatives are moving into the *tanjū,* that is, people who have never experienced working in the mines for themselves.

The interviews

After we were invited into the Hari house, seated at the low table under the *kotatsu* (a heated quilt with which the people sitting at the table cover the lower part of their bodies), with cups of steaming green tea and rice biscuits in front of us, I was able to start the interview with Tazuko. Hari was out, presumably moonlighting, according to a later remark of Oguchi.

In the latter part of this chapter there are extracts from interviews with Hari, Tazuko and Oguchi. I shall employ a dramatic structure, using the interviews with the Hari family as the base, and adding the relevant parts of Suzuki's interview into the text to present a picture of his perceptions of the same issues.

> T: When we first claimed welfare, my husband was ill and unable to work, so we thought that it was our obvious right to get on the dole, because we were unable to make ends meet. That was when he was injured, in February.
> O: He fell down the stairs. (*Laughs.*)
> M: How exactly was he injured?
> T: It was his back and hip. He'd hurt his back at work before, you see. Anyway, he got some nerve damage this time, and his legs became numb so he was hospitalised. He was in hospital for a month or so. He'd been working for a dry-cleaner up till then.
> As far as the welfare was concerned, there was a problem, you see, which affected us later on. About six months before that my grandmother had put her savings into our bank account because she thought that her great-grandchild could use it when she grew up.

Tazuko's grandmother worked in the local relief program and had her retirement pay in a savings account. In order to qualify for the pension she was required to dispose of her savings. Hence she put the savings (600,000 yen) into Tazuko's account for the child. When Hari lost his job they weren't eligible for welfare themselves because they had too much money in her savings account. It was only after they had exhausted the money that they became eligible for the welfare.[8]

> T: If we had admitted that it was her money, she would not have been able to claim pension benefits for more than a year. So we thought that it couldn't be helped and lived with it.

S: Legally the applicant is allowed to have one-third of the minimum monthly amount, as dictated by the government's directive governing this, as savings. For example, for a three-person family the minimum wage is set at between 120,000 and 130,000 yen a month. So in this case the applicant is allowed to have 35,000 or so in savings and still be entitled to welfare if they meet the other criteria. If they have more than this amount in savings, their application will be refused.

For example, if a person earns or has saved 70,000 yen, it is the difference between that amount and the minimum that is used to determine his need. Therefore, if this person applies for welfare and the minimum level for supporting life is decided to be 120,000, he receives 50,000 yen from the welfare. (*Laughs.*) I don't think that you can believe this, can you? But that's the way it works here.

The 123 Legislation is of considerable importance in determining whether an applicant is eligible for benefits. The case worker from the welfare office comes to the applicant's house and asks which relatives are able to assist them.

T: The caseworker discussed the structure of the family with us. That is, he asked about our parents, our relatives generally, whether or not there was someone who would be able to help us out. Basically all he wanted to know was whether there some people who would be able to give us some money so that we would be able to live.

Living in the housing estate, which is rather isolated, the Haris had owned a car, but they had heard that if they were to receive welfare they had to dispose of it. Realising that if they were without a car they would be totally isolated, they disposed of it illegally, assuring themselves of its use.

We had a car, but we knew that if we had a car when we applied for welfare the money would be refused. It was only an old car, but it gave us some freedom of movement. So we registered the car in my younger brother's name. We thought that even if we sold it we would get hardly any money for it, so we might as well get some use from it. It would be a waste to just get rid of it after all. Anyway, it sits around at my brother's place and we use it when we need it.

Suzuki corroborates the information that the Haris had about the car, and makes the welfare bureaucracy's stance on this matter very clear:

S: To be quite concrete about it, the first thing that the caseworker looks for is whether the applicant has a car. As far as the government is concerned, the applicant, apart from in special circumstances, is not allowed to own a car.

The exceptions are in the case of physically handicapped people, and when a car is being used as a means of transport to get the applicant to work. Apart from these exceptions an applicant cannot receive welfare if he owns a car. A car is regarded as being personal property, which can be disposed of for cash, you see.

M: I see. So if an applicant had an old car, for example, and said that they would scrap it, and then reapplied for the welfare they would have the potential of receiving it, is that right?

S: Yes, that's it.

The caseworkers

Tazuko describes her contact with the local caseworkers:

T: The first man who came around was pretty easygoing. He was very young, though. He looked as though he had just graduated from university and started work. When I say he was easy going what I mean is that he seemed to believe our story. But we have seen a number of case workers — two or three, anyway. They are often changing. When you tell some of them what has happened, what you're trying to do, they just seem not to be listening half the time, and when they look at you, they seem to be saying that you're a liar. The new caseworker's visits are rather frequent. He pressures my husband into working, even though physically he is unable to. The sort of thing that he says, and the way he says it is a violation of our privacy.

Suzuki first explains the discretion that an individual caseworker has, and then critically describes the sort of person who is employed by the welfare office these days. He makes a point of criticising government policy, which is aimed at reducing welfare expenditure at the expense of people who really need it.

S: The caseworker does have a little discretion, but not a lot. Just a little. The caseworker decides how far to investigate the application. As a supervisor, I find that I have to decide what is applicable in each case based on the material that I receive. We take the position of the applicant into consideration, and we think about not doing the immoral thing by the person who has applied. However, there are many caseworkers who do not think like this, and will follow the rules that the government has made to the limit. They are devoted to the government, these people. If the caseworker thinks like this, then the investigation that they make into the applicant's case is necessarily tough. These people have become overwhelmingly numerous actually.

From where I stand, it seems that the young caseworkers are generally very keen to do their jobs in the spirit in which they are employed, which means that they are quite devoted to the government's position. But perhaps they do not really consider what welfare is all about.

Suzuki describes the unthinking complicity of new, inexperienced caseworkers as a tool of current government policy to reduce welfare. Over time, as government policy on welfare expenditure gets tighter, those who stay within a particular welfare office can see the changes in policy as part of the course of history. These caseworkers are more likely to be sympathetic to the hardships that people like the Haris endure. The new breed of welfare workers, however, are recruited from universities outside the region and often have no previous training in welfare, little sympathy for the sometimes singularly local conditions of employment, and no recognition of either the way welfare distribution has been conducted in the past, or the historical circumstances that have given rise to the contemporary welfare-related problems.

> S: They follow the rules if they can, and the things that obstruct them in the fulfilment of their duty are the only things that they are really concerned about. However, the rules change as we enter a new era. If you work in the welfare office for a long time you can see the process of change.

To prevent the young caseworkers getting too sympathetic with local welfare recipients, the prefectural government has adopted a policy of transferring them to other districts every five years.

> S: It's the prefecture's human relations strategy. To speak quite frankly here, it is best to have as much experience as possible in the one area when dealing with welfare in general, but in Japan right throughout the country the same thing applies: the work transfer cycle is extremely fast.
> This is one of the human resources strategies that applies to the welfare service with the aim of constraining the distribution of welfare payments. In Fukuoka prefecture the cycle is five years.

In connection with the caseworkers, Tazuko says that her husband has a 'bad back', but it is a sporadic thing, which sometimes cripples him and at other times allows him relative freedom of movement, so it is difficult for the caseworkers to understand the nature of his pain. Consequently they put extreme pressure on him to return to work.

> T: If he's not at home and he's not at the hospital, the caseworkers think that he is at work pulling the wool over their eyes (that is, claiming benefits even though he is working). The caseworker comes two or three times a week. The same caseworker. Sometimes he comes in the morning, sometimes during the day. It's completely random. We are never told when he is coming, so it's not possible always to wait for him. I mean we sometimes have to go out and do things.
> They never tell us when they are coming. You see, they think that if he is secretly working, then if they come around at odd times they might catch him when he is at work. Get him while he's ripping the system off. That's what they think. So they come without warning. When they come, we talk in the *genkan*. They don't say they are going to cut the welfare, but they tell us to hurry up and quit applying for it. They say, 'Go to work, do something.' They tell us that even if a month's pay for the work he does is not enough to

support the family, they will supply the difference so that we will be able to survive.

Hari comes home and joins in the discussion.

H: O.K. As far as I am concerned, if I was to become totally dependent on the welfare, it would be the end of me. I've had a taste and I can tell you that it has already disgraced me. Because of this, all I wanted to do was to give up living.

I think that young people on welfare are picked out for special treatment by the caseworkers. I was asked to get work of any sort, and I know that I should take some work, but because I have a back injury I just can't get any. It's the same everywhere. It's a really vexing situation [because I want to work] and the hardest thing about it is that I have to stand there and take it [the caseworkers' scorn].

Hari displays a sound, working knowledge of current welfare policy, and of the caseworkers' attitudes in particular:

H: It's not really that the caseworker always disbelieves me about the pain I have in my back. The fact is that they just want to make the numbers work out right. You see, if I give up welfare and take work regardless of how badly it pays, the numbers are balanced for the caseworker. It doesn't really matter that I've got a bad back.
M: It's been said that people on welfare view the caseworker as their enemy and vice versa. How do you feel about them yourself?
H: (*Long pause.*) I suppose you could say that I have these feelings about them, but I couldn't say it aloud. It's partly because the caseworkers are afraid of us, I think, afraid that we're going to do something to them. Enemies don't get away with coming to certain areas, and this is one of them: Kawasaki.

You know Omine [a suburb in Kawasaki]? After the last caseworker was chased out of there by welfare recipients, no one has wanted to go there, and I don't blame them. I think that the people gang up on them. So over there the caseworkers contact them by phone and ask them what's happening.

Just as they are starting to know the people and the conditions in which people live, they are transferred to other areas. As a person who has had the experience of being on welfare, as far as the caseworkers go, I think that it's only a job to them, but to us it's the opposite. There's all this pressure. As far as they're concerned, they want to change the position I am in, to get me to work, regardless of what I do. It's the welfare bosses, you see. The aim is to make me stop applying for welfare, no matter what is required.

Suzuki supports Hari's comments to a certain extent, but qualifies them, saying that people like himself apply a more liberal interpretation to the letter of the law.

S: The caseworkers seem to feel that they have to be hard in their application of the laws, but ... well, they feel that they must be businesslike in their dealings with the people. However, caseworkers like myself, who have studied something of the welfare system at university, are quite different, I think. We listen carefully to the way that the person describes their household and to what they have to say, and on the basis of what they say we develop a relationship of trust. We then suggest to them how they could work, for example. However, the way that this social work is being done at present is not like this at all.

These caseworkers listen only to what they regard as being necessary. Apart from that, they don't listen to what the applicant has to say. They ask only questions that are necessary to the performance of the investigation into the circumstances of the applicant. They perform the investigation and then decide on this basis whether it is necessary to give out the welfare. In this case there is no human relationship involved at all — no understanding.

As far as I am concerned, of course we have to look into the way that welfare applications should or shouldn't be handled, but we also try to develop some sort of depth of understanding with the applicant. Of course, whether this is successful or not is another story, but we have to try our best to do this. In this area the way things are done is a little different.

According to Suzuki, caseworkers *are* subjected to pressure to reduce welfare expenditure, and moreover, more senior welfare workers like himself are also pressured. This in turn increases the pressure to which the caseworkers are subjected. He describes the process:

S: I don't get told not to give out welfare. However, the welfare rate here is very high, so there are a lot of ways in which I am asked to lower the welfare rate where possible. We are never told to reduce the welfare spending in as many words. But we are told to lower the welfare rate. It's the same thing, but in different words. There is a sort of pressure.

The pressure comes from the national government I think. The national government develops these policies, which the prefecture is bound to follow, and in turn this is made into a form of action that affects each welfare office. Then the head of the individual welfare office is told to follow these directions. He tells the *kacho* to do the same, and eventually it is passed on to me. To speak quite frankly, it is a policy to reduce welfare spending that the national government has made.

It's a case of *honne* and *tatemae*. As far as the meaning that I get from this system of buck-passing goes, it is a simple matter of the fact that I am being told to reduce welfare spending.

Suzuki is as cynical as Hari about the reasons for reducing welfare expenditure. The need to reduce the statistics of welfare dependency is mentioned by both Hari and Suzuki, although Suzuki displays a more sophisticated understanding of the problem.

S: Last year in April or May the national figures for welfare reached less than one per cent. This is extremely low when compared with any other developed capitalist country. When the rate fell to 0.99 per cent for the first time, even though the national government said that the economy was performing well, I could not believe that, given the actual state of affairs, welfare conditions had really improved at all. Therefore you can say that the lowering of the rate of welfare was just a strategy to show statistically that the economy was performing better than it actually was.

Welfare, the Kawasaki work ethos and the *yakuza*

An alternative work ethos has developed in Kawasaki over the years since the coalmining days, something that is related to the limited opportunities for employment in the region. Following the withdrawal of the H-san mine and the other coal companies, many ex-miners became dependent on welfare as their main form of subsistence. The development of the town's economic infrastructure was slow, and apart from day labouring on building sites and in the public works programs initiated under the TCRB, employment opportunities for skilled miners were rare.

The new-found dependence on welfare left many people with the consciousness that, even after they had found work, they had the right to remain on the welfare. In fact, as in the halcyon days of the coal companies' presence, the local community developed an alternative consciousness to that of the authorities of where they fitted into the scheme of things. A series of welfare scams was implemented, which involved many Kawasaki employers, *yakuza* personnel and many government bureaucrats. To a certain extent, many of these scams are still perpetrated today.

Old habits died hard, and especially the habits traditionally associated with coalmining (gambling and drinking) were expensive. In order to maintain these luxuries on greatly reduced incomes, many people turned to unofficial suppliers for capital, the loan sharks. The loan sharks were often *yakuza* or *yakuza*-connected, and could be relied on not to inform the welfare office of a person's financial commitments or status. The *yakuza* also ran almost all the gambling in town, from SP bookmakers to the *pachinko* parlours, and they controlled the booming love motel and prostitution businesses. Moreover, they had diversified interests in the construction industry, one of the only industries to employ ex-miners in the harsh local economic climate. They were therefore able to monitor the movements of many people's leisure activities, and could determine how people actually earned, spent, borrowed and lost money.

Given the limited opportunities for many ex-miners to earn money, apart from labouring and gambling, the *yakuza* were in favour of a system of government-subsidised payments for the masses. By guaranteeing the people a steady base income, the gangsters were able to estimate with great accuracy how much money they could afford to lend to whom, when the money would be returned (based on the day of the month when welfare cheques were dispensed), and how the money would be spent in town. The welfare system, then, lent itself to abuse.

Apart from their obvious crime-related interests, the *yakuza* also had interests in politics. In the formative days of welfare distribution in Kawasaki in the 1960s, when it was conducted virtually without prefectural government interference under the 'Scrap and Build' program, the local *yakuza* were able to offer local government officials percentages as incentives to allow almost any applicant free rein to receive benefits. On occasions the welfare cheque would be paid to the *yakuza* directly, the amount owed for services deducted, and the remainder, if there was any, passed on to the official recipient. If there was still money owed, the recipient would be forced to borrow more money until the next welfare cheque arrived. It was a vicious circle. Further, the *yakuza* themselves were also on the welfare payroll, because they were not officially working.

However, the introduction of the 123 Legislation seriously affected the system. The national and prefectural governments identified some of the problems associated with what was becoming an excessive welfare bill in the area, and moved to create a much stricter environment, as I have described in the previous chapter. It has been suggested by one of my *yakuza* informants that although the appearance of the welfare distribution system has changed, the same processes still exist. Having identified the case worker as the weak link in the bureaucratic chain of command, they are targeted by the *yakuza*. That is, they are threatened with personal violence if they will not support the application of a person whom the *yakuza* has recommended.

Suzuki supports the argument that 'in the past' these sort of occurrences were common, but says that they have largely disappeared today. This may be either naive or very well informed. Certainly, few caseworkers seemed prepared to discuss this issue. Hari, on the other hand, suggests that many people who are living quite comfortably on welfare, and are working or using the money to gamble, owe it to the influence of the *yakuza*. Certainly the incidence of direct *yakuza* involvement is decreasing, just as the influence of the gangsters in society in general is waning, but there is a strong link between the mentality caused by their intervention in the formative days of welfare distribution in Kawasaki and the contemporary work ethos. Hari explains his interpretation of the Kawasaki work ethos:

> H: The problem conditions from the past have continued on into the present. What I mean is that there are many people in Kawasaki who get welfare support (*seikatsu hogo*) and take the money and use it on the racetrack, or in gambling generally. It's part of Kawasaki's language — the welfare. (*Laughs.*)

In Kawasaki there are other, different sorts of pressure placed [on the case workers]. I'd say, you know, like the *yakuza* used to do. When all the people in a small area get welfare, there is a sort of group solidarity. Everyone boasts about how easy it is to get on the welfare, and I suppose that there is a sort of consciousness that it is everyone's right, not a privilege. They sort of use it to balance their wages so that they make a good living.

Oguchi describes it more succinctly:

O: Around here, you see, because there are so many people in the same boat, if you went to work in a factory there is a good chance that many of the others who are working there would also be on the dole. Because everyone is in the same position no one says anything and the caseworkers never find out. If someone known by everyone becomes *minseiin* (volunteer town welfare investigation officer), he knows what everyone is doing, but because he wants to keep his position of respect among the people, he knows that there is little he can do to make people report their 'secret work'.

You see, everyone around here likes to think that they're equal, and if others are working on the dole there is no reason why they can't. It's a form of egalitarianism. If someone has no money then he thinks that he is below everyone else, and that is not how things are around here. That's the sort of character that this place has. It's important for everyone to feel about the same level.

Searching for work

The availability of work is of critical importance in determining whether or not a person is eligible for unemployment welfare. Formally the government employment system consists of an office called the *shokugyō anteisho*, a publicly funded 'job introduction centre', to which applicants are referred by the caseworker. The caseworkers, like many others in the public service, appear ignorant of the way the centre functions, and therefore place their trust in its capacity to gainfully employ welfare recipients. Welfare recipients, on the other hand, thanks to experience gained from having to deal with the centre, are aware of its shortcomings and are appropriately cynical of its capacity to solve their unemployment dilemmas. Hari, for example, says that there is a 'pecking order' of regulars at the centre who always get the good jobs, and that people like himself are offered only casual day-labouring. Because this is not the sort of work he wants, he often refuses to take it.

There have been times when he has been asked to go to interviews with big companies that may have been able to employ him on a full-time basis, but he has not managed to get past the first interview because of his back problem. It seems that the companies were not willing to employ a person with a medical history, the introduction from the job centre notwithstanding.

In Tagawa-gun, as in most areas in Japan, once a person has passed
the initial 'recruiting age' (usually after they leave university or school),
there is a limited job market, and this market is dependent, to some
extent, on personal contacts. In Hari's case, he has few contacts who are
able to offer him anything other than the advice that he should stay on
the dole and work 'secretly' as other people in town do.

> H: I hate being on welfare. Once you've been on the dole there is no way that
> you can get back your sense of self-esteem. When I look at the people around
> here who basically do nothing other than lie around a couple of days a week,
> gamble a bit, maybe work a day or two on a construction site and take the
> dole money, I get really pissed off.
> And they all put pressure on me to be like them. They think that we're
> arrogant because I really want to work, and because I'm not playing any
> games with the dole. They're just lazy, useless bastards who only want to
> preserve their selfish ways of life. That's why we get pressured. It's to make us
> conform to what they are, so that we won't tell. Of course we won't tell
> anyone [except foreigners, obviously], but I hate it all the same.

Discussion

There are a number of contradictory values expressed in the preceding
section, which need further clarification. I would like to look at some of
the issues raised individually, so that the respective attitudes of the
informants are made clear within the context of the discussion.

When the Haris decided that it was essential to apply for the welfare
they were well aware of how the relevant sections of the welfare regulations affected them. They were quite aware, for instance, that they
would have to dispose of their car and of their savings before they
would become eligible to receive any benefits. They chose to 'dispose'
of the car in a rather simple and effective way, which allowed them to
have the use of it, yet not be penalised for what they regarded as a
stupid regulation, a regulation that served only to restrict their movements and their independence and to make their lives more difficult.
They justified this, while still condemning others in town for receiving
welfare benefits in an 'immoral manner'. This was because of their
strongly held belief that they were 'in the right', that they were trying to
work, and not abuse the system, and that owning the car was important
if Hari was to find work, because public transport was so bad in the
area. In other words, bending the law, as they did in this instance, could
be justified on the grounds that the law in respect of car-ownership was
unfair for people living in rural areas, and was a law made for people on
welfare in the cities where car-ownership *was* a luxury.

In subsequent conversations, Suzuki said that he could not understand that a car could be considered a means of making finding work

easier for welfare recipients. He perceived the situation as simply that, if an applicant had a car, it didn't matter where they lived, or how poor public transport was, it was essential that they transfer this property into cash, and so realise their full financial potential. This was because he believes that welfare exists for those who need it, and if there is any superfluous property it should be converted into cash.

The issue of savings also caused Suzuki some difficulty. He was aware that the law provided only for those who had nothing, and that the applicant had to demonstrate that he or she was basically penniless before claiming benefits. This meant that applicants who had used up their resources so that they qualified for welfare had absolutely nothing left. Because the welfare benefits take about two weeks to process, applicants are forced to borrow money to make ends meet over that period, sometimes from relatives, rarely from the welfare office, and most commonly from loan sharks, who charge high rates of interest. This forces the applicant into a debt cycle from which it is hard to escape. Suzuki was opposed to this strict method of means testing, but was in the position where he was unable to offer any way of modifying it within the framework of the overall welfare system.

Opinions varied regarding the young welfare workers. Both the Haris and Suzuki agreed that they were inexperienced and not given a chance to gain the experience necessary to perform their jobs with distinction. They both agreed that the young caseworkers were brash and abrupt on the whole, and that they lacked empathy with their clients.

However, Hari said that the reason the caseworkers were so hostile towards them was that the caseworkers were afraid of the people of the area. This was because the locals had developed a powerful network of welfare contacts, and had connections with the *yakuza*. The caseworkers tried to compensate for the uneven and unfair distribution of welfare funds by putting pressure on those welfare recipients who were unable to resist. This meant that some who did not need benefits received allowances, and others who desperately needed funds were ineligible. Hari saw this to be a result of pressure brought to bear on the welfare workers by the welfare office to reduce the number of people on the dole.

Although Suzuki was in agreement about some of these comments, he disputed the notion that those who should not be receiving welfare were, in fact, getting benefits. He said that the *yakuza* were no longer able to exert pressure on the young welfare workers, because they were 'politically aware these days'. However, I was told on many occasions by both welfare workers and *yakuza* members alike, that if a person who knew a senior man in the *yakuza* wanted to be on the dole, then it was arranged. The Tagawa and Kawasaki police also corroborated this in part by informing me that all the records they had of the *yakuza* personnel in Kawasaki and Tagawa showed that, with the exception of the top level 'bosses' the men were on the dole.[9]

Conclusion

It is quite clear that the perceptions that Hari and his wife, Takuzo, have of the social welfare system are very different to those of the welfare workers. Hari believes that there is a need for the welfare distribution process to be amended so that only the people who need welfare support from the government would get benefits, a situation that Suzuki says already exists. There is an ideological difference between the recipients and the distributors of welfare that is not easily reconciled, but which is quite predictable.

The ambiguity that Hari displays about the nature of the local community is also noteworthy in the context of the discussion. He emphasises the closed nature of the community, and says that he feels sorry for the caseworkers who are forced to deal with the recalcitrant welfare recipients. On the other hand, he agrees with Oguchi that there is a strong community spirit, which has extended from the past coal-mining days to the present. It might be maintained that this spirit had its negative aspects, if one is to take his comments about his own self-worth at face value.

Both Hari and his wife emphasise the pressure brought to bear on them not only by the caseworkers, but also by the community in general. The difficulties he had in finding work that was reasonably well paid and held some intrinsic interest for him were exacerbated by the bureaucracy, and by the *shokugyō anteisho* in particular. The job introduction centre is a local government organisation that gets some of its funding (30 per cent) from Tokyo. The charter of this organisation is to secure employment for all those without jobs who are actively seeking work. As Hari described the situation, the bureaucrats who run this service are not concerned with what sort of work is available for qualified people. They are concerned primarily with reducing the number of people who come to them seeking work. They are more concerned with finding jobs for known acquaintances and discouraging individuals such as Hari from approaching them, thus making the unemployment figures for the area appear lower than they actually are. For example, in Hari's case, although he had been on the *seikatsu hōgo* for some time, because he hadn't registered at the *shokugyō anteisho*, the fact that he was unemployed was officially ignored in the statistical breakdown of unemployment in the region. According to Suzuki, there is little or no co-ordination between the respective welfare agencies.

Of more interest to an anthropological inquiry is why Hari decided not to register with the *shokugyō anteisho* in the first instance. When I asked him about this, he was rather direct, saying that they were 'a useless group of bureaucratic idiots who didn't care what happened to those who were forced to come to see them'. He extended this comment to say that 'They give all the good jobs to the men they know the best — their old school friends, work mates — you know.' Hari maintained that the best way to find a decent job was to use the network of contacts a person develops over the years. In his case, because he felt 'stigmatised' by his 'lack of social worth', he was reluctant to call on his contacts at first, but as the necessity for further income became more evident, he decided that he would have to take whatever work he could find. At least through contacts there was no problem of his working being reported to the authorities, so he was able to earn a little extra pocket money without fear of losing his welfare benefits.

As Tazuko explained, they both know the system and are prepared to manipulate it to their own ends, but they draw the line at the welfare excesses that occur in Kawasaki. In some ways this may seem hypocritical, but to the Haris there is no conflict. They feel that he is making a concerted effort to find work that is suitable, given his back injury, and that the majority of people who are living on the welfare are people who are abusing the system so that they can continue to support a lifestyle of gambling and sloth. It is probably not unreasonable to suggest that the attitude of this family is more vehemently anti-welfare state than the attitudes of the population at large.

Within the local community, Hari has adopted the role of voluntary pariah, shunning contact with most of their neighbours, partly in shame because he feels that he cannot hold his head up in public knowing that he is not contributing to society, and partly because he reviles the type of people who are their neighbours. This increases the pressure on both himself and his family, who are left alone, in turn, by the community. Reciprocal ostracism has been an integral part of village life in Japan for hundreds of years, according to well-documented sources,[10] and the pressure to conform to social stereotypes, whether they be positive or negative, is intense within the context of *on* and *giri*. When, on top of the financial and social pressures, caseworkers demand that welfare recipients either transfer the responsibility for their support to their relatives, through the 123 Legislation, or withdraw voluntarily from the scheme, the pressures to which the welfare recipients are subjected become extreme. In particular, the social stigma which attaches to welfare recipience in a nation that emphasises from a young age the need for all Japanese to conform to a so-called standard Japanese work ethic is debilitating.

In this case, perhaps one of the more interesting aspects is the notion of reverse stigma, the concept that by not claiming the dole and working, Hari has become an outsider in his own community. The small community which depends on inside allegiances and contacts, has all but shunned the Hari family, even though their background is similar to their own. Oguchi remarked in private that people in the *tanjū* thought that the Hari family regarded themselves as superior, and that there was a lack of mutual trust.[11] As he said:

> It's the fault of the welfare office that Hari's in such trouble in the *tanjū*. Those bastards should come here to see what's going on for themselves. They send kids out here who don't know what they're doing, and when they make a mistake, they get transferred, and another new idiot replaces them. Everyone around here knows how to screw the system, and when someone like Hari, who genuinely needs support, applies for welfare, he gets dragged over the coals by enthusiastic, dumb kids. It's all crazy.[12]

What does this say about welfare in Chikuho then? It is apparent that welfare recipience has become a way of life for many people in the area. The majority of these recipients are old-age pensioners with no private superannuation. But there is still a high proportion of relatively young people receiving benefits, most of whom are unemployed. Although the national unemployment statistics are the lowest in the developed world (in 1991, the Bank of Japan noted Japan had 2.1 per cent unemployment[13]) it is undeniable that areas such as Chikuho are disproportionately disadvantaged. In other words, the area has a disproportionately high percentage of unemployed and welfare dependent people (over 25 per cent).

The 'Kawasaki work ethic' has taken root in parts of Chikuho as a response to the lack of business opportunities and public interest, the poor infrastructure, the history of organised crime, and the reputation of the area as a 'trouble spot'. This situation is unlikely to be ameliorated while the government pursues the current policies towards welfare. As Idegawa says:

> The area's problems have not been solved, although the government takes the view that they have been. The responsibility for the decline of Chikuho lies with the government and the coal companies for their neglect of the people who lived and worked in the area.[14]

The lack of interest from government in the region, apart from the apparently monolithic concentration on reducing welfare payouts, has led to a situation where alternatives to the system are needed if the situation is to change for the better.

NOTES TO CHAPTER 15

1 Idegawa, Ishizaki, Takashima, Chikara, interviews.
2 See for example, Fukuoka Prefecture Annual Welfare Statistics, 1980 to 1989; Tagawa *Kotoshi no Tōkei*, Tagawa City, 1989; Otoma Report on Welfare, 1986.
3 Otoma, 1986, pp.78–9
4 Aoyama, interview, 1989.
5 Fukushiro (government employee), interview, 1988.
6 Ogata, interview, 1988
7 Otoma, 1986, p.34.
8 When her grandmother put the money into their account, her husband was working, so it was seen as a way for the grandmother to contribute something towards her great-granddaughter's upbringing, and still, by claiming the *seikatsu hōgo*, allow her to maintain a reasonable standard of living. Further, it increased the sense of obligation that the children felt for her. Unfortunately, although it was well thought out, she didn't take into consideration Hari becoming unemployed. This effectively meant that the gesture, and the ploy to deceive the authorities by transferring the funds, became meaningless. The money was soon discovered, and the Haris had to spend all the money over a period of six months in a 'proper and responsible manner', providing receipts to the welfare office before they became eligible for welfare.
9 Kawano (a detective with the Tagawa Police) interview, 1989.
10 See Nakane, 1971, for example.
11 Oguchi, personal communication, 1989.
12 Oguchi, interview, 1989.
13 Bank of Japan, Comparative International Statistics, 1992, *Keizai Tōkei Geppo*.
14 Idegawa, interview, 1988.

CHAPTER 16

A Yakuza *Story*

'Four beers', he says, holding up one finger. The waitress looks bemused, and asks him if he wanted one beer. 'No, stupid woman', he says, '*four* beers. Are you blind? Count them. One. Two. Three. Four'. Winking at me, he counts off each non-existent finger of his left hand. Only then does the truth penetrate: he only has one full finger on his left hand, the others have been severed at the last joint. Blanching noticeably the waitress murmurs her apologies and rushes to the refrigerator where she gets the beers. Bringing them back, she says that they are 'on the house'. All four of us wait silently until she has left, then Chikara bursts into raucous laughter. 'It works every time', he informs us.

Chikara and I are sitting in a dimly lit bar in Tagawa City where we have come to discuss the political direction of a small Kawasaki municipality. Chikara, the headman of the village, is concerned that the new government policy to restrict welfare payments is having a detrimental effect on the old people in the village.

A member of the *yakuza* for more than 25 years, Chikara gives the impression of a coiled spring about to release. Everything he says and does is committed and powerful. His energy seems boundless, although it is probably related to the copious quantities of amphetamines he pumped straight into his system over 15 years. As a junior member, or *chimpira*, of the *yakuza*, he often disobeyed orders and, following the rules of the organisation, he was required to sever a joint of a finger for each infraction. On both hands altogether he has five full fingers left, including the thumbs. The general public is aware of the *yakuza* custom of severing fingers, and in this case, when the waitress finally realised that she was dealing with a gangster, she became instantly attentive and ingratiating. Seeing her pale demeanour underneath her powdered and painted mask, as she served us beer after beer, reinforced the idea that the power of the *yakuza* is still very much in evidence in Chikuho.

Chikara was born in 1932 in Kawasaki Town. He dropped out of school at the age of ten and went to work in the mines. By the time he was 15, he decided that mining involved too much physical labour and joined a local gang as the lowest-level *chimpira*.

Throughout his professional career with the *yakuza* it is claimed that Chikara killed more than 50 people. The group he belonged to was informally contracted to the mining company renowned for owning H-san mine among other reputedly dangerous holdings. He maintains that the people he killed were generally those who escaped from the mines: that is, Koreans. They had broken the rules, and rule-breakers were always unmercifully punished according to local *yakuza* and company directives.

Chikara has been married twice and has a son who is now 18 years old from the earlier marriage. He has also had a long-term relationship with amphetamines, particularly speed, which he used intravenously for more than 15 years. Although for the last eight years or so he has kept clear of drugs, he says that if he didn't have the support of his wife in helping him stay 'clean', then he would be using again. When he 'retired' from the *yakuza* nine years ago, he made a decision to give up not only the violent lifestyle but also drugs. Although he drinks considerable quantities of Scotch, *shōchū* and beer, he says that he has not wanted to touch amphetamines for many years, and that this has happened because his wife has threatened to leave him if he does drugs again.

By getting out of the *yakuza* Chikara took the first in a number of steps that were to take him from the realm of the criminal to the realm of the respectable (although he maintains that in reality they are the same). He bought into the construction business with money that he made from his gangster activities, paid off his debts to the *oyabun* (*yakuza* boss), and became a rare example of a senior gangster who has made the transition into legitimate society. As partner in a construction company, he is able to control who is employed within the industry locally, and he looks to give young local people the opportunity to work in the area when possible. Involvement within the construction industry gave him some experience with local government bureaucracy. On the basis of this experience, he decided that it was badly run and more corrupt than any *yakuza* gang, and incapable of providing industry support. Always an ardent supporter of the LDP, he changed allegiance to the JSP after a series of run-ins with local politicians and

bureaucratic obstruction to his plans to encourage more local involvement in industry. Never short of confidence, he campaigned successfully with his usual tactics of intimidation and charm to become
headman in his local village in 1983.

In his village in these days there is widespread participation in
community projects. Chikara initiated programs that encourage local
children to understand their natural environment through nature
camping trips. These trips often include the *kami shibai* man, who tells
stories about the old coalmining days, reinforcing the cultural link with
the past. Monthly trips for both children and adults to different towns
and cities, which aim to broaden perspectives, are also organised by
Chikara and Oguchi. In addition to the standard rentpayers' association, the old people's groups, the farmers' association, the village
planning committee and the local council, there are groups that
promote the development of local culture and art, and the sports and
activities group, of which most children are members. The community
has a roster system to organise parents to take the children to the
weekly activities in the village minibus.

Apart from organising these committees and groups, and purchasing
the minibus, through 'voluntary' contributions from every household
in town, Chikara has two roles for which he is well respected. First, he is
the representative of the village at the regional government; and
second, he is the arbitrator in disputes between local people.

In the first role Chikara has been successful in gaining funding for a
number of local building activities: paving the roads, installing new
drainage pipes, erecting road signs extolling the virtues of safe driving,
and building a new public hall. He has also extracted from the Coal
Villages Rebuilding Committee funds to keep the houses in good repair
and a promise to maintain the rents at their current level. Furthermore,
he actively lobbies federal politicians to push the government to
increase compensation to the coal communities in Chikuho. To a large
extent through intimidation, Chikara has been able to increase the
local politicians' commitment to reviving the area.

In the second role Chikara has played a formative part in developing
community consciousness about their past, the common origins, the
pride of the coal communities and the dangers of allowing things to just
happen. His involvement at the community level as an informal justice of
the peace has helped eliminate many traditional rivalries among residents. He constantly draws on his own experience with the *yakuza* to for-
mulate tactics with which to deal with problems. Furthermore, his loyalty,
which was once so fiercely partisan towards the *yakuza*, is now directed
towards the people with whom he lives. His energies have been devoted to
improving the quality of life for most of the people in the village.

A man who is used to getting his own way, Chikara is a persuasive and somewhat intimidating speaker. He compels one to listen to him. His shaven, bullet-shaped head and powerful wrists and forearms lend him credibility when he talks so casually of the violent deaths of tens of men in the mines. His eyes, which are small, black and bright, remind one of a ferret, and unlike many Japanese who regard it as rude to look directly at a person's eyes and hence gaze at or around one's chin, Chikara stares directly at one's eyes, unblinking.

Describing a confrontation with the local Member of the Diet over the lack of government compensation, which had been promised the village following further land subsidence, Chikara said:

> I said, 'Do something about this, you slack bastard. The people are relying on you and you just sit on your arse in your office doing nothing. Get them their money!' I wouldn't take 'no' for an answer, so I just kept at him. He kept making excuses that for the sake of Tagawa-gun they couldn't afford to pay up because it was the whole region that would have to support us. I had heard this crap from government many times before, just like everyone else. You know, the old line that we all have to do our duty for the government, be considerate.
>
> Fuck that. I told him that we all had had enough bullshit, and that if he didn't do something very quickly I would come into the office and kill him where he sat. He was such a lazy animal. It worked though. Within a week we got our special compensation payouts.[1]

The double standards that he employs are worth expanding upon, because they are surprisingly successful. In a society where bureaucracy is overwhelmingly powerful, and its actions, or inactions, hinder and obstruct the implementation of legislation designed to improve the quality of people's lives, Chikara is anathema. When he needs to achieve something that operating within mainstream social values cannot achieve, he operates outside 'normal' social boundaries. In other words he switches to his *yakuza* role, threatening violence and eschewing social strictures. In this sense he moves from being on the inside to being on the outside, in much the same manner as the traditional *kami shibai* men. However, while the *kami shibai* men were restricted by their role as enter-tainers to what sort of information and gossip they could disseminate throughout the community, Chikara is virtually unrestrained. Not only does he have credibility on a political level, thanks to his involvement in village politics, he also has credibility on the level of being an accom-plished assassin through the contacts he has maintained with the gangs.

However, although he maintains contact with the gangs, he believes that the spirit has disappeared from the gangs and that the *yakuza* are now a bunch of dispirited bullies with little real individual power. He says that in the past, when the *yakuza* held real political control in

Chikuho, an individual *yakuza* was as tough as three policemen, but now they are weak, and one policeman could arrest three *yakuza*. Chikara says that what he is doing politically is only typical of the traditional *yakuza*, who, while they were prone to extremely violent behaviour, also performed many socially cohesive functions. Sasaki, a Tagawa coalminer, reinforces this position:

> In the old days a man could walk around the *tanjū* at night with no fear of attack, even if he was drunk and carrying his monthly pay packet. This was not due to any great community spirit or to a high police presence. The *yakuza* were the ones who looked after social problems and kept the peace. Up until the war they were honourable men, and then for some reason, after the war ended, they became bitter, less traditional, more involved with drugs and money-lending. They changed.[2]

Regardless of whether or not traditionally the *yakuza* were really philanthropists in gangsters' clothing, Chikara's loyalty to and concern for the community, his ability to stand up to local and prefectural government bureaucracies, and his success in motivating the community to be more assertive about its rights guarantees that his village does still have a future, unlike many in Chikuho. However, it is faced by the same structural constraints that are apparent in most of the small towns and villages in the region. There are few job opportunities in or around the village. Chikara's personal influence does not extend to the major Kyushu cities, and if and when young people are forced to leave the village to search for work, they take with them the disadvantages of their background: poor education, a lack of vocational skills, 'rough' mannerisms and language, and few contacts in the cities. Many young people from Chikuho are not successful in competing for jobs in difficult-to-enter industries, and subsequently return. In these circumstances, welfare, petty crime and the welfare scams are appealing options.

It is these larger issues that, even given the charisma and personal influence of Chikara and other revivalists, are massive impediments to improving the situation over the longer term.

Conclusion

This book has been concerned with how people seek to achieve both self-determination and dignity during a crisis in economic and social confidence. However, although a number of committed people have dedicated their lives to improving the image of the region in both local people's and outsiders' eyes, the economics of the situation still work to undermine their efforts. Welfare dependence, a result of the economic policies implemented following the decision to replace coal with oil in the 1950s, has become a Chikuho-wide social and economic problem in the 1980s and 1990s. Certainly, most Chikuho economies are relatively static and appear unlikely to change in the near future, given the poor prospects for underdeveloped regions such as Chikuho in plans for future Japanese economic development. In this sense the story of the coalfields is the story of the underdevelopment of a region in a highly developed society.

The region's decline is related not only to the macro-economic decision to replace coal with oil, but also to the micro-economic structure of the coal industry while it was operating. The dependence of the population on the coal industry, and the culture of violence within which many miners worked, created great tensions between labour and management. In fact these tensions were stretched so taut that even the ruthless *rōmu* were unable to quell the tide of rebellion that heralded the unruly and disorganised demise of the industry in Chikuho. However, the miners' protests in the twilight of the coal era, contrary to their expectations, only hastened the departure of the coal companies: that is, when the companies realised that workers' protests against the closure of mines were going to continue, rather than facing the

263

disruption that the protests would cause, they took preventative action by closing down the mines as soon as possible.

Labour action, which reached its climax in the M-san Miike strike of 1960–61, was largely ineffectual in either improving the working conditions of the remaining miners or in saving the industry. However, although the action at Miike led to few concessions from M-san, the publicity surrounding the protest did provide the impetus for activists from outside the region to become involved in labour-management actions on behalf of local Chikuho people.

As I intimated in the introduction, this book has concentrated on the activities of a group of people who are attempting to reverse the trend of economic and social deprivation that had its roots in the coal industry of the past, and has continued through to the 1990s. The role of the revivalists in the current challenge to orthodoxy, as seen in the attempts to revitalise interest in the coalmining era, is of some importance in understanding conflict and resolution of conflict in the coalfields of Chikuho. Through many of the revivalists' current agendas of attempting to reconstruct the history of the coalfields, the intention of integrating Chikuho more into the mainstream of society is becoming closer to reality. Yet there are numerous obstacles, which need to be overcome; not least are the welfare dependence and the attitudes of the local communities towards the status quo.

Throughout the narrative I have been sympathetic to the position of the revivalists in attempting to challenge the more dominant views of Chikuho history. There is a reason for this. I too think that it is necessary to understand some of the historical complexities of the coalmining communities if one is to come to terms with the past, and hence develop appropriate plans for the future. The storytellers I have sketched have an important role to play in the reconstruction of Chikuho's history, because they are themselves part of the history of the region. Moreover, their stories transmit the past to those who care to listen.

The development of a counter ideology to that which is dominant in mainstream society is of considerable importance in understanding the nature of the coalfields in the 1990s. This ideology in turn is predicated upon the notion that there is little hope that people from the coalfields can compete with those who have access to good education, the work contacts that evolve from education, social advancement, opportunities for well paid work and so on. The success of organised crime in the region, and the opportunities for material advancement that are offered by becoming involved with the *yakuza*, on the one hand, and in the absence of sound vocational options, the opportunities for a relatively comfortable existence afforded by living off welfare, gambling and petty crime, on the other, provide the foundations for a radically different interpretation of the role of an individual in society than is seen elsewhere in Japan. The notion of a vertically integrated society, as described by Nakane (1967, 1970, 1971), where individuals are motivated by the need to conform to group expectations may well hold true, but the values of the group, itself isolated from the wider society, are quite different to the values of society outside Chikuho.

The culture of violence that dominated the lives of individuals within the coalmines, and the incidence of often daily violence, rather than causing a wave of protests, resulted in relatively few labour disturbances. This is not related to talented and competent management, as I have shown in the chapters on K-san, H-san, D-san and Y-san; it was related rather to the institutionalised powerlessness of the miners who lived in a spatially, culturally, socially and economically isolated environment, where the mores of mainstream society were seldom able to penetrate. Coercion rather than consensus, corruption and castigation rather than co-operation, and incompetence rather than competence were the governing values of mine management in Chikuho.

By the 1950s, working conditions in the Chikuho mines had deteriorated to such an extent that it was no longer feasible to consider coalminers as anything other than human capital (*jinzai*). Their lives were dominated by the companies, and the companies were not prepared to jeopardise their own viability for the sake of their employees in the harsh and highly competitive economic climate engendered by the arrangement between the larger coal companies and the government to allow the phasing out of the industry. Miners were expendable, their employability dependent only on their capacity to dig coal cheaply. To further reduce costs so that some continuity of production would occur, mining companies took steps to limit not only the expenditure on safety measures, but also on training for the miners. In the extremely violent and repressive small mines (*asseiyama*), the companies reinforced the physical isolation of the miners by coercing them to work, through the efforts of the *rōmu*, and by restricting their contact with the outside world. Yet these less-than-ideal circumstances notwithstanding, the companies provided food and shelter for their miners, which in itself engendered a form of dependence on the company within the rank and file.

The geographical isolation of the communities further allowed the mining companies to pursue draconian policies in their largely successful attempts to maintain the acquiescence of the coalminers. However, the companies alone were unable to provide the structures within which these abuses of power occurred. There was tacit agreement with other industries, with government, both local and prefectural, and with government agencies, in particular the police, which fostered an environment where miners were rendered powerless in the face of continued company aggression; that is, so long as coal was produced and there was little overt dissent from within the coalfields, there was no reason for outsiders to intervene; at least this was the rationale employed. The concept of human rights was neither developed, nor abuses protested against by the miners with any degree of co-ordination, and in the absence of publicity of their plight, government agencies were content to allow the situation to continue unchanged.

With the K-san action, attention was focused on the coalfields for a short time; in fact, just long enough to allow *Tanrō* to enter the dispute and to wield its political muscle. However, as I have described, the K-san action was basically futile. The mine closed soon after the labour action, working conditions were not ameliorated, and wages improved by only a minuscule amount (two yen per day) after 101 days of striking. Yet although few concessions were gained from the company, the K-san case provides some rather startling contrasts to the situation that emerged following the flooding disaster at H-san, where miners and their families were left without compensation, employment or the right to protest against the company.

At H-san, fear of company retribution even after the accident meant that miners and their families were either unable or unwilling to protest against the human rights abuses that routinely occurred in the day-to-day running of the company. Compensation was a non-issue, as the company was able to enforce among the workforce the concept that the future of the miners and their families lay in the hands of management. In this case, the lever was the supply of housing following the closure of the mine. It was made quite clear that those who showed dissent would be excluded from access to company housing. The isolation of the community and the disjointed aims of individuals within the labour force contributed to acquiescence about the depressed living standards. Indeed, few miners were aware of their rights under the law, and even fewer were prepared to make a stand against the blatant abuses of power by the company-employed hoodlums. In this sense, the company was able to forestall challenges to the status quo, both during and after the days of coalmining. This situation is similar to that described by Gaventa (1980) in his work on the Appalachian coal communities. Faced with few alternative employment opportunities, acquiescence was maintained, and the process of challenge prevented. The culture of violence that was endemic within the mines supported this position.

The revivalists

It was to deal with these human rights issues that the revivalists first appeared. As the central focus of this study, the views, written works and actions of the revivalists provide a window through which the mechanisms of power within the region can be clearly seen. By examining their activities over time, the historically determined reasons for their activities and the reasons for their successes in dealing with their opponents in the past and their failures in the present, the importance of economic rationalism and the ideology that fosters this attitude can be seen.

Following the H-san disaster, a number of these outsider revivalists, mainly from Tokyo, moved to Chikuho. Their activities, which were based on strong political views, were to become the focus of a series of protests against the mining companies and the abuses of human rights in the dying days of the industry and in the post-coal period. Effectively, there have been three stages of revivalist involvement in Chikuho. First, as protesters concerned with the above agendas, they became involved in the fight to save jobs and to ameliorate working conditions within the mines. Second, following the closure of the mining industry, they were concerned with securing rights to compensation, welfare and housing for the miners. Third, following the government's decision to produce 'plans for the future', they became involved in challenging the image of Chikuho constructed by local governments and coal companies, and have attempted to secure both welfare for the needy and jobs for the communities.

In the first stage, which was typified by the D-san action, revivalists penetrated company unions and became involved in attempting to improve working conditions in the mines, as the mines moved to close down operations in the wake of the new energy policies. This was consistent with the leftist ideology of the outsider activists. As it became obvious that no amount of protest and dissent would result in the industry remaining solvent, the tone of the protests changed, and the actions revolved around recouping losses and attempting to win for the miners the right to a dignified existence in the post-coal era. To some extent, the protest at D-san was able to achieve this goal. However, the sophisticated methods used to disrupt production and to challenge the authority of the mine-owners were able to secure changes only following a protracted legal battle with the company and police.

The second stage was exemplified by the legal action of the Y-san widows, who, with the support from the Sonos and their action group, were able to ensure that changes to the status quo did eventuate. Like the D-san action, this movement was also destined to be based around a protracted and bitter struggle between the company and the miners' families. That the courts ruled in favour of the widows was a watershed in the development of citizens' protests, and led to a more comprehensive understanding of the processes of legal action and the potential rewards of such actions among the mining communities. However, as with the D-san action, the compensation that was finally settled upon was not generous, given that the case took 11 years to resolve. As the Sonos remarked, it was a case of 'too little too late' for the miners and their families. The mining industry had ceased to exist in Chikuho by the time the case was resolved, and although there were many other instances of similar abuses of power in the region during the 1960s and 1970s, none had the success of the Y-san case, which was based on criminal charges proved against the company.

It is the third stage of the actions on which I would now like to concentrate, because it is the situation of welfare dependence and crime that has become synonymous with the image of Chikuho in the 1990s. The revivalists in the 1990s now have as their focus the rewriting of the history of Chikuho. This is to improve the image of the region in the eyes of both local people and outsiders. There are three main agendas here.

First, by improving the image of the region in the eyes of outsiders, the revivalists want to attract industry from other parts of Japan to Chikuho. This, they believe, will provide jobs and income for many of the younger people of the region. In this, they have similar aims to those who support the *machi-zukuri* movement. However, although the aim is similar, the means by which they attempt to revive interest in the region are quite dissimilar. Whereas those who support the *machi-zukuri* movement are attempting to distance the region from the dark image of the past, the revivalists intend to make the past central to their interpretation of events. They believe that the construction of history is flawed, and that it exists in this case to suit the needs of coal companies, local and central governments exclusively. By correcting what they see as a biased and inaccurate version of the past, another aspect (the miners' strength of character in being able to withstand the pressures to which they were subjected) should provide potential investors with confidence in the capacity of Chikuho people to perform in the economic environment of the 1990s.

Second, in rewriting the history of Chikuho and in describing the abuses to which miners and their families were routinely subjected, the revivalists hope that a record of the morally reprehensible actions of the coal companies and the government will emerge. Once this occurs, it is assumed that the government will accept responsibility for the welfare of the region. This will encourage government agencies to treat the people of Chikuho with the respect that they believe is due to them. Moreover, the attitude of government, which supports the notion that the 'Chikuho problem' is solved, will be subjected to review, and those who are living on welfare will be able to continue to do so in the absence of suitable vocational opportunities.

Third, the revivalists believe that the development of large-scale economic policies that do not consider the lives of people in industries targeted for closure should be mitigated, so that local people have some input in deciding what is to become of them. So far, the concept of self-determination is basically undeveloped in Chikuho, and the region is largely dependent on the charity of government and outside organisations. Some revivalists are involved in agitating for political change, which would allow this concept to develop further.

Although these aims are laudable, if somewhat idealistic, there remain a number of structural impediments to the achievement of these goals. The development of a 'welfare mentality', whereby many young appear to be inheriting the attitudes of parents about the inevitability of receiving welfare for most of their lives, is one such impediment. For some of these young and relatively poorly educated people, their best hope for 'success' lies in exploiting contacts with organised crime. Becoming a member of a *yakuza* gang provides good alternative opportunities for social and economic advancement, certainly better opportunities than if one worked as a day-labourer, part-time shop assistant or factory worker. For others, gambling offers enticements. As for many of the older ex-coalminers, there are few possibilities for alternative employment within the area, and, given their redundant skills, they appear to be destined to live off charity of one form or another until they die.

Welfare, poverty, the coalminers and Chikuho

Within the coalmining villages, the camaraderie and group support developed during the 1950s and 60s are still present, as once more the residents face erosion of their incomes and their dignity. This time, however, it is not mine management that is forcing a repressive system of living on them. It is rather the national and prefectural governments. Their collective inability either to solve or attempt to solve the economic problems of the area arising from the decline of the coal industry has an equally powerful and oppressive effect on communities in Chikuho.

Today, although there is a government-sponsored move to cauterise the past and to develop an image of a newly revived, rebuilt, energetic area that is facing the challenge of the twenty-first century head on, the image of the city-planners is somewhat unconvincing, given the scale of social, economic and legal deviancy involved. Although towns such as Nogata and Iizuka have new shopping centres and train stations, parks landscaped with hedges and fountains complete with statues of miners depicting the glory of the days of the coalmines, just around the corner are the *tanjū*, ramshackle reminders of the coal days. Soaring above the plains of the Chikuho Basin are the slag-heaps, some slowly disintegrating, others consolidating and sprouting trees and grass on the sides. These *bota yama* still symbolise Chikuho for many people, including the revivalists, who demand that Chikuho people understand the past in order to invent the future.

Yet the past is fading, obscured by a film of technology. Even those living on welfare, who do not seem aware that they are undergoing a process of change, are absorbing the images and values that go with the twenty-first century 'megalopolis', the dream of the city councils. As Suzuki from the welfare office said, 'Where are their priorities?', referring to the councils' inability to solve the welfare problems and their high-profile, no-holds-barred leap into the future. As he might have said, what about the human garbage, those thrown out after the coalmines closed? Will they just be jettisoned? When the rest of Japan is comfortably settled in their futuristic megalopolis, what will the poor in Chikuho coalmining villages be doing?

In 1986 Otoma highlighted the incidence of second- and third-generation welfare dependence in Chikuho in an attempt to bring the plight of the region into the public forum. In doing so, he demonstrated the inadequacy of current economic and welfare policies. The rates of unemployment, poverty and crime in Chikuho continue to mock the rhetoric of national associations that maintain that these problems are largely solved in Japan. However, the situation in Chikuho has not been solved, and the imposition of the 123 Legislation will serve only to make the current problems more severe, by tightening the economy of the region. Rather than offering companies tax incentives to invest in the area, creating job-training programs, improving education facilities so local children can absorb the technological developments to which children from other regions have access, and increasing fiscal expenditure on local infrastructure, for example, the government has attempted to transfer the burden of welfare expenditure to the families of the poor.

As the situation stands, the people of Chikuho to some extent have been left as victims of a wrinkle in time. While as a nation Japan advanced economically and socially, moving in line with the developed countries, Chikuho remains stuck in the 1950s. Although technology did slowly penetrate the region, the close ties between the miners and the families of the miners bound the people both geographically and spiritually. The source of their work, their incomes, their pride, their culture and their energy was lost when the mines closed, and although the mines were pernicious working environments, there is still more than a twinge of nostalgia apparent when the mining days are discussed.

Revival?

The material conditions of life in Chikuho are considerably less comfortable than the conditions in which the majority of Japanese live. Although the *tanjū* in Tagawa are being bulldozed to make way for new, five-storeyed apartment estates (*danchi*) it seems unlikely that the city will be able to rid itself of slums. Inhabitants of *tanjū* in other towns and cities which have replaced the old wooden 'barns' with concrete apartment blocks have already experienced a more densely populated type of ghetto, with new and less human rules. A life in the concrete *danchi* slums appears to be the future for those who worked in the coalmines, as their housing and the lifestyle which went with it is torn down and replaced by the new.

No doubt the welfare situation will continue to deteriorate, and the old people in particular will be forced to look for charity from their relatives as the welfare screws are tightened and they are no longer able to meet their new expenses (the rent in the new apartments is six times that in the old *tanjū*). However, there are some strong characters who still care about what happens to Chikuho. Oguchi, with his irrepressible appetite for stories, singing, food and alcohol; Chikara, quietly threatening his way into the hearts of local politicians and citizens alike; Ogata and Sasaki, who will tell their stories to anyone who listens (although their forum, the public baths at M-san Ita *tanjū*, was closed at the end of 1992); and Idegawa and Ishizaki, with their boundless enthusiasm and talented writing, will continue to influence the way many people perceive, and identify with, their past.

The threads of power apparent today are those that were dominant throughout the coalmining period. The institutionalised ability to turn away from unpleasantness, to refuse to publicly acknowledge controversy, to counter overt challenge to the status quo with whatever means are available, to press economic rationalism as ideology on the population and to constrain the organs of information dissemination are still evident in today's society.

Historically, it is apparent that the culture of violence and its corollary powerlessness have helped to maintain the miners and their families in relationships of financial dependence, in these days with respect to welfare. Although there were cases where the desires of individuals within local communities to break free from the relations of dependence became clear, and although the revivalists have worked to improve the image of the region, many people are still dependent on the goodwill of the government in maintaining their existence. With the state's current agenda of reducing welfare expenditure, it appears that once more the people of Chikuho will be forced to assimilate negative changes to their lives, their dignity compromised in the face of a flood of economically rationalist policies. The underdevelopment of a region in a developed nation continues, and, given current political and economic agendas of government, is likely to continue for some years to come.

Bibliographical Essay

The intention of this essay is to provide a reader with further readings on topics that are dealt with, sometimes peripherally, in the body of this text.

In the years since 1945 Western interest in Japan has increased dramatically, largely as a response to the rapid economic development of the nation, the so-called 'Japanese economic miracle'. In recent years a wide range of disciplinary studies of Japan have appeared, and most researchers have attempted to situate their work within the framework of either Western theory, or theory that emphasises the 'uniqueness' of Japan, the so-called 'Nihonjinron' perspective. Economic theorists, both from Japan and from overseas, often employ interpretations of either neo-classical or neo-mercantilist theory to explain the success and relatively even distribution of economic wealth following the rise of Japan to international economic power. Other Japanese economists, also from within current theoretical constructs, choose to emphasise the role of economic policy, formed through the tight relationship between government and business, in providing the framework for entrepreneurial skills to ascend to economic excellence. Yamazawa (1990), Nakamura (1981), Ohkawa (1972), Ohkawa and Rosovsky (1973), Kosai (1986) and Minami (1986) are good examples of these approaches. Alternative macro-economic and political-economic scenarios are painted by Marxist, neo-Marxist and other radical analysts. Halliday (1975), Halliday and McCormack (1973), Mouer and Sugimoto (1986) and Nester (1990, 1991, 1992) provide some of the more entertaining and well-written works of this genre.

Finer-grained studies of Japanese companies — by Abegglan (1958, 1973), Dore (1973, 1986, 1987), Fruin (1989), Kamata (1982b), Morita,

Reingold and Shimomura (1986) and Lo (1990), for example — have concentrated on the way in which companies are structured and operate. These studies range from those that laud the type of operation, market penetration techniques and labour management, to those that condemn the nature of Japanese management practices. Critical interpretations of Japanese work practices are quite common in both Japanese and English — see Kamata (1980, 1982a), Nakayama (1974), Ohashi (1971), Ono (1973), in Japanese, and Kamata (1982b), Moore (1983), Saso (1990) and Yamamura (1990), in English, for example — and emphasise the problems of workplace socialisation, labour repression, the employment of women in part-time capacity and the employment of seasonal labour in companies.

From a macro-political-economic perspective, it is difficult to argue against the notion that global communication, the presence of multinational corporations, and the emergence of regional trading blocs has changed irrevocably the nature of international economics. (See Johnson 1987, Maswood 1989, Nester 1990, Sato 1989 and Steven 1990 on Japan and its role in the developing international political economy.) Through trade, the establishment of production facilities overseas, the employment of cheap labour in newly industrialising countries (NICs) and newly exporting countries (NECs), and the continuing reliance on international technology transfers, exogenous relations are made quite apparent. It is in relation to the endogenous factors that distinctions between nations become clearer.

Many authors have shown that they believe Japanese corporate culture and practice is significantly different to other capitalist countries. (See Abegglan 1958, Clarke 1989, Dore 1986 and 1987, Friedman 1988, Johnson 1982, and Rohlen 1974, for example.) The Confucian work ethic, the existence of the Shinto religion in forming people's attitudes towards family and nation, the perception that the nation is a further extension of the 'traditional' extended family, and the over-arching concept that groups in Japan are more important than individuals provide the backbone for studies that claim this bias. The differences between Japanese and non-Japanese companies and their activities are stressed in these studies, which tend to suggest that either non-Japanese companies have a lot to learn from the Japanese or that the 'alienness' of the Japanese companies means that without understanding of the phenomenon of 'Japaneseness' non-Japanese companies are destined to wallow in the wake of their 'successful' competitors.

From a sociological perspective, however, a major dilemma which reflects that within economic and business studies of Japan dominates the literature. That is, within Japanese society, is the search for consensus within the group the organising principle (see De Vos 1973,

Doi 1973, Lebra 1976, 1984 and 1989, Marsella, De Vos and Hsu 1985, Nakane 1967, 1970, 1971 and Reischauer 1970, 1978, for example)? Or is conflict and its resolution an important theme in understanding the nature of the society (see Befu 1980 and 1989, Eisenstadt and Ben-Ari 1990, McCormack and Sugimoto 1986 and 1988 and Mouer and Sugimoto 1986, for example)? This study has attempted to shed light on a number of issues that are central to this dilemma, by focusing on instances of conflict in the coalfields.

Within the literature on Japan, produced in recent years by sociologists and anthropologists, a number of analysts have concerned themselves with interpreting the socio-psychological profiles of urban and non-urban dwellers, the creation of selfdom and the deconstruction of social fictions that perpetuate current roles, both gender and occupational (see, for example, Ben-Ari, Moeran and Valentine 1990, Brinton 1989, Coleman 1983, De Vos 1973, Gluck 1985, Hendry 1981 and 1986, Kondo 1990, Lebra 1984, Lo 1990, Ohnuki-Tierney 1987, Plath 1983, Rohlen 1974, Rosenberger 1991, and Smith 1983). More recently, Bestor (1989) and Robertson (1991) have introduced fascinating ethnographical material, which deals with the construction and consolidation of community values in response to social pressures.

There have also been some excellent attempts to deal directly with the issue of conflict in Japanese society from a number of approaches. In particular, Ishida and Krauss (1989), Krauss, Rohlen and Steinhoff (1984), and Steiner, Krauss and Flanagan (1980) have convincingly displayed familiarity and insight in dealing with the issue of conflict and conflict resolution at the community level, while focusing on the applicability of their case studies with current liberal theoretical models. Representing a quite different and radical perspective is the work of Chalmers (1989), Ishida (1989), McCormack and Sugimoto (1986), McCormack and Sugimoto (1986), Mouer and Sugimoto (1988) and Najita and Koschmann (1982). These approaches, which stress class distinctions, unequal social relations, and the structural and superstructural limitations of Japan's economic and social development, support intepretations suggesting that Japanese society is governed by similar pressures to other developed societies, and thus are intrinsically critical of the work cited above in this paragraph. A further approach to conflict resolution rests on the assumption that there is a tendency in Japan to reduce the incidences of conflict, and that the nation is structured to achieve a high degree of internal cohesion, based on the homogeneity of society. According to this approach, conflict is largely avoided, and when it is unavoidable is amicably and fairly settled. De Vos (1973), Doi (1973) and Nakane (1970) are good examples of this approach.

Violence in Japan, as a topic, has not had much currency among Western authors, presumably because it is well hidden. However, some works on the *yakuza* over recent years have challenged the perception that Japan is a highly integrated and harmonious society. In particular, writings by Kaplan and Dubro (1986) and Steinhoff (1989) have provided some insights into, respectively, the workings of organised crime and violence in Japan.

With respect to works on Japan that challenge the relatively static interpretations of the 'Japan Inc' arguments so common in the 1970s and 1980s (see Kahn 1970, Reischauer 1970 and 1978, and Vogel 1980), recently a new wave of what have been called 'Japan-bashing' books has emerged, mainly from the United States, and mainly concerned with economics. Burstein (1989), Emmott (1989), Prestowitz (1989), Tsurumi (1988) and Van Wolferen (1989) provide good examples of this approach, which has generated considerable criticism from within Japan; in fact, so much so that Ishihara (1989), among others, has written highly critical interpretations of United States' economic policy in both English and Japanese.

Coalmining in Japan, for the most part, has been ignored by sociologists and anthropologists. Yet coalmining in other countries has received considerable attention. Since the 1950s, when Dennis, Henriques and Slaughter (1956) wrote about Ashton, a town in the north of England, a considerable amount of anthropological and sociological research in this area has been conducted. Nash (1979), in her influential study of tin miners in Bolivia, used powerful prose to describe the relationship between the miners and their capacity to transform commodity fetishism into an idiosyncratic synthesis of culture and history, while still emphasising the relations of an exploitative capitalist economy that depended on the extraction of minerals. In the United States, Gaventa (1980) described an Appalachian coalmining community, supporting Stephen Lukes' thesis of power relations. In Australia, Metcalfe (1988) has recently produced a sophisticated interpretative account of coalmining in Kurri, using a Marxist frame of analysis, and Williams (1981) has produced a sociological account of the working class in a north Australian open-cut mining town. In Great Britain, Douglass and Krieger (1983) wrote a seminal ethnographic account of how coalminers perceive their world and their work.

Perhaps because mining is seen as one of the more archetypal examples of capitalist exploitation of workers, most anthropology of this industry has been couched in Marxist terms. Indeed it is hard to avoid coming to the conclusion that workers are tied to the means of production in a more obvious, physical manner than in most other industries. In Japan, where there is a strong tradition of Marxist thought, it is surprising that so little work has been done on the mining industry, which was the cornerstone of the economy for many years of the twentieth century. Of the work that has been done in this area, the writing of Hayashi (1987), Ishizaki (1987), Matsumoto (1974), Shinfuji (1985) and Ueno (1960, 1985 a-e) has emphasised the Marxist tradition within an anthropological framework. Other writing on the subject has tended to view the coal industry as being part of the overall economy within which Japan has moved to change its status from 'developing country' to 'industrial power'. (See, for example, Nagasue 1973, Samuels 1987 and Yada 1975, 1977 and 1981.) While acknowledging the role of the coal industry in Japan's economic development, this interpretation of coalmining has inevitably overlooked the nature of work within the industry, and has conspicuously bypassed the role of the people of the coalmining communities.

The above-mentioned books should provide a reader who has an interest in these topics with some preliminary information. It should be noted that most of the materials dealt with in this small essay are books, rather than journal articles. It is recommended that for further reading on any of these topics, the reader should consult appropriate journals for current literature. Moreover, Kelly's (1991) work provides an excellent overview of anthropological research conducted, and being conducted in Japan.

Bibliography

Abegglan, James (1958) *The Japanese Factory: Aspects of its Social Organisation.*
Glencoe, Ill.: Free Press.
——(1970) 'An Anatomy of Japan's Economic Miracle.' *Washington Post,*
15 March.
——(1973) *Management and Worker: The Japanese Solution.* Tokyo: Kodansha.
Aruga, Kizaemon (1943) *Nihon Kazoku Seido to Kōsaku Seido* (The Japanese
Family System and Tenant System). Tokyo: Iwanami Shoten.
Asahi Shinbun (articles) (1960) 3 September, 2 June; 16 November.
——(1961) 14 January, 16 December.
——(1962) 11 October.
——(1965) 2 June.
——(1988) 23 February.
Bank of Japan (1992) *Comparative International Statistics, 1992. Keizai Tōkei Geppo,*
Keizai Koho Center.
Befu, Harumi (1980) 'The Group Model of Japanese Society, and an Alter-
native'. *Rice University Studies,* 66 (1):169–87.
——(1989) 'Four Models of Japanese Society and their Relevance to Conflict',
in Yoshio Sugimoto and Ross Mouer (eds), *Constructs for Understanding
Japan.* London: Kegan Paul International.
Ben-Ari, E., Moeran, B., and Valentine, I. (eds) (1990) *Unwrapping Japan: Society
and Culture in Anthropological Perspective.* Honolulu: University of Hawaii
Press.
Benedict, Ruth (1946) *The Chrysanthemum and the Sword.* Boston, Mass.:
Houghton Mifflin.
Benjamin, Walter (1977) *Illuminations.* Glasgow: Fontana/Collins.
Bestor, Thomas (1989) *Neighbourhood Tokyo.* Stanford, Calif.: Stanford University
Press.
Brinton, M. (1988) 'The Social-institutional Base of Gender Stratifica-
tion: Japan as an Illustrative Case'. *American Journal of Sociology,* 94:
300–34.
——(1989) 'Gender Stratification in Contemporary Japan', in *American
Sociology Review,* 54: 549–564.

278

Burstein, Daniel (1989) *Yen: The Threat of Japan's Financial Empire*. Sydney: Bantam.

Chalmers, Norma (1989) *Industrial Relations in Japan: The Peripheral Workforce*. London: Routledge.

Chikuhō Tsūshin Series 1977 to 1982 (1977-82) *Chikuhō Karaban Hōjo* (The Chikuho Caravan News). Tagawa *Chikuhō Tsushin* Publications.

——(1978) *Chikuhō Nōto*, June 1978. Tagawa: *Chikuhō Tsūshin* Publications.

Chikuhō Fukkō Kyōtō Kaigi (1966) *Yomigaere Chikuhō no Sōgoteki Fukkō no Dō*. (Restore Chikuho: The Road to a United Recovery). Fukuoka: Yugen.

Clark, Rodney (1989) *The Japanese Company*. New Haven, Conn.: Yale University Press.

Clifford, James and Marcus, George E. (eds) (1986) *Writing Culture: The Poetics and Politics of Ethnography*. Berkeley, Calif.: University of California Press.

Coleman, Samuel (1983) *Family Planning in Japanese Society*. Princeton, N.J.: Princeton University Press.

Davidson, Alastair (1968) 'Antonio Gramsci: The Man, His Ideas'. *Australian Left Review*. Sydney:

Dazai, Hirokuni (1986) *Social Welfare Services in Japan*. Tokyo: Japanese National Committee, International Council on Social Welfare Organizing Committee.

Dennis, N., Henriques, F. and Slaughter, C. (1956) *Coal Is Our Life: An Analysis of a Yorkshire Mining Community*. London: Eyre & Spottiswoode.

De Vos, George A. (1973) *Socialisation for Achievement: Essays on the Cultural Psychology of the Japanese*. Berkeley, Calif.: University of California Press.

——(1975) 'Apprenticeship and Paternalism.' In *Modern Japanese Organisations and Decision-Making*, Ezra Vogel (ed.). Berkeley, Calif.: University of California Press.

Doi, Takeo (1962) 'Understanding Japanese Personality Structure.' In Robert Smith and Richard Beardsley (eds), *Japanese Culture: Its Development and Characteristics*, Chicago, Ill.: Aldine.

——(1973) *The Anatomy of Dependence*. Translated by John Bester. Tokyo: Kodansha.

Dore, Ronald (1973) *British Factory Japanese Factory: The Origins of National Diversity in Industrial Relations*. Berkeley, Calif.: University of California Press.

——(1978) *Shinohata: A Portrait of a Japanese Village*. London: Allen Lane.

——(1982) 'Introduction' in Satoshi Kamata, *Japan in the Passing Lane: An Insider's Account of Life in a Japanese Auto Factory*. New York: Pantheon.

——(1986) *Flexible Rigidities: Industrial Policy and Structural Adjustment in the Japanese Economy 1970–80*. Stanford, Calif.: Stanford University Press.

——(1987) *Taking Japan Seriously: A Confucian Perspective on Leading Economic Issues*. Stanford, Calif.: Stanford University Press.

Douglass, David and Krieger, Joel (1983) *A Miner's Life*. London: Routledge & Kegan Paul.

Eccleston, Bernard (1989) *State and Society in Post-War Japan*. Cambridge: Polity Press.

Eisenstadt, S. and Ben-Ari, E. (eds) (1990) *Japanese Models of Conflict Resolution*. London: Kegan Paul International.

Embree, John (1972) *Suye Mura: a Japanese Village*. Chicago, Ill.: University of Chicago Press.

Emmott, Bill (1989) *The Sun Also Sets: The Limits to Japan's Economic Power*. New York: Times Books.

Forgacs, David (ed.) (1988) *A Gramsci Reader.* London: Lawrence & Wishart.
Friedman, David (1988) *The Misunderstood Miracle: Industrial Development and Political Change in Japan.* Ithaca, N.Y.: Cornell University Press.
Fruin, W. Mark (1992) *The Japanese Enterprise System: Competitive Strategies and Cooperative Structures.* Oxford: Clarendon Press.
Fukuoka-Ken (1980–89) *Kotoshi no Seikatsu Hōgo ni okeru Tōkei* (Fukuoka Prefecture Social Welfare Statistics). Fukuoka: Adoron.
——(1980–89) *Kotoshi no Tōkei Fukuoka* (Fukuoka Prefecture Annual Statistics). Fukuoka: Adoron.
——(1990) *Fukushi ni Tsuite no Tōkei* (Statistics Concerning Welfare). Fukuoka: Adoron.
Fukuoka Kōsan Hōan Kensakyoku (FMSC) (1961) *Fukuoka Kōsan Hōan Kensakyoku Hōkoku* (Fukuoka Mine Safety Commission Report). Fukuoka: photocopy.
——(1966) *Fukuoka Kōsan Hōan Kensakyoku Hōkoku* (FMSC Report). Fukuoka: photocopy.
——(1974) *Fukuoka Kōsan Hōan Kensakyoku Hōkoku* (FMSC Report). Fukuoka: photocopy.
Gaventa, John (1980) *Power and Powerlessness: Quiescence and Rebellion in an Appalachian Valley.* Oxford: Clarendon Press.
Geertz, Clifford (1973a) *The Interpretation of Cultures.* New York: Basic Books.
——(1973b) 'Deep Play: notes on a Balinese Cockfight.' In *The Interpretation of Cultures.* New York: Basic Books.
Girard, R. (1977) *Violence and the Sacred.* Baltimore, Md: Johns Hopkins University.
Gluck, Carol (1985) *Japan's Modern Myths: Ideology in the Late Meiji Period.* Princeton, N.J.: Princeton University Press.
Halliday, Jon (1975) *A Political History of Japanese Capitalism.* New York: Pantheon.
Halliday, J. and McCormack, G. (1973) *Japanese Imperialism Today.* London: Penguin Books.
Hasegawa, Nyozekan (1966) *The Japanese Character: A Cultural Profile.* Translated by John Bester. Tokyo: Kodansha.
Hayashi, Eida (1987) *Chikuhō Furyoki* (Memories of the Chikuho Captives). Kyoto: Akishobo.
Hendry, Joy (1981) *Marriage in Changing Japan.* New York: St Martin's Press.
——(1986) *Becoming Japanese: The World of the Pre-School Child.* Honolulu: University of Hawaii Press.
Hidaka, Rokuro (1986) 'The Crisis of Postwar Democracy.' In Gavin McCormack and Yoshio Sugimoto (eds), *Democracy in Contemporary Japan.* Sydney: Hale & Iremonger.
Hoare, Quinton and Nowell Smith, Geoffrey (eds) (1972) *Selections from the Prison Notebooks of Antonio Gramsci.* New York: International Publishers Ltd.
Hunter, Janet (1984) *Concise Dictionary of Modern Japanese History.* Berkeley, Calif.: University of California Press.
Idegawa, Taiko (1984) *Hi no Unda Hahatachi: Jōkōjō kara no Kikishō* (The Mothers Who Gave Birth to Fire. Stories from Women Miners). Fukuoka: Yoshishobo.
Ikeda, Ko (1978) *Mitsui o Utsu Chitei kara no Kokuhatsu* (An Indictment from the Underground's Attack on Mitsui). In *Chikuhō Tsūshin* Series. Tagawa: *Chikuhō to Kyōtō suru kai.*

Ishida, T, and Krauss, E (eds) (1989) *Democracy in Japan*. Pittsburgh, Pa: University of Pittsburgh Press.

Ishihara, Shintaro (1989) *The Japan That Can Say No*. New York: Simon & Schuster.

Ishizaki, Shigeko (1987) *Inochi no Sōkō ga Nuketa Ko onna to Tennō no Kuni* (Less Than the Dregs of Life: A Girl and the Emperor's Country). Tokyo: Keishobo.

Japan Update: Autumn 1990 No 17. Tokyo: Keizai Koho Center. pp. 21–4.

Johnson, Chalmers (1982) *MITI and the Japanese Miracle: The Growth of Industrial Policy, 1925–1975*. Stanford, Calif.: Stanford University Press.

——(1987) *Japan and the North Asian NICs: Implications for World Trade*. Kensington, NSW: Centre for Applied Economic Research, UNSW.

Journal of Japanese Trade and Industry: October/November 1992, vol. 8, No. 17.

Kahn, Herman (1970) *The Emerging Japanese Superstate: Challenge and Response*. Englewood Cliffs, N.J.: Prentice Hall.

Kamata, Satoshi (1974) *Rōdō genba no hanran-hachi kigyō miru gorika to rōdō no Kaitai* (Rebellion on the Job: Rationalisation and the Disorganisation of Labour at Eight Companies). Tokyo: Daiyamondosha.

——(1980) *Rōdō genba: zōsenjo de nani ga okotta ka* (What Goes on at the Shipbuilding Yards?). Tokyo: Iwanami Shoten.

——(1982a) *Kyoiku kōjō no kodomotachi* (Children of the Education Factories). *Sekai* 440: 224–39.

——(1982b) *Japan in the Passing Lane: An Insider's Account of Life in a Japanese Auto Factory*. New York: Pantheon.

Kaplan, David and Dubro, Alec (1986) *Yakuza: the Explosive Account of Japan's Criminal Underground*. Reading, Mass.: Addison-Wesley.

Kawasaki Chō (various authors) (1951) *Kawasaki Chōshi* (Kawasaki Town History). Kawasaki: Yasuda.

Kelly, William (1991) 'Directions in the Anthropology of Japan'. *Annual Review of Anthropology.*, 20: 395–431.

Kondo, Dorinne (1990) *Crafting Selves: Power, Gender, and Discourses of Identity in a Japanese Workplace*. Chicago, Ill.: University of Chicago Press.

Kosai, Yutaka (1986) *The Era of High-Speed Growth: Notes of the Postwar Japanese Economy*. Tokyo: University of Tokyo Press.

Krauss, E., Rohlen, T. and Steinhoff, P. (eds) (1984) *Conflict in Japan*. Honolulu: University of Hawaii Press.

Kyōsei Renkō (1980–89a) *Kyōsei Renkō Kyokaisho* (Korean Forced Labourers' Society Papers). Osaka: private papers.

——(1980–89b) *Kyosei Renko Bulletin* (private papers).

Lebra, Takie (1976) *Japanese Patterns of Behaviour*. Honolulu: University Press of Hawaii.

——(1984) *Japanese Women: Constraint and Fulfillment*. Honolulu: University of Hawaii Press.

——(1989) 'Adoption among the Hereditary Elite of Japan: Status Preservation Through Mobility'. *Ethnology* 28:185–218.

Lo, Jeannie (1990) *Office Ladies and Factory Women: Life and Work at a Japanese Company*. Armonk, N.Y.: M. E. Sharpe.

Lukes, Steven (1974) *Power: A Radical View*. London: Macmillan.

McCormack, Gavin and Sugimoto, Yoshio (eds) (1986) *Democracy in Contemporary Japan*. Sydney: Hale & Iremonger.

————(1988) *The Japanese Trajectory: Modernisation and Beyond.* Cambridge: Cambridge University Press.

Maeda, Shintaro (1977) *Chikuhō Mondai wa Owatta no ka?* (Has the Chikuho Problem Ended?). In *Chikuhō Tsūshin* Series. Tagawa: Chikuho to Kyoto suru kai.

Marsella, A., De Vos, G. and Hsu, F. (eds) (1985) *Culture and Self: Asian And Western Perspectives.* New York: Tavistock.

Maswood, Syed Javed (1989) *Japan and Protection: The Growth of Protectionist Sentiment.* London: Routledge Nissan Institute.

Matsumoto, Yoichi (1974) *Bakuhatsu no Ato* (After the Explosion). Kita Kyushu: Asahi Shinbunsha.

Metcalfe, Andrew (1988) *For Freedom and Dignity: Historical Agency and Class Structures in the Coalfields of NSW.* Sydney: Allen & Unwin.

Miike Tanko Rōdōkumiai (1985a) *Miike Tōsō no Kinen* (Anniversary of the Miike Struggle). Fukuoka: Yugen.

————(1985b) *Miike Tankō Rōdōkumiae Nōto* (Miike Coal Union Notes). Fukuoka: photocopy.

Minami, Ryoshin (1986) *The Economic Development of Japan: A Quantitative Study.* London: Macmillan.

Moore, Joe (1983) *Japanese Workers and the Struggle for Power, 1947–1949.* Madison, Wis.: University of Wisconsin.

Morita, Akio with Reingold, E. and Shimomura, M. (1986) *Made in Japan: Akio Morita and Sony.* New York: Dutton.

Mouer, Ross and Sugimoto, Yoshio (1986) *Images of Japanese Society: A Study in the Structure of Social Reality.* London: Routledge & Kegan Paul.

Nagasue, Jujiyu (1973) *Chikuhō: Sekitan no Chiiki Shi* (Chikuho: History of the Coalfields). Tokyo: NHK Books.

Najita, T. and Koschmann, V. K. (eds) (1982) *Conflict in Modern Japanese History: The Neglected Tradition.* Princeton, N. J.: Princeton University Press.

Nakamura, Takafusa (1981) *The Postwar Japanese Economy: Its Development and Structure.* Tokyo: University of Tokyo Press.

————(1985) *The Economic Development of Modern Japan.* Tokyo: Ministry of Foreign Affairs.

Nakane, Chie (1967) *Kinship and Economic Organisation in Rural Japan.* London: Athlone Press.

————(1970) *Japanese Society.* London: Weidenfield & Nicolson.

————(1971) *On the Characteristics of the Japanese and Japanese Society.* Tokyo: Nihon Kokusai Kyoiku Kyokai.

Nakayama, Ichiro (1974) *Rōshi kankei no keizai shakaigaku* (The Socio-Economic Study of Labour–Management Relations). Tokyo: Nihon Rodo Kyokai.

Nash, June (1979) *We Eat the Mines and the Mines Eat Us: Dependency and Exploitation in Bolivian Tin Mines.* New York: Columbia University Press.

National Coal Board (British) (1984) *British NCB Report on Absenteeism.* London: NCB Publications.

Nester, William (1990) *Foundation of Japanese Power: Continuities, Changes, Challenges.* London: Macmillan.

————(1991) *Japanese Industrial Targeting: the Neomercantilist Path to Economic Superpower.* London: Macmillan.

————(1992) *Japan and the Third World: Patterns, Power, Prospects.* New York: St Martin's Press.

Nishi Nihon Shinbun (Articles) (1960) 28 June; 21, 22, 23, 25 and 27 September, 4 and 5 October.

——(1961) 12 August.
——(1962) 25 November.
——(1988) 17 January, 6 July.
Noguchi, Yukio (1986) 'Overcommitment in Pensions: the Japanese Experience'. In R. Rose and R. Shiratori (eds), *The Welfare State, East and West.* Oxford: Oxford University Press.
Ohashi, Ryuken (1971) *Nihon no Kaikyū Kōsei* (Japan's Class System). Tokyo: Iwanami Shoten.
Ohkawa, Kazushi (1972) *Differential Structure and Agriculture: Essays and Dualistic Growth.* Tokyo: Kinokuniya Bookstore.
Ohkawa, Kazushi and Rosovsky, Henry (1973) *Japanese Economic Growth: Trend Acceleration in the Twentieth Century.* Stanford, Calif.: Stanford University Press.
Ohkawa, Kazushi and Shinohara, Miyohei (eds) (1979) *Patterns of Japanese Economic Development: A Quantitative Appraisal.* New Haven, Conn.: Yale University Press.
Ohnuki-Tierney, Emiko (1987) *The Monkey as Mirror: Symbolic Transformations in Japanese History and Ritual.* Princeton, N.J.: Princeton University Press.
Onishi, Keisuke (1975) *Gisei no Tō* (The Tower of Self-sacrifice). Tagawa: private papers.
Ono, Akira (1973) *Sengo Nihon no chingin kettei: rōdō shijō no kōzō henka to sono eikyō* (Wage Determination in Postwar Japan: The Effect of Structural Change on the Labour Market). Tokyo: Toyo Keizai Shimposa.
Otoma, Shinmasa and the Otoma Zeminaru (1986) *Chikuhō: Kyūsantan chiiku: Chikuhō ni okeru Shakai Fukushi Chōsa Hōkokusho* (Chikuho: The Past Coalfields: Publications Concerning the Incidence of Social Welfare in Chikuho). Nagoya: Nihon Fukushi Daigaku.
Pellicani, Luciano (1976) *Gramsci: An Alternative Communism.* California: Hoover Institution Press.
Plath, David (ed.) (1983) *Work and Life-Course in Japan.* Albany: State University of New York Press.
Prestowitz, Clyde (1989) *Trading Places: How We Are Giving our Future to Japan and How to Reclaim it.* New York: Basic Books.
Reischauer, Edwin (1970) *Japan: The Story of a Nation.* New York: Knopf.
——(1978) *The Japanese.* Cambridge, Mass.: Harvard University Press.
Riches, David (ed.) (1986) *The Anthropology of Violence.* Oxford: Basil Blackwell.
Robertson, Jennifer (1991) *Native and Newcomer: Making and Remaking a Japanese City.* Berkeley, Calif.: University of California Press.
Rohlen, Thomas (1974) *For Harmony and Strength: Japanese White-Collar Organisation in Anthropological Perspective.* Berkeley, Calif.: University of California Press.
Rose, R. and Shiratori, R. (eds) (1986) *The Welfare State, East and West.* Oxford: Oxford University Press.
Rosenberger, Nancy (ed.) (1991) *The Japanese Sense of Self.* New York: Cambridge University Press.
Samuels, Richard J. (1987) *The Business of the Japanese State: Energy Markets in Comparative and Historical Perspective.* Ithaca, N.Y.: Cornell University Press.
Saso, Mary (1990) *Women in the Japanese Workplace.* London: Hilary Shipman.
Sato, Ryuzo (1989) *Beyond Trade Friction: Japan–U.S. Economic Relations.* Cambridge: Cambridge University Press.
Shinfuji, Toyoshi (1985) *Akai Botayama no Hi: Chikuhō: Miike no Hitobito* (Fire on the Red Slagheap: The People of Chikuho and Miike). Tokyo: Sanshodo.

Smith, Robert (1983) *Japanese Society: Tradition, Self and the Social Order.* Cambridge: Cambridge University Press.

Sonoda, Minoru (1970) *Sengo Sekitan Shi* (History of Coal in the Postwar Period). Fukuoka: Sekitsu.

Steiner, K., Krauss, E. and Flanagan, S. (eds) (1980) *Political Opposition and Politics in Japan.* Princeton, N.J.: Princeton University Press.

Steinhoff, Patricia (1989) 'Hijackers, Bombers, and Bank Robbers: Managerial Style in the Japanese Red Army'. *Journal of Asian Studies,* 48(4): 724–40.

Steven, Rob (1990) *Japan's New Imperialism.* Armonk, N.Y.: M. E. Sharpe.

Sugino, Yunichi (1978) *Chiiku no Jūmin Jidai ga Tsukuru 'Kyōiku' no Undo* (The Movement to Develop the Area's Populist 'Education'). In *Chikuhō Tsūshin* Series. Tagawa: 'Chikuho to Kyoto suru kai'.

Tagawa Shi (various authors) (1979) *Tagawa Shishi. Geka.* (Tagawa City History. Final Series). Kyoto: Gyosei.

Tagawa Shi (1988) *Tagawa Shi Dai San-ji Sango Keikaku* (Tagawa City Third Overall Plan). Tagawa: Yugen.

——(1988) *Unyu mondai no kensa* (Survey of Transport Problems). Tagawa: Yugen.

Tagawa-Shi Fukushi Jimusho (Tagawa City Welfare Office) (1987–89) *Kotoshi no Tōkei* (This Year's Statistics). Tagawa: Tagawa shiyakusho.

Takashima, Susumu (1986) *Shakai Fukushi no Riron to Seisaku: Gendai Shakai Fukushi Seisaku Hihan* (The Theory and Policy of Social Welfare: A Critique of Recent Social Welfare Policy). Kyoto: Mineruba.

——(1988) *The Outline and Problems of the Social Welfare System in Japan.* Paper for the International Welfare Symposium in Sweden.

——(1989) *Unemployment and its Impact on Social Work in Japan.* Paper for the International Welfare Symposium in London.

Takazaki, Yoshifume (1961) *Sekitan Chiiki no Hōkokusho* (Report on the Coalfields). Kurate: private papers.

——(1966) *Sekitan to Jinsei* (Coal and Human Life). Kurate: private papers.

Taussig, Michael (1987) *Shamanism, Colonialism and the Wild Man: A Study in Terror and Healing.* London: University of Chicago Press.

Tsurumi, Patricia (ed.) (1988) *Other Japan: Postwar Realities.* Armonk N.Y.: M. E. Sharpe.

Ueno, Eishin (1960) *Chi no Tei no Waraibanashi* (Underground Jokes). Tokyo: Iwanami Shinsho.

——(1985a) *Hanashi no Koguchi* (The Mine Entrance of Stories). Tokyo: Keishobo.

——(1985b) *Naraku no Seiun* (The Nebula of Hell). Tokyo: Keishobo.

——(1985c) *Moyashitsukusu Hibi* (Every Day Rekindling the Fire). Tokyo: Keishobo.

——(1985d) *Yami o Sai toshite* (Darkness is the Stronghold). Tokyo: Keishobo.

——(1985e) *Chokon no Fu* (A Tribute of Long-Standing Hatred). Tokyo: Keishobo.

US–Japan Working Group (1990) *Interim Report and Assessment on the Structural Impediments Initiative.* Tokyo: US Embassy. 5 April.

Van Wolferen, Karel (1989) *The Enigma of Japanese Power.* London: Macmillan.

Vogel, Ezra (1963) *Japan's New Middle Class.* Berkeley, Calif.: University of California Press.

——(1980) *Japan as Number One: Lessons for America.* Tokyo: Charles E. Tuttle.

Williams, Claire (1981) *Opencut: The Working Class in an Australian Town.* North Sydney: George Allen & Unwin.

Yada, Toshifumi (1975) *Sengo Nihon no Sekitan Sangyō* (The Postwar Japanese Coal Industry). Tokyo: Shinhyoron.
——(1977) *Sekitan Gyōkai* (The Coal Industry). Tokyo: Kyoikusha.
——(1981) *The Abandonment and Renovation of Coal Reserves in Japan.* In Proceedings of UNU-TGS Symposium. Tokyo: Hosei University.
Yamamura, Kozo (1990) *The Political Economy of Japan.* Stanford, Calif.: Stanford University Press.
Y-san Accident Inquiry (1978) *Fukuoka Jiko Chōsaren* (Fukuoka Accident Investigation Committee). Fukuoka.
Y-san Izokukai (Y-san Widows' Movement) (1978) *Chitei: Gasu Daibakuhatsu.* (Underground: A Huge Gas Explosion). Fukuoka: Y-san Izokukai.
Yamazawa, Ippei (1990) *Economic Development and International Trade: The Japanese Model.* Honolulu: Resource Systems Institute, East-West Center.
Zenkoku Fukushi Kyōgikai (1990) *Zenkoku Fukushi Kyōgikai no Tōkei* (National Association of Welfare Statistics). Tokyo: Fukushi Jimusho.

List of Informants

Name	Age	Occupation
Aoyama Junichi	67	Tagawa optometrist.
Chikara Konosuke	60	Headman of village near Kawasaki, ex-*yakuza* assassin.
Fujimori Tadeo	47	Tagawa City bureaucrat.
Fukushiro Ken-ichi	46	Tagawa City bureaucrat.
Hamasaki Takashi	44	Forklift driver, former coalminer M-san Miike.
Hanatsuki Masayuki	52	Retired M-san coalminer.
Hanno Eiichi	66	Retired coalminer, K-san.
Hari Nobuhiro	32	Welfare recipient.
Hari Tazuko	29	Welfare recipient.
Hayashi Akira	65	Director, Coal Resources Allocation Board, Iizuka, ex-leader K-san union.
Idegawa Taiko	59	Author, social historian, museum curator.
Ikeda Osamu	41	Social historian, photographer.
Inoue Masaki	42	Drainage supervisor, M-san Engineering; ex-coalminer, Y-san Mine.
Ishiguchi Saburo	68	Leader, U-san Buzen Mine union.
Ishizaki Shigeko	61	Author, social rights activist.
Iwai Michio	60	Retired coalminer, M-san Tagawa.
Kashihama Isao	61	Retired head of construction unit at H-san Mine, company museum curator.
Kawano Junichi	35	Tagawa police detective.
Kazuko	63	Pensioner, retired coalminer, M-san Tagawa.
Kim Pak Sung	67	Author, Korean Rights activist.
Kubota Shigeaki	68	Retired M-san company union representative.
Kuroyama Tazuko	53	Author, housewife.

286

Matsumoto Shuntaro	57	Ex-office manager, Y-san Mine.
Mishima Noriko	38	Social welfare worker, Fukuoka regional office.
Miyoshi Mitsuko	43	Social welfare women's caseworker, Tagawa-gun welfare office.
Mizuno Hideo	45	Acupuncturist, herbalist, ex-leader, D-san Mine union.
Mori Hideaki	59	Leader, M-san Miike 'Old' union.
Nakano Mizuo	62	Tagawa dentist.
Nakayama Hiroshi	58	Tagawa doctor.
Nishiguchi Hanako	48	Tagawa factory worker.
Ogata Shigeru	62	Pensioner, retired coalminer, Tagawa M-san and H-san.
Oguchi Hanako	41	Potter.
Oguchi Keisuke	45	*Kami shibai* man.
Omoi Toshiki	51	Former coalminer, M-san Miike coalmine.
Otani Naoki	66	Former coalminer, K-san mine.
Sasaki Yoichi	64	Pensioner, retired coalminer, M-san Tagawa.
Sato Hideo	32	*Yakuza chimpira* (footsoldier), Tagawa.
Shiroiwa Yoichi	32	Social welfare caseworker, Tagawa-gun welfare office.
Sono Kenichi	45	Alternative community leader, ex-radical student activist.
Suzuki Noboru	46	Social Welfare Section Chief; caseworkers' section, Tagawa-gun welfare office.
Suzuki Ryosuke	59	Former coalminer, K-san mine.
Tajima Jun	38	Tokyo photographer.
Takashima Susumu	64	Professor, Japan University of Welfare Studies.
Takazaki Yoshifume	70	Author, retired bureaucrat.
Yada Toshifumi	63	Author, academic Kyushu University Coal Research Centre.

Index

288